N Black
ARCHS.UK
March 07

D0494147

Corporate Citizenship in Developing Countries

Mahad Huniche & Esben Rahbek Pedersen
Editors

Corporate Citizenship in Developing Countries

– New Partnership Perspectives

Copenhagen Business School Press

Corporate Citizenship in Developing Countries – New Partnership Perspectives

© Copenhagen Business School Press
Printed in Denmark by Narayana Press, Gylling
Cover design by Morten Højmark
First edition 2006

ISBN 87-630-0141-1

This book has been published with financial support from Danida and Nordic Consulting Group a/s.

Distribution:

Scandinavia
DJOEF/DBK, Mimersvej 4
DK-4600 Køge, Denmark
Phone: +45 3269 7788, fax: +45 3269 7789

North America
Copenhagen Business School Press
Books International Inc.
P.O. Box 605
Herndon, VA 20172-0605, USA
Phone: +1 703 661 1500, fax: +1 703 661 1501

Rest of the World
Marston Book Services, P.O. Box 269
Abingdon, Oxfordshire, OX14 4YN, UK
Phone: +44 (0) 1235 465500, fax: +44 (0) 1235 4656555
E-mail Direct Customers: direct.order@marston.co.uk
E-mail Booksellers: trade.order@marston.co.uk

All rights reserved. No part of this publication may be reproduced or used in any form or by any means - graphic, electronic or mechanical, including photocopying, recording, taping or information storage or retrieval systems - without permission in writing from Copenhagen Business School Press at www.cbspress.dk

Table of Contents

Table of Contents

Part Two: New Partnership Perspectives

Introduction

Esben Rahbek Pedersen

Ph.D. Fellow, Copenhagen Business School, Denmark

Abstract

Corporate citizenship has come from nowhere to be practically everywhere: An infinite number of scholars and practitioners sing its praise in annual reports, conference papers, journal articles and magazines; there has been an impressive growth in companies that formulate codes of conduct and publish social and environmental reports; more and more socially responsible investors place huge amounts of money in good corporate citizens; and, last but not least, a wide range of private consultants, NGOs, international organisations and governmental bodies have been involved in the development of social and environmental management standards, labelling schemes and reporting systems. Corporate citizenship and related terms (such as corporate social responsibility (CSR) and sustainable development) have swept across the world and become catchwords of the new millennium.[1]

How on earth did it come to that?

---

[1] Some see corporate citizenship as a replacement of CSR and treat the two concepts as synonyms, whereas others reserve the use of 'corporate citizenship' to philanthropy or the company's relationships with the local community (Andriof & McIntosh 2001; Wood et al. 2002; Wood & Logsdon 2001; Matten & Crane 2005). This introduction adopts the former approach. The introduction will adopt the view of Waddock (2004, p. 9), who defines corporate citizenship as: "(…) the strategies and operating practices a company develops in operationalizing its relationships with and impacts on stakeholders and the natural environment." It is outside the scope of this chapter to discuss whether this definition is in accordance with other authors' use of 'corporate citizenship'. The important matter is that the definition above acknowledges the close ties to the stakeholder theory and accepts the eclectic nature of corporate citizenship by refraining from limiting itself to specific strategies, specific stakeholders and/or specific social and environmental issues.

From 'Commie Plot' to Core Business

Despite its current popularity, corporate citizenship is by no means a new phenomenon. For instance, the phenomenon of philanthropy existed long before companies began to donate money for schools, libraries, sport facilities etc. (cf. Cannon 1994; Carroll & Buchholtz 1999; Smith 2003; Wulfson 2001). In fact, philanthropic giving to alleviate hunger was reported in Mesopotamia some 4400 years ago (Eson & Webb 1991).[2] Elements of altruism, philanthropy and benevolence can also be found in most religious traditions. In their role as 'communities of memory', religious institutions have produced and reproduced concern for others as a central value and a precondition for a healthy society for centuries (ibid.). However, in the wake of the industrial revolution, these ideas were brought into the realm of economy (cf. Cannon 1994). It is therefore the word 'corporate' we have to pay attention to if we want to understand the current fuss about corporate citizenship.

Before and during the early phases of industrialisation, the boundaries between individual and corporate citizenship were blurred, because the companies were often founded, owned and managed by the same person. When one man (as it usually was) personified the company instead of representing it, the *noblesse oblige* - the obligation of the privileged to be generous – of the individual was inseparable from that of the company. However, the industrial revolution and the increasing size, power and wealth of private corporations soon challenged the traditional systems of authority and responsibility.

Today, the private sector is often not dominated by individual tycoons. The management of companies is often delegated to a new group of professional leaders, whereas the ownership is divided between a diverse group of more or less passive and anonymous stockholders (cf. Cannon 1994; Post et al. 2002). The new business structure implies that societal expectations to the private sector also have to be redirected to the more abstract and artificial category - 'the company'. Combined with the growing importance of the private sector, it is not difficult to understand how the idea of corporate citizenship could emerge and become an important issue on the public agenda.

---

[2] Moreover, both Western and non-Western thinkers advocated for controlling the greed of businessmen centuries BC (Blowfield & Frynas 2005).

In the beginning, however, concepts like corporate citizenship and corporate social responsibility were met with a great deal of scepticism. They were regarded with suspicion and not something profit-oriented managers were expected to be interested in, let alone do something about. Some even argued that social and environmental responsibility could destroy democracy, the capitalist system and the free society (cf. Mintzberg 1983, Moir 2001; Friedman 1970). Even though some still consider corporate citizenship as a 'Commie Plot'[3], the concept has in general become much less controversial, not only in academia but also among companies, consultants, governmental bodies, NGOs and community-based organisations. The growing popularity of corporate citizenship is also manifested in the mushrooming of social and environmental management standards, labelling schemes and reporting systems. It is increasingly argued that corporate citizenship has (or should be) changed from being a peripheral add-on to the companies' everyday activities to being integrated in all core business functions (Cowe 2004; Tantram 2004; Dickson 2004).[4]

Corporate Citizenship in a Globalised World

Today, discussions on corporate citizenship are often linked to the phenomenon of globalisation (Matten & Crane 2005). Powered by the liberalisation of world trade, privatisation, breakthroughs in information technology and reduced transportation costs, the number of multinational corporations (MNCs) has increased from some 37,000 in 1990 to more than 60,000 today – with millions of foreign affiliates and suppliers (WEF 2005; Farrell 2004; Locke 2002). This de-territorialisation of the economy is a two-edged sword. On the one hand, globalisation can stimulate economic, social, and environmental growth in developing countries through industry development, job creation, technology transfer etc. On the other, globalisation makes it difficult for governmental institutions to effectively exert regulatory

---

[3] For instance, Bergkamp (2002, p. 146) notes that: "[ ]it is ironic that we see a revival in "social responsibility thinking shortly after the communist system almost completely collapsed. In a way, imposing social responsibilities is importing communism."

[4] As noted by Warhurst (2005, p.154): "Increasingly, international companies are embracing the concept of corporate citizenship, and are developing principles, policies, strategies and reporting procedures that define a completely different way of working – and not simply a nice to have 'add-on' like much environmental protection in the 1980s."

influence, because MNCs are able to exploit national differences in social and environmental legislation (cf. Jenkins 2001; McEwan 2001; Neergaard & Pedersen 2003). Moreover, some governments, especially in less developed countries, may also have an incentive to enforce low social and environmental standards in order to speed up industrialisation and development (Christmann & Taylor 2001; Selassie & Hill 1998).

Even though the empirical evidence of this 'race to the bottom' hypothesis is inconclusive[5], it has nonetheless led to more calls for corporate citizenship. When nation states are unable to regulate the global economy, companies are increasingly expected to self-regulate, e.g. by adopting social and environmental management systems, labelling schemes and reporting standards.[6] Moreover, MNCs are increasingly formulating codes of conduct, i.e. a set of written principles, guidelines or standards, which are intended to improve the company's social and environmental performance. According to the World Bank (2003), approximately 1,000 of these codes are estimated to be in existence today.

Corporate Citizenship and the Development Agenda

In the wake of globalisation, development issues are also increasingly incorporated in the corporate citizenship literature. Globalisation has also exposed national differences in standards, rights and responsibilities and drawn attention to the severe social and environmental problems facing a wide range of developing countries (see Table 1). In consequence, development is now a key issue on the corporate citizenship agenda and a growing number of especially

---

[5] For instance, some argue that MNCs actually help raise the social and environmental standards in developing countries. According to the International Finance Corporation (IFC) (2000, p. 17): "Multinational corporations also tend to abide by local laws and regulations more strictly than do local firms – often exceeding locally mandated standards – partly out of concern for their international reputations." Based on the results from 14 case studies, Farrell (2004, p. 52) concludes that: "(…) contrary to what critics charge, our case studies showed that foreign companies paid higher wages and were more likely to follow local labor laws than domestic companies in the same sector."

[6] However, it can be difficult to see how corporate citizenship can be the solution to problems caused by lack of corporate citizenship (especially when it is still unclear whether pollution prevention, social investments etc. always pay off). The boom in corporate scandals regarding e.g. violation of union rights, polluting production, use of child labour, dangerous working conditions and discrimination. clearly illustrate that problems caused by a lack of public regulation cannot be solved just by encouraging self-regulation.

MNCs make commitments to fight poverty, pollution, corruption, social exclusion, HIV/AIDS, malaria, etc. Some address development issues because they think it is the right thing to do, some because they believe that their stakeholders expect it, and some because they are aware that political, economic and social instability is a barrier to the realisation of the unutilised business opportunities in developing countries.

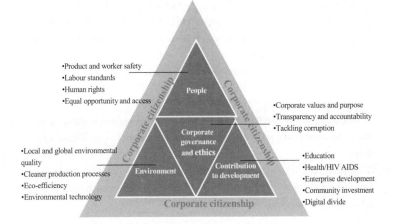

Figure 1 Key Corporate Citizenship Issues
Source: WEF (2003, p. 20)

Just as development issues have made their entrance on the corporate citizenship agenda, corporate citizenship is also beginning to take hold in the donor community (cf. Fox 2002; Michael 2003, Jenkins 2005). Corporate citizenship is increasingly seen as the private sector's contribution to development, and even though the term is not always used explicitly, a wide range of development agencies are now promoting responsible business practices in developing countries (cf. Vives 2004; Moberg 2004; Fox & Prescott 2004). This development is probably inspired by the current Zeitgeist and the fact that the private sector is increasingly seen as the 'engine of growth', the motor which is expected to push forward social and economic progress in developing countries (cf. Schulpen & Gibbon 2001; UN 1999). Private companies have become a key alliance partner in international development, whether it concerns conflict prevention, anti-corruption, human rights, healthcare or infrastructure development.

- The population of the 49 least developed countries is expected to grow by more than 1 billion in the next 50 years (Grayson & Hodges 2004).
- More than one billion people still live for less than one dollar per day, and poverty causes the death of 20,000 people each day (UN 2005).
- The number of internally displaced people is roughly 25 million (UN 2005).
- 2.4 billion people have inadequate sanitation and 1.2 billion have no access to clean drinking water (Grayson & Hodges 2004).
- It is estimated that 42 million adults and children are living with HIV/AIDS - 29 million in Sub-Saharan Africa. The population in 38 African countries greatly affected by HIV/AIDS will be 91 million (10%) smaller by 2015 than it would have been without AIDS (UN 2004).
- The world's rain forests will disappear within the next 100 years if the current rate of deforestation continues (NASA 1998).
- Malaria kills 3,000 people a day (WEF 2005).
- In 1999, approximately 115 million school-age children worldwide did not attend school. An estimated 94% of these children lived in developing countries (UN 2004).
- 120 million children aged between 5 and 14 work full-time (Waddell 2003).
- Pregnancy and childbirth cause the death of 585,000 women each year, of which 99% occur in developing countries (UN 2004).

Table 1 Examples of Development Issues

In other words, the private sector plays an important role in development thinking, and donor agencies and development finance institutions are now supplementing the economic instruments with corporate citizenship initiatives. Poverty reduction is still the main objective, but 'soft' issues, like working environment, training and technical assistance, gender equality and sustainable development, have found their way into policy papers and country strategies. In addition, development agencies have launched a wide range of pro-corporate citizenship programmes, which are intended to promote responsible business practices - either directly, by offering incentives for companies, or indirectly, by providing an enabling environment for sustainable business (cf. Schulpen & Gibbon 2001).

New Partnership Perspectives

In other words, we are beginning to see the contours of a merger between the agendas of development agencies and private companies (Moberg 2004; Pedersen 2005). Both business and donors seem to agree that the private sector is important in addressing development challenges. Moreover, there is also an emerging consensus on the means: partnerships.[7] Throughout the world, partnerships between business, governments, donor agencies and civil society are now playing an important role in addressing economic, social and environmental challenges in developing countries. For instance, partnerships were a key issue at the 2002 World Summit on Sustainable Development in Johannesburg and are a crucial element in achieving the United Nations Millennium Development Goals (UN 2003; UN 2004; MFA/DANIDA 2004). Moreover, in recent years a growing number of international organisations, donor agencies and development finance institutions have launched partnership initiatives as a means to promote responsible business practices. As noted by Covey and Brown (2001, pp. 1-2):

"Intersectoral partnerships are promoted by a diverse chorus of advocates, from multilateral agencies like the UN Global Compact and the Business Partners for Development (a business, civil society, World Bank partnership) to bilateral aid agencies such as USAID and DFID, to business support organisations such as the Prince of Wales Business Leaders Forum and The World Business Council for Sustainable Development. Many large international NGOs, such as CARE, ActionAid and Save the Children, are actively engaging with multinational and local corporations to support development programmes. Similarly local NGOs, business and governments are cooperating in a range of joint initiatives at the local level."

---

[7] I have chosen the neutral term 'partnerships' to describe the formal relations between representatives from the state, the market and/or the civil society. However, I am aware that there are wide range of related concepts that all try to capture the essence of the increased cooperation between the state, the market and/or the civil society, such as multi-stakeholder initiatives, tri-sector partnerships, cross-sector partnerships, intersectoral partnerships, public-private partnering, new social partnerships, global action networks etc. (Michael 2003; Utting 2001; Warhurst 2001; Zadek et al. 2001; Waddell 2003).

Figure 2 The State, the Market and the Civil Society Source: Pedersen (2005)

- The Deutsche Gesellschaft für Technische Zusammenarbeit (GTZ) has introduced a Public-Private Partnership (PPP) programme that covers a wide range of partnerships between GtZ, private companies, and/or associations. Over the years, the PPP programme has generated more than 300 partnerships in 60 countries (see: www.gtz.de).

- As a follow-up to the World Summit on Sustainable Development in Johannesburg, the Danish International Development Assistance (DANIDA) has also launched a PPP initiative that is expected to contribute to poverty reduction and sustainable development in developing countries. The PPP initiative includes a training programme for social responsibility, capacity building for researchers in developing countries, a programme for management cooperation, and a Business Linkage Programme between Denmark and Vietnam (MFA/DANIDA 2004).

- The United Nations Industrial Development Organization (UNIDO) is involved in a business partnership programme, as well as public-private partnership (PPP), cluster and networking programmes with MNCs and SMEs throughout the world. The work is based on the principles of the United Nations Global Compact (see: www.unido.org)

Continued on next page

> • The Global Development Alliance (GDA) is an initiative of the US Agency for
> International Development (USAID) that is intended to generate positive
> development impact through public-private alliances between USAID, NGOs,
> foundations and private companies (USAID 2003). According to USAID (2003), the
> objective of the GDA is to: *"(…) encourage economic growth, develop businesses
> and workforces, address health and environmental problems and expand access
> to education and technology"*.

Table 2. Examples of Partnership Initiatives

The Pros and Cons of Partnerships

The growing emphasis on partnerships does not only concern actors
operating in developing countries. On the contrary, partnerships have
become the universal solution to practically all problems - whether we
talk about healthcare, arts, social inclusion, poverty reduction, human
rights, post-conflict resolution or SME development. Some even argue
that we have entered the 'age of partnerships' and the 'partnership
society' (Googins & Rochlin 2000; Zadek 2001). The much talk about
partnerships, dialogue, participation, empowerment, involvement and
engagement reflects the overall societal tendency towards inclusion,
i.e. that people can and should be involved in decision-making
processes that affect their life. Moreover, partnerships can also be seen
as an ideological compromise in the ongoing regulation vs. self-
regulation debate. Partnerships essentially reflect a disillusion with
both the state and the market as the guarantor of social and economic
wealth. The basic premise seems to be that collaboration between
representatives from all sectors is required because existing approaches
to problem solving have failed to solve the complex problems of
today's society (cf. Waddell 2003; Covey & Brown 2001; Zadek et al.
2001).

At least two questions spring to mind. The first is: Why do
partnerships matter? Even though the partnership literature makes the
right diagnosis - that both state regulation and market self-regulation
are unable to solve the problems emerging in the wake of globalisation
- it does not necessarily follow that hybrid forms of organisation are
the cure. In order to be sufficiently alternative, it must be expected that
partnerships can potentially alleviate the weaknesses of each sector
while at the same time cultivate the strengths. However, there are few
guidelines when it comes to describing under which circumstances the
synergy between the three sectors will manifest itself. Partnerships
often remain at the level of lofty rhetoric and the root of the problem is

perhaps that they are often treated in theory and practice as something that is good by definition, a goal in itself, and not as one method out of many that are well-suited to solve only a limited set of problems (Googins & Rochlin 2000; Ostrower 2005).[8] The best example is probably the Millennium Development Goals, which explicitly consider partnerships between stakeholders from different sectors as an independent goal. There is a need to better understand when partnerships are the best means to achieve economic, social and environmental goals, and when they are not. Failing to do so will inevitably lead to an inefficient use of resources.

The second question is: Why should each sector get involved in partnerships with the others? This is a relevant question because partnerships essentially do not break with the voluntary nature of corporate citizenship and other types of self-regulation. It is almost a contradiction in terms to talk about mandatory partnerships. They might be a response to societal pressure, but they are still voluntary in the sense that they are not the product of state regulation. In consequence, there is a risk that partnerships will fail to deal with economic, social and environmental issues of a more controversial nature. Partnerships are unlikely to attract actors who do not see some benefits from these cooperative arrangements.

Summing Up: The Limits of the New Leviathan

Looking back, the period from the Second World War until the late 1970s was dominated by the idea that the state was the prime mover of economic, social and environmental development. From the early 1980s, however, the state was increasingly seen as the cause rather than the solution to practically all problems (Adelman 2000; Peters 1996; Schulpen & Gibbon 2001). This ideological transformation was followed by a wide range of more market/less government reforms and especially Ronald Reagan and Margaret Thatcher came to personify a new era characterised by self-regulation, privatisation, deregulation, trade liberalisation and commercialisation (cf. Neergaard & Pedersen 2003; Utting 2001). The wave of market-friendly initiatives in the 1980s also had a positive impact on the corporate citizenship movement (Windsor 2001; Utting 2001). After all, if there was great confidence in governmental institutions and their ability to regulate the

---

[8] In a study of 1,192 grantmakers, 42% responded that partnering was a precondition for funding (Ostrower 2005).

economy, there would be little reason why scholars and practitioners should devote so much time and energy to discussions of corporate citizenship.

However, the idea that companies could self-regulate soon started to attract criticism (Jenkins 2005; Utting 2001). The corporate scandals in the 1990s and the mixed blessings of market-friendly regimes experienced by some developing countries made more people question the free and unregulated capitalism. However, the apparent failure of both the state and the market to be the hegemonic actor, able to regulate the economic, social and environmental development, created a vacuum waiting to be filled by a new central authority. This disillusion with existing forms of governance has prepared the ground for the current wave of partnerships. When globalisation makes public regulation difficult and market failures place limitations on the benefits that can be expected from self-regulation, private companies, public authorities and/or civil society organisations have to join forces in order to achieve social, environmental and economic goals. In these partnerships, the dichotomy between voluntary self-regulation and mandatory regulation is dissolved and what we see instead is a wide range of more complex governance structures.

However, it is difficult to see how partnerships can be the new Leviathan. After all, there is a fine line between cliquishness and cooperation, and partnerships can both become a forum for participatory and inclusive democracy as well as an arena for very undemocratic and highly exclusive decision-making processes (Pedersen 2005; Zadek 2001). Moreover, the voluntary character of partnerships implies that this type of governance is unlikely to rule out economically, socially and environmentally irresponsible behaviour.

In conclusion, partnerships can hardly be seen as a panacea that is capable of eliminating all social and environmental challenges in today's globalised and polycentric world. However, this does not mean they are without importance. Even if partnerships were just castles in the air, they are still important because they are perceived as such. When private companies, policy-makers, civil society organisations etc. increasingly embrace the concept of partnerships, it is reasonable to expect that these partnerships will sooner or later have an impact on the way we organise society. Like the old saying: "(…) if people define a situation as real, it tends to become real in its consequence" (W.I. Thomas, in Bauman 2001, p. 101).

Moreover, it is also important to emphasise that partnerships inevitably offer many interesting potentials. The list is exhaustive and I will only mention a few of the *potential* benefits from partnerships in relation to corporate citizenship:

- Partnerships can have positive reputation effects for companies.
- Partnerships can lever more resources for promoting responsible business practices.
- Partnerships can be a trust-building instrument for the participants.
- Partnerships can improve the legitimacy of corporate citizenship initiatives.
- Partnerships can improve the quality of monitoring and verification.
- Partnerships can generate synergies by alleviating some of the weaknesses and nurturing the strengths of the individual partners.
- Partnerships can make it easier to solve multidimensional problems that are caused by a wide range of economic, political and social factors.
- Partnerships can optimise the allocation of resources spent on corporate citizenship.
- Partnerships expand the networks of the actors involved in the partnerships.
- Partnerships open possibilities for skill-sharing, learning and capacity-building.
- Partnerships between representatives from the state, the market and/or the civil society can help obviate overlap and duplication.
- Partnerships can increase the commitment to responsible business practices and ensure that corporate citizenship initiatives do not become isolated events.

In consequence, there are many good reasons to examine when, how and why partnerships can contribute to the solution of the problems facing the world today. Hopefully, this book can make a small contribution here.

The Objective of this Book

This book is about corporate citizenship in developing countries. It covers a wide range of contributions from scholars and practitioners with an interest in corporate citizenship, CSR, environmental management, private sector development etc. The book presents different perspectives on corporate citizenship in developing countries, paying special attention to the new partnerships between business and development agencies.

Some of the contributors have a critical approach to corporate citizenship, whereas others adopt a more positive view. This is intentional on the part of the editors because the objective of this book is to stimulate discussion rather than to try to build consensus. Hopefully, this book will contribute to the ongoing debate of corporate citizenship in developing countries and the role of partnerships as a means to address the development challenges of the world today.

Happy reading!

Bibliography

Adelman, I. (2000). The role of government in economic development, p. 48-55 in Tarp, F. (ed.), Foreign aid and development. London: Routledge.

Andriof, J. and McIntosh, M. (2001). Introduction, p. 14-24 in Andriof, J. & McIntosh, M. (eds.), Perspectives on Corporate Citizenship. Sheffield, UK: Greenleaf Publishing Ltd.

Bauman, Z. (2001). Community: Seeking Safety in an Insecure World. Cambridge: Polity Press.

Bergkamp, L. (2002). Corporate Governance and Social Responsibility: a New Sustainability Paradigm? European Environmental Law Review, [May 2002], p. 136-152.

Blowfield, M. & Frynas, J. G. (2005). Setting new agendas: critical perspectives on Corporate Social Responsibility in the developing world, International Affairs, 81[3], p. 499-513.

Cannon, T. (1994). Corporate Responsibility. Edinburgh Gate, Harlow, England: Pearson Education Limited.

Carroll, A. B. & Buchholtz, A. K. (1999). Business & Society - Ethics and Stakeholder Management. Cincinnati, Ohio: South-Western College Publishing.

Christmann, P. & Taylor, G. (2001). Globalization and the Environment: Determinants of Firm Self-Regulation in China, Journal of International Business Studies, 32[3], p. 439-458.

Covey, J. & Brown, L. D. (2001). Critical Cooperation: An Alternative Form of Civil Society-Business Engagement, IDR Reports, 17[1], p. 1-18.

Cowe, R. (2004). CSR hits the boardroom, European Business Forum [Summer 2004], p. 7-9.

Dickson, T. (2004). CSR: moving on to the front foot, European Business Forum [Summer 2004], p. 2.

Eson, M. E. & Webb, E. J. (1991). Altruism and Philanthropy: Religious and Secular Approaches. 1991. Stanford: Stanford University/Graduate School of Business.

Farrell, D. (2004). The Case for Globalization, The International Economy [Winter 2004], p. 52-55.

Fox, T. (2002). Development Agency Round Table on Corporate Social Responsibility - Round Table Report. London: International Institute for Environment and Development (IIED). http://www.iied.org/docs/cred/cred_roundtable.pdf

Fox, T. & Prescott, D. (2004). Exploring the role of development cooperation agencies in corporate responsibility. London: International Institute for Environment and Development (IIED). http://www.iied.org/docs/cred/report.pdf

Friedmann, M. (1970). The social responsibility of business is to increase its profits, New York Times Magazine, p. 32-33.

Googins, B. K. & Rochlin, S. A. (2000). Creating the Partnership Society: Understanding the Rhetoric and Reality of Cross-Sectoral Partnerships, Business and Society Review, 105[1], p. 127-144.

Grayson, D. & Hodges, A. (2004). Corporate Social Opportunity! Seven Steps to make Corporate Social Responsibility work for your Business. Sheffield: Greenleaf Publishing.

IFC (2000). Paths out of Poverty: The Role of Private Enterprise in Developing Countries. Washington, D.C.: International Finance Corporation (IFC).

Jenkins, R. (2005). Globalization, Corporate Social Responsibility and Poverty, International Affairs, 81[3], p. 525-540.

Jenkins, R. (2001). Corporate Codes of Conduct: Self-Regulation in a Global Economy. Geneva, Switzerland: United Nations Research Institute for Social Development (UNRISD).

Locke, R. M. (2002). Note on Corporate Citizenship in a Global Economy. Cambridge, MA: Industrial Performance Center, Massachusetts Institute of Technology.

Matten, D. & Crane, A. (2005). Corporate Citizenship: Toward an Extended Theoretical Conceptualization, Academy of Management Review, 30[1], p. 166-179.

McEwan, T. (2001). Managing Values and Beliefs in Organisations. Harlow: Financial Times/Prentice Hall.

MFA/DANIDA (2004). Public-Private Partnerships in the Development Cooperation: Five New Programmes. Copenhagen: Ministry of Foreign Affairs (MFA)/Danish International Development Assistance (DANIDA).

Michael, B. (2003). Corporate Social Responsibility in International Development: An Overview and Critique, Corporate Social Responsibility and Environmental Management, 10[3], p. 115-128.

Mintzberg, H. (1983). The Case for Corporate Social Responsibility, The Journal of Business Strategy, 4[2], p. 3-15.

Moberg, J. (2004). How Sida promotes responsible business practices, a fact-finding study. Stockholm, Sweden: Sida.

Moir, L. (2001). What do we mean by corporate social responsibility? Corporate Governance, 1[2], p. 16-22.

NASA (1998). Tropical Deforestation, NASA Facts, November 1998. National Aeronautics and Space Administration (NASA). http://eospso.gsfc.nasa.gov/ftp_docs/Deforestation.pdf

Neergaard, P. & Pedersen, E. R. (2003). Corporate Social Behaviour: Between the Rules of the Game and the Law of the Jungle, Journal of Corporate Citizenship, 12, p. 43-57.

Ostrower, F. (2005). The Reality Underneath the Buzz of Partnerships: The Potentials and Pitfalls of Partnering, Stanford Social Innovation Review [Spring 2005], p. 34-41.www.ssireview.com

Pedersen, E. R. (2005). Guiding the Invisible Hand: - The Role of Development Agencies in Driving Corporate Citizenship, Forthcoming in Journal of Corporate Citizenship.

Peters, B. G. (1996). Governing: Four emerging Models. Lawrence: University Press of Kansas.

Post, J. E., Preston, L. E. & Sachs, S. (2002). Redefining the Corporation: Stakeholder Management and Organizational Wealth. California: Stanford University Press.

Schulpen, L. & Gibbon, P. (2001). Private Sector Development: Policies, Practices and Problems. Copenhagen: Centre for Development Research (CDR). www.cdr.dk

Selassie, H. & Hill, R. (1998). The Business Environment for IJV Formation in LDCs: A Case Study, p. 238-253 in Hooley, G., Loveridge, R. & Wilson, D. (eds), Internationalization: Process, Context and Markets. Hampshire: Macmillan Press Ltd.

Smith, N. C. (2003). Corporate Social Responsibility: Whether or How? California Management Review, 45[4], p. 52-76.

Tantram, J. (2004). CSR: drivers and challenges, European Business Forum, [Summer 2004], p. 20-21.

UN (1999). Looking Ahead - A Common Country Assessment of Viet Nam. Hanoi: United Nations.

UN (2003). Partnership for Sustainable Development. New York: United Nations (UN)/Department of Public Information and the UN Department of Economic and Social Affairs.

UN (2004). Development and Globalization: Facts and Figures. New York and Geneva: United Nations (UN). http://www.unctad.org/en/docs/gdscsir20041_en.pdf

UN (2005). In larger freedom: towards development, security and human rights for all. New York: United Nations. http://daccessdds.un.org/doc/UNDOC/GEN/N05/270/78/PDF/N05270 78.pdf?OpenElement

USAID (2003). The Global Development Alliance: Expanding the Impact of Foreign Assistance through Public-Private Alliances. Washington D.C.: U.S. Agency for International Development.
http://www.usaid.gov/our_work/global_partnerships/gda/pnact008com pliant.pdf

Utting, P. (2001). Regulating Business via Multistakeholder Initiatives: A Preliminary Assessment, Voluntary Approaches to Corporate Responsibility - readings and resource guide. Geneva: UN Non-Governmental Liaison Service, NGLS.
http://www.unsystem.org/ngls/Section%20II.pdf

Vives, A. (2004). The Role of Multilateral Development Institutions in Fostering Corporate Social Responsibility, Development, 47[3], p. 45-52.

Waddell, S. (2003). Global Action Networks: A Global Invention Helping Business Make Globalisation Work for All, Journal of Corporate Citizenship, 12, p. 27-42. 2003.

Waddock, S. (2004). Parallel Universes: Companies, Academics, and the Progress of Corporate Citizenship, Business & Society Review, 109[1], p. 5-42.

Warhurst, A. (2005). Future roles of business in society: the expanding boundaries of corporate responsibility and a compelling case for partnership, Futures, 37[2-3].

Warhurst, A. (2001). Corporate Citizenship and Corporate Social Investment: Drivers of Tri-Sector Partnerships, Journal of Corporate Citizenship, 1[1], p. 57-73.

WEF (2005). Partnering for Success: Business Perspectives on Multistakeholder Partnerships 2005. Geneva: World Economic Forum (WEF).

Windsor, D. (2001). The Future of Corporate Social Responsibility, The International Journal of Organizational Analysis, 9[3], p. 225-256.

Wood, D. J., Davenport, K. S., Blockson, L. C. & Van Buren III, H. J. (2002). Corporate Involvement in Community Economic

Development: The Role of U.S. Business Education, Business & Society, 41[2], p. 208-241.

Wood, D. J. & Logsdon, J. M. (2001). Theorising business citizenship, p. 83-103 in Andriof, J., McIntosh, M. (eds.), Perspectives on Corporate Citizenship. Sheffield: Greenleaf Publishing.

World Bank (2003). Strengthening Implementation of Corporate Social Responsibility In Global Supply Chains. Washington: The World Bank Group.

Wulfson, M. (2001). The Ethics of Corporate Social Responsibility and Philanthropic Ventures, Journal of Business Ethics, 29, p. 135-145.

Zadek, S. (2001). Partnership alchemy: engagement, innovation and governance, p. 200-214. in Andriof, J. & McIntosh, M. (eds.) Perspectives on Corporate Citizenship. Sheffield, UK: Greenleaf Publishing Limited.

Zadek, S., Hojensgard, N. & Raynard, P. (2001). The New Economy of Corporate Citizenship, p. 13-29 in Zadek, S., Hojensgard, N. & Raynard, P. (eds.), Perspectives on the New Economy of Corporate Citizenship. Copenhagen: The Copenhagen Centre.

PART ONE

CORPORATE CITIZENSHIP IN DEVELOPING COUNTRIES

CHAPTER 1

REVISITING CARROLL'S CSR PYRAMID

AN AFRICAN PERSPECTIVE

Wayne Visser

Ph.D. Fellow, The University of Nottingham, United Kingdom.
Special Advisor, Sustainability Services, KPMG South Africa

"African poverty and stagnation is the greatest tragedy of our time."
Commission for Africa, 2005

Abstract

This chapter explores the nature of corporate social responsibility (CSR) in an African context, using Carroll's CSR Pyramid as a framework for descriptive analysis. Carroll's CSR Pyramid is probably the most well-known model of CSR, with its four levels indicating the relative importance of economic, legal, ethical and philanthropic responsibilities respectively. However, the exploration of CSR in Africa is also used to challenge the accuracy and relevance Carroll's CSR Pyramid. If Carroll's basic four-part model is accepted, it is suggested that the relative priorities of CSR in Africa are likely to be different from the classic, American ordering. However, it is also proposed that Carroll's CSR Pyramid may not be the best model for understanding CSR in general, and CSR in Africa in particular.

Introduction

This chapter has two primary objectives: 1) to use Carroll's corporate social responsibility (CSR) Pyramid to illustrate the nature of CSR in Africa; and 2) to use the context of Africa to demonstrate the limitations of Carroll's CSR Pyramid as a framework for understanding CSR. Anglo American is used as a case study to illustrate the debate.

The African Context

The debate over Africa's future has taken centre stage recently, with the publication of *Our Common Interest*, the report of the Commission for Africa (2005). The report calls for improved governance and capacity building, the pursuit of peace and security, investment in people, economic growth and poverty reduction, and increased and fairer trade. It is not hard to see that business has a key role to play in this transformation process, with much of its contribution capable of being framed in terms of CSR.

Despite generally negative press, there has been significant progress on the continent over the past decade. Fifteen countries, including Uganda, Ethiopia and Burkina Faso, have been growing on average more than 5% per year since the mid-1990s. And foreign direct investment (FDI) rose to $8.5 billion in 2004, up from $7.8 billion the previous year (World Bank, 2005a). Africa's new generation of leaders, through initiatives like the New Partnership for Africa's Development (NEPAD)[9], the African Union[10] and the East African Community[11], are taking responsibility for development (Lundy & Visser, 2003).

Nevertheless, Africa remains a marginal region in global terms. With 12% of the world's population (around 750 million people) in 53 countries, Africa accounts for less than 2% of global gross domestic product (GDP) and FDI, and less than 10% of FDI to all developing countries (African Development Bank, 2003, 2004). Of the 81 poorest countries prioritised by the International Development Association, almost half are in Africa (World Bank, 2005a). And even within Africa, there is highly skewed development, with the largest ten economies accounting for 75% of the continent's GDP (African Development Bank, 2004).

---

[9] http://www.nepad.org/
[10] http://www.africa-union.org/
[11] http://www.eac.int/

The extent of the challenge for CSR in Africa becomes even clearer when we are reminded of the scale of social needs that still exist, despite decades of aid and development effort: life expectancy in Africa is still only 50 years on average (and as low as 38 years in some countries), Gross National Income per capita averages $650 (and drops as low as $90 in some countries) and the adult literacy rate is less than 20% in some countries (World Bank, 2004). At the current pace of development, Sub-Saharan Africa would not reach the Millennium Development Goals[12] for poverty reduction[13] until 2147 and for child mortality[14] until 2165; and as for HIV/AIDS and hunger, trends in the region are heading up, not down (UNDP, 2004).

The Role of Business

The track record of big business in Africa is mixed at best. There is certainly no shortage of examples of corporate complicity in political corruption, environmental destruction, labour exploitation and social disruption, stretching back more than 100 years (Christian Aid, 2004; Malan, 2005; Pakenham, 1992; Transparency International, 2005; UN Security Council, 2002). Equally, however, there is voluminous evidence of the benefits of business bringing capital investment, job creation, skills transfer, infrastructure development, knowledge sharing and social responsibility programmes to countries throughout Africa (African Development Bank, 2004; Fourie & Eloff, 2005; IBLF, 1995, 2002a; SustainAbility, 2002; Visser, 1999, 2005a).

Despite this polarisation of the debate, there is general agreement that the private sector remains one of the best placed institutions to make a significant positive contribution towards improving social, economic and environmental conditions in Africa. Recognition of this role is especially evident in the recent spate of publications on the potential of business to impact on development (IBLF & WBCSD, 2004; Nelson & Prescott, 2003) and poverty alleviation (IBLF, 2002b; Prahalad, 2004; Prahalad & Hammond, 2002; WBCSD, 2004). These envisaged corporate contributions are most often discussed in terms of CSR. This begs the question: CSR according to what (or whose) definition? And is it a definition that is relevant to the African context?

---

[12] http://www.developmentgoals.org/

[13] Target 1: Halve, between 1990 and 2015, the proportion of people whose income is less than one dollar a day; Target 2: Halve, between 1990 and 2015, the proportion of people who suffer from hunger. http://www.developmentgoals.org/

[14] Target 5: Reduce by two-thirds, between 1990 and 2015, the under-five mortality rate. http://www.developmentgoals.org/

Carroll's CSR Pyramid

Defining CSR

According to Carroll (1983), "corporate social responsibility involves the conduct of a business so that it is economically profitable, law abiding, ethical and socially supportive. To be socially responsible then means that profitability and obedience to the law are foremost conditions when discussing the firm's ethics and the extent to which it supports the society in which it exists with contributions of money, time and talent" (p.608). By Carroll's (1999) own admission, this is only one of countless definitions which have proliferated in the literature since the 1950s.

This diversity of conception is testimony to Moon's (2002) observation that CSR, similar to other important concepts like democracy and justice, is "essentially contested". Moon (2002) also makes the point that CSR "is only one of several terms in currency designed to capture the practices and norms of new business-society relations. There are contending names, concepts or appellations for corporate social responsibility" (p.3).

This is confirmed by a survey of CSR education in Europe, which found 50 different labels for CSR modules, 40 different labels for CSR programmes and numerous CSR synonyms, the most popular of which were: business ethics, corporate citizenship, sustainability or sustainable development, corporate environmental management, business & society, business & governance, business & globalisation, and stakeholder management. Reviews of CSR literature by Carroll (1994; 1999) and Garriga & Mele (2003) reach similar conclusions regarding multiplicity of aligned terms.

Nevertheless, common ground between these nuanced concepts and CSR is widely acknowledged (Madsen & Ulhoi, 2001; Moon, 2002; Van Marrewijk, 2003; Wheeler, Colbert, & Freeman, 2003). The definition of corporate responsibility by Sustainability (2004) is a good illustration of this confluence and interdependence of terms, describing it "an approach to business that embodies transparency and ethical behaviour, respect for stakeholder groups and a commitment to add economic, social and environmental value" (p.4).

For the purposes of this chapter, therefore, CSR is viewed as an umbrella concept, which includes corporate citizenship, corporate sustainability, stakeholder management, environmental management, business ethics and corporate social performance. However, it is Carroll's definition of CSR which will serve as the framework for further analysis and discussion.

Despite the plethora of CSR definitions over the last 50 years, Carroll's four-part conceptualisation has been the most durable and widely cited in the literature (Crane & Matten, 2004). Some of the reasons for this could be that:

1. The model is simple, easy to understand and has an intuitively appealing logic;
2. Over the 25 years since Carroll first proposed the model, it has been frequently reproduced in top management and CSR journals, mostly by Carroll himself (Carroll, 1979, 1983, 1991, 1994, 1998, 2000, 2004);
3. Carroll has sought to assimilate various competing themes into his model, e.g. corporate citizenship (Carroll, 1998) and stakeholders (Carroll, 2004);
4. The model has been empirically tested and largely supported by the findings (Aupperle, Carroll, & Hatfield, 1985; Pinkston & Carroll, 1994); and
5. The model incorporates and gives top priority to the economic dimension as an aspect of CSR, which may endear business scholars and practitioners. In fact, Carroll (1991) goes so far as to point out how little his definition of CSR differs from Friedman's (1970) view of the responsibilities of the firm.

Representations of CSR

Carroll (1979) first delineated the now-familiar four categories of CSR in a paper on corporate social performance, depicting them as ordered layers which he labelled economic, legal, ethical and discretionary responsibilities (see Figure 1:1).

Carroll (1979) explained that the four classes "are simply to remind us that motives or actions can be categorised as primarily one or another of these four kinds" (p.500). The order and relative weighting was "to suggest what might be termed their fundamental role in the evolution of importance" (p.500). In its first conception, therefore, the framework took a retrospective developmental perspective, based on the claim that "the history of business suggests an early emphasis on the economic and then legal aspects and a later concern for the ethical and discretionary aspects" (p.500).

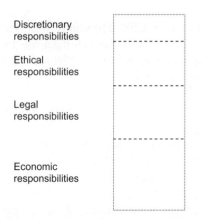

Figure 1:1 Social Responsibility Categories (Carroll, 1979)

In 1991, Carroll (1991) first presented his CSR model as a pyramid, as shown in Figure 1:2. He once again uses his original historical explanation for the relative weighting, saying: "To be sure, all these kinds of responsibilities have always existed to some extent, but it has only been in recent years that ethical and philanthropic functions have taken a significant place" (p.40). He also introduces dependence as a rationale, "beginning with the basic building block notion that economic performance undergirds all else" (p.42). Finally, he suggests that, although the components are not mutually exclusive, it "helps the manager to see that the different types of obligations are in a constant tension with one another" (p.42).

Figure 1:2 The Pyramid of Corporate Social Responsibility (Carroll, 1991)

Carroll (1998) appeared to briefly retract his dubious equating of philanthropy with corporate citizenship and to abandon his pyramid concept by reconceiving his model as "the four faces of corporate citizenship", but soon returned to his original construct (Carroll, 2000). Most recently, Carroll (2004) reproduced his 1991 CSR pyramid once again, but this time attempted to incorporate the notion of stakeholders, in terms of which economic responsibility contains the admonition to "do what is *required* by global capitalism", legal responsibility holds that companies "do what is *required* by global stakeholders", ethical responsibility means to "do what is *expected* by global stakeholders", and philanthropic responsibility means to "do what is desired by global stakeholders" (author's original emphasis).

Empirical Evidence

Aupperle, Hatfield & Carroll (1985; 1983) performed the first empirical test of the four part CSR model by surveying 241 Forbes 500-listed CEOs using 171 statements about CSR. The statistical analysis supported the model in two ways: 1) by confirming that there are four empirically interrelated, but conceptually independent components of CSR; and 2) by giving tentative support to the relative weightings Carroll earlier assigned to each of the four components. It is worth noting, however, that in this second conceptualisation, Carroll's framework reflects the perceptions of business leaders about the current relative importance of the four CSR categories, rather than an historical or dependence perspective.

In an effort to extend the earlier empirical analysis (Aupperle et al., 1985), Pinkston & Carroll (1994) performed a similar survey among top managers in 591 US subsidiaries of multinational chemical companies with headquarters in England, France, Germany, Japan, Sweden, Switzerland and the USA. Aggregate findings once again confirmed Carroll's four-part weighted model but interestingly showed Germany and Sweden to be exceptions, where legal responsibilities were ranked the highest priority followed by economic, ethical, and philanthropic aspects respectively. Comparison with the Aupperle, Hatfield & Carroll's (1985) findings also showed that in the intervening ten years the gap between the relative weightings of economic and legal responsibilities had decreased while ethical responsibilities had appeared to increase. Philanthropic responsibilities, on the other hand, had decreased in importance during this same period (Pinkston & Carroll, 1996).

Another study tested Carroll's CSR Pyramid on a sample of 503 large, black-owned businesses in the USA, suggesting the importance of culture (Edmondson & Carroll, 1999). The survey found that, while the economic component was rated as most important, ethical responsibilities were prioritised above legal responsibilities, and the differential between philanthropic and legal responsibilities was relatively small. A further study with a cultural dimension compared the views of 165 Hong Kong and 157 US students on CSR and found that Hong Kong students emphasised economic aspects more strongly than their US counterparts, and gave no difference in weighting between legal and ethical dimensions of CSR (Burton, Farh, & Hegarty, 2000).

The table below summarises the mean values of these various empirical studies.

Studies	Mean values			
	Economic orientations	Legal orientations	Ethical orientations	Philanthropic orientations
Aupperle, Carroll & Hatfield (1985)	3.50	2.54	2.22	1.30
Pinkston & Carroll (1994)	3.28	3.07	2.45	1.15
England	*3.49*	*3.15*	*2.29*	*0.98*
France	*3.60*	*3.04*	*2.35*	*0.98*
Germany	*2.86*	*3.21*	*2.46*	*1.42*
Japan	*3.34*	*2.76*	*2.42*	*1.41*
Sweden	*3.27*	*3.30*	*2.43*	*1.00*
Switzerland	*3.11*	*3.04*	*2.70*	*1.10*
USA	*3.11*	*2.96*	*2.48*	*1.19*
Edmondson & Carroll (1999)	3.16	2.12	2.19	2.04
Burton, Farh & Hegarty (2000)	-	-	-	-
Hong Kong	*3.11*	*2.32*	*2.32*	*1.84*
USA	*2.81*	*2.42*	*2.51*	*1.99*

Table 1:1 Comparison of CSR Studies Using Carroll's Pyramid Concept

Africa's CSR Pyramid

Most of the research on Carroll's CSR Pyramid has been in an American context. Nevertheless, several of the empirical studies already discussed suggest that culture may have an important influence on perceived CSR priorities (Burton et al., 2000; Edmondson et al., 1999; Pinkston et al., 1994). Crane & Matten (2004) address this point explicitly by discussing CSR in a European context using Carroll's CSR Pyramid. They conclude that "all levels of CSR play a role in Europe, but they have different significance, and furthermore are interlinked in a somewhat different manner" (p.46).

In the same way that Crane and Matten (2004) have used Carroll's pyramid to describe CSR in Europe, this section will use the four-part construct to look at how CSR manifests itself in an African context. Although no comparative empirical study has been conducted, it is speculatively argued that the order of the layers in Africa – if they are taken as an indicator of relative emphasis assigned to various responsibilities – differs from Carroll's classic pyramid. In Africa, economic responsibilities still get the most emphasis. However, philanthropy is given second highest priority, followed by legal and then ethical responsibilities. This is illustrated in Figure 1:3.

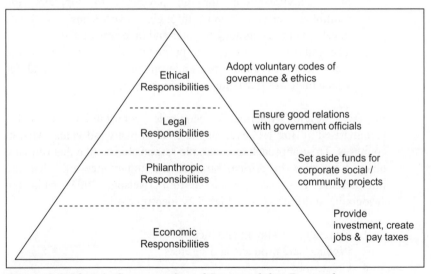

Figure 1:3 Africa's Corporate Social Responsibility Pyramid

Economic Responsibilities

As already pointed out in the introduction, Africa suffers from a shortage of foreign direct investment. Furthermore, many African countries suffer from high unemployment – the most recent consolidated statistics (1997) show that only 43% of Africa's labour force participates in the continental economy (African Development Bank, 2003). Poverty is also widespread (the proportion of the population living on less than $1 a day is as high as 70% in some countries) and external debt is crippling (in some countries exceeding Gross National Income) (African Development Bank, 2004).

It is no surprise, therefore, that the economic contribution of companies in Africa is highly prized, by governments and communities alike. Crane & Matten (2004) claim that economic responsibility in the USA is strongly focused on profitability and returns to shareholders, while companies in continental Europe tend to define this contribution much more widely. The latter could also be said of African companies. To use Anglo American (2003) as an example, they emphasise in their *Report to Society 2003* (a form of CSR reporting) that "our economic contribution extends far beyond the profits we generate and can be divided into:

1. Value added in the course of production and the wider effects of these activities (e.g. through payments to suppliers and multiplier effects) and through investments in staff development, technology transfer and investment; and
2. The value to society of our products, which are used in the manufacture of goods that underpin our way of life and for which there are few ready substitutes" (p.53).

In fact, Anglo American's economic contribution in Africa (summarised in Box 1:1) exceeds the GDP of many individual African countries. Their approach to economic responsibility, like that of many other companies in Africa, stresses the importance of what the International Business Leaders Forum (Nelson, 2003) calls the "economic multipliers", of which they identify eight:

1. Generate investment and income
2. Produce safe products and services
3. Create jobs
4. Invest in human capital
5. Establish local business linkages
6. Spread international business standards
7. Support technology transfer
8. Build physical and institutional infrastructure

Employment:	135,000 employees
Value added*:	$3.3 billion
Distribution of economic benefits -	
Employees:	$1.9 billion
Suppliers:	$4.2 billion
Tax and related payments to governments -	
South Africa:	$606 million
Mali:	$24 million
Capital expenditure:	$1.8 billion
Black economic empowerment -	
Procurement from black-owned companies:	$411 million
Value of empowerment transactions:	$424 million
Proportion of South African management from historically disadvantaged groups	35%
Shareholders:	Mostly institutional; 32% are resident in South Africa
National presence:	Botswana, Guinea, Mali, Namibia, South Africa, Tanzania, Zimbabwe

* Value added is the difference between the value received for the sale of products and the cost of the materials required for production. Source: (Anglo American, 2003)

Box 1:1 Anglo American's Economic Contribution in Africa (2003)

In a country like South Africa, where business is being actively encouraged (and in some cases required) to redress the inequities of the past, economic contribution takes on the added dimension of black economic empowerment and employment equity (affirmative action). For example, Anglo American is now subject to the South African Mining Charter, which is a legally binding commitment by the industry to increase the access of previously disadvantaged individuals to the mineral resources of the country and their associated economic benefits. They do this through prioritised development and promotion of previously disadvantaged staff, entering into financial partnerships with empowerment companies and prioritised procurement from black-owned firms. In addition, Anglo American has established the $5.3 million Anglo Khula Mining Fund to promote the entry of black economic empowerment participants into junior mining companies.

It is worth noting as a caveat to conclude this section that, in Africa, economic responsibility has two faces – economic contribution on the one side and economic dependence on the other. To use a different example, as a result of BHP Billiton's construction of the Mozal aluminium smelter in Maputo, Mozambique's export earnings went from \$220 million to \$1 billion, and the net positive impact on the country's balance of payments was around \$100 million. In 2002, Mozal accounted for 53% of Mozambique's exports, 28% of imports and added 2.1% real GDP growth to the economy (BHP Billiton, 2003). The economic contribution is clear, but so is the dependence. What would be the economic impact if they were to withdraw from the country, for whatever reason (as did Anglo American from Zambia in 2002)? And what are the implications for legal compliance and ethical conduct, when the government is so dependent on a single company?

Philanthropic Responsibilities

Crane & Matten (2004) note that philanthropic responsibility in Europe tends to be rather more compulsory via the legal framework than discretionary acts of successful companies or rich capitalists like in the USA. In this respect, Africa has more in common with the American model, although philanthropy generally gets an even higher priority as a manifestation of CSR in Africa. This is the case for a number of reasons. In the first instance, the socio-economic needs of the African societies in which companies operate are so great that philanthropy is an expected norm – it is considered the right thing to do by business. Companies also realise that they cannot succeed in societies that fail, and philanthropy is seen as the most direct way to improve the prospects of the communities in which business operates.

Secondly, many African societies have become reliant on foreign aid. In 2002, Sub-Saharan Africa received around \$19 billion of official development assistance (ODA), which equates to \$28 per capita, compared with an average of \$11 for the world (African Development Bank, 2004). A study of philanthropy by US Foundations showed that in 2002, Sub-Saharan Africa received around \$150 million from American grantmakers alone (Foundation Centre, 2004). Hence, there is an ingrained culture of philanthropy in Africa. Fox (2004) also argues that "the contemporary CSR agenda is skewed by the dogma that often limits it to voluntary business activities, by its domination by actors in the North, and its focus on large enterprises" (29).

A third reason for Africa's philanthropy prioritisation is that it is generally still at an early stage of maturity in CSR, sometimes even equating CSR and philanthropy, rather than the more embedded approaches now common in developed countries. Southern African

Grantmakers' Association[15] typifies this corporate emphasis on philanthropy, with its membership comprising corporations with social responsibility programmes, international donor organisations, local private foundations, grantmaking non-governmental organisations, community foundations and government funding agencies. A similar (but US-based) organisation is the Africa Grantmakers' Affinity Group.[16]

There are no consolidated figures for corporate philanthropy in Africa. However, Trialogue (2004a) estimates that the total corporate expenditure on corporate social investment (CSI) in South Africa for the 2003 financial year was R2.35 billion (around $385 million), 6.8% higher than in 2002. Based on the total CSI budget of a sample of 100 leading corporate grantmakers, the average CSI budget per company in South African in 2003 was R13 million ($2.1 million). In terms of the priority issues, education funding made up 39% of CSI spent in 2003, up from 35% in 2000, while spending on health (including HIV/AIDS) is up to around 10% in 2003, and a similar proportion to support for job creation initiatives. Other areas, in order of declining budget proportion, were training, social development, arts and culture, community and rural development, environment, sports development, safety and security, and housing.

Anglo American is once again a good example, typifying the philanthropic approach taken by many companies in Africa. In their *Report to Society 2003,* Anglo American (2003) support the main contention of this section when they say that "in developing countries there is still a significant role for philanthropic programmes" (p.48). Their primary vehicle for charitable engagement in Africa is the Anglo American Chairman's Fund, which was established in 1975 and aims "to enable people to take greater control over their daily lives" (p.48). The largest proportion of the $10 million distributed in 2003 went to education (51%). Further details of their philanthropic contribution are summarised in Box 1:2.

---

[15] http://www.donors.co.za/
[16] http://www.africagrantmakers.org/

Corporate social investment (Southern Africa) Anglo American Chairman's Fund	More than $20 million
Number of projects supported (past decade)	7,800
Extent of contribution (past decade)	$66 million
Number of grants (2003)	442
Value of grants (2003)	$10 million
HIV/AIDS	
HIV wellness programme enrolment (2003)	3,300 employees
Donation to LoveLife AIDS charity	$4 million
Voluntary Aids testing programme	10% of employees
Free antiretroviral treatment to employees	94% back at normal work

Source: (Anglo American, 2003)

Box 1:2 Anglo American's Philanthropic Contribution in Africa (2003)

In Africa, however, philanthropy goes beyond simple charitable giving. HIV/AIDS is a case in point, where the response by business is essentially philanthropic (HIV/AIDS not being an occupational disease), although clearly in companies' own medium to long-term economic interest. A survey of 8,719 business executives in 104 countries on HIV/AIDS notes that in areas where the prevalence of HIV/AIDS is above 20%, such as in Southern and Central Africa, 72% of companies now have formal and informal policies to tackle the disease (World Economic Forum, UNAIDS, and Harvard School of Public Health, 2004). The survey cites Anglo American as a global benchmark for implementing extensive voluntary counselling and testing for HIV infection, coupled with antiretroviral therapy for employees. The result is that over 90% of the 2,200 Anglo American employees who have accessed and remained on treatment are well and have returned to normal work.

Legal Responsibilities

In Africa, legal responsibilities have a lower priority than in developed countries. This does not necessarily mean that companies flaunt the law, but it is far less of a pressure for good conduct. There are several reasons for this. Firstly, in much of Africa, the legal infrastructure is poorly developed and often lacks independence, resources and administrative efficiency. Many African countries also lag behind the developed world in terms of incorporating human rights and other issues relevant to CSR into their legislation (Mwaura, 2004).

For example, the Nigeria Law Reform Commission (1987) declined to recommend the adoption of a provision obliging directors to have regard to the interests of employees on the basis that it would adversely affect the developing economy of the country by deterring foreign investors and, in turn, lead to job losses. This approach seems more similar to the American view of legislation as interference with private liberty than the European approach of a strong state role in regulating corporate practice (Crane et al., 2004). In Africa, however, there is the further suggestion that Carroll's (1991) assumption that the law is a form of "codified ethics", where changing values are "the driving force behind the very creation of laws and regulations" (41), may not always hold true.

Admittedly, over the past ten years some countries in Africa have seen significant progress in strengthening the human rights and CSR aspects of their legislation – South Africa (Visser, 2005b) and Kenya (Mwaura, 2004) being two cases in point. However, government capacity for enforcement remains a serious limitation and reduces the effectiveness of legislation as a driver for CSR. This view is supported by a survey of South Africa's top companies, in which only 10% cited "abiding by laws and regulations" as their one principal motivation for pursuing corporate citizenship (Trialogue, 2004b).

The weak influence of the law as a deterrent against unethical behaviour was also illustrated in a survey of 1,026 public and private sector organisations in South Africa (KPMG, 2002). The study found that 67% of respondents believed fraud was a problem in their organisations, and 66% cited a lack of adequate penalties and law enforcement, as well as inefficiencies in the justice system, to be the reason for the increase in fraud.

Not surprisingly, Anglo American (2002) claim legal compliance as one of their fundamental business principles, saying "we respect the laws of host countries" (2) and "we will comply with all laws and regulations applicable to our businesses and to our relationships with our stakeholders" (3). Nevertheless, in 2003, legal actions against the company for breaches of safety legislation resulted in fines of $235,000 and environmental incidents resulted in fines of $40,000. The point is not so much the company's commitment to legal compliance, but rather that it is given relatively less importance as a driver in the pursuit of CSR, compared with economic and philanthropic pressures.

Ethical Responsibilities

Crane & Matten (2004) suggest that ethical responsibilities enjoy a much higher priority in Europe than in the USA. In Africa, however, ethics seems to have the least influence on the CSR agenda. This is not to say that Africa has been untouched by the global trend towards improved governance. In fact, the 1992 and 2002 King Reports on Corporate Governance in South Africa have both led the world in their inclusion of CSR issues. For example, the 1992 King Report was the first global corporate governance code to talk about "stakeholders" and to stress the importance of business accountability beyond the interests of shareholders (IoD, 1992). Similarly, the 2002 King Report (King II) was the first to include a section on "integrated sustainability reporting", covering social, transformation, ethical, safety, health and environmental management policies and practices (IoD, 2002).

Although adoption of the code remains voluntary, the Johannesburg Securities Exchange (JSE) has subsequently made King II a listing requirement. In terms of compliance, South Africa's large companies seem to have responded well. For instance, a survey of the 154 companies listed on the JSE's All Share Index showed that 65% now report annually on sustainability-related issues and 77% reference some form of internal code of ethics (KPMG, 2004). Similarly, research of the top 200 JSE-listed companies revealed that nearly 60% claim to have already fully adopted the requirements of King II, while more than 90% claim they will fully comply in the future (Trialogue, 2004b).

This progress is certainly encouraging, although on the broad scale of Africa it is still the exception rather than the rule. Even among large South African companies where a basic ethics infrastructure is in place (such as codes of conduct and whistle-blower mechanisms), ethics training and senior management responsibility for ethics still appears to be lacking (KPMG, 2001). The critical question is whether corporate governance practices have since filtered down to the broad mass of companies in Africa. In this respect, global statistics on corruption in Africa suggest that, in practice, ethics remains the lowest CSR priority.

For instance, in Transparency International's (2004a) Corruption Perception Index, in which 145 nations are surveyed (where 1st is least corrupt and 145th is most corrupt), only two African countries are in the top 50 (Botswana 31st and South Africa 44th), while 31 are ranked lower than 50th, and 17 are ranked lower than 100th. Similarly, in Transparency International's (2004b) Global Corruption Barometer, more than half of all respondents in the African countries surveyed indicated that corruption affects business to a large extent. The World Bank's Investment Climate Survey paints a similar picture of Africa (World Bank, 2005b).

One of the attempts to address corruption in Africa has been the UK-led Extractive Industries Transparency Initiative (EITI), which aims to increase transparency over payments by companies to governments and government-linked entities, as well as transparency over revenues by those host country governments. Here there is perhaps more cause for optimism, with countries like Nigeria and Ghana having taken the lead on publishing extractive industry revenues.

Anglo American (2003) notes its support for the EITI "as a means of increasing stakeholder confidence, reducing opportunities for embezzlement and stimulating debate around how revenues are allocated most effectively in resource-dependent economies" (p.10). In their statement of business principles Anglo American (2002) also insist that "we are implacably opposed to corruption. We will not offer, pay or accept bribes or condone anti-competitive practices in our dealings in the marketplace and will not tolerate any such activity by our employees" (3). In 2003, they launched a whistle-blowing facility in order to allow employees to anonymously report any violations of Anglo American's business principles or any legal or ethical concerns.

Hence, in Africa, we see a gap between the generally high ethical stance taken by a minority of companies – typically large multinationals like Anglo American – and the widespread reality of corruption that remains entrenched in many countries on the continent. The recently launched African Union Convention on Preventing and Combating Corruption is a further attempt to change this malaise and instil a new culture of ethical responsibility. But with eight outstanding ratifications of the fifteen needed for it to enter into force, there appears to still be a lack of political will.

Revisiting Carroll's CSR Pyramid

As this chapter has shown, Carroll's CSR Pyramid is both a durable and useful model for defining and exploring CSR. However, it has some serious limitations. These can be grouped into two categories:

1) Conceptual clarity - i.e. what is the model trying to say? and
2) Descriptive accuracy - i.e. does the model describe reality?

Conceptual Clarity

Carroll is not consistent in his explanation of why CSR is depicted as a hierarchy. Sometimes, he suggests it is the way CSR has developed historically (Carroll, 1979, 1991), other times he uses it to depict an order of dependence (Carroll, 1991, 2004), and his empirical evidence implies yet another rationale, namely that it reflects the relative perceived importance assigned by managers (Edmondson et al., 1999; Pinkston et al., 1994, 1996). He even suggests at one point that the model was simply conceived to make the point that these various obligations (economic and ethical) should be fulfilled simultaneously (Carroll, 2000).

Another criticism is that, in his attempt to conflate various allied concepts such as business ethics, corporate citizenship and stakeholder management into his own CSR Pyramid, Carroll fails to do justice (or seemingly even to properly understand) these competing themes. As previously mentioned, at one point he equates corporate citizenship with philanthropy (Carroll, 1991), then he suggests it is essentially the same as CSR (Carroll, 1998; Pinkston et al., 1994), before reverting back to his original view of it only representing the discretionary element at the top of his pyramid (Carroll, 2004). Scholars of corporate citizenship (Matten & Crane, 2005; McIntosh, Thomas, Leipziger, & Coleman, 2002) certainly do not share Carroll's narrow interpretation.

This begs the question: what is Carroll's model trying to depict? What is the scope of coverage he envisages? His attempts at incorporating related themes certainly suggests that he is trying to establish an umbrella concept for the relationship between business and society, and Aupperle et al. (1985) praise its "comprehensive quality" (455). But what then of the whole field of environmental management or corporate sustainability? This is perhaps the most glaring content omission in Carroll's CSR Pyramid and especially conspicuous given the recent trend towards integrating the social, economic and environmental aspects of corporate responsibility (Elkington, 1994, 1997; Visser & Sunter, 2002). The fact that managers are increasingly likely to use the banner of sustainability or the triple-bottom-line approach to describe their CSR activities suggests Carroll's pyramid has limited instrumental value.

It is also not clear whether Carroll is using the pyramid as a descriptive or normative model. The retrospective and dependence explanations suggest a descriptive bias, while his empirical and simultaneity arguments tend towards the normative. If it is intended as a normative framework, there are many in Africa and elsewhere outside America who would not agree with Carroll's ordered elements as representative of their CSR aspirations (De Jongh & Prinsloo, 2005; Springett, 2003; Visser, 2003; Welford, 2003).

Descriptive Accuracy

Carroll is striving for universality with his model, but it has not been properly tested in contexts outside of America. What evidence there is to date suggests that different cultures and sub-cultures not only give different nuances to the meaning of each component, but may also assign different relative importance (Burton et al., 2000; Crane, 2000; Edmondson et al., 1999; Pinkston et al., 1994). Although this chapter has not followed Carroll's positivist empirical approach to test his CSR Pyramid in Africa, one might speculate that such research would add further evidence of the variability of CSR in different cultural contexts.

Carroll's pyramid is also very simplistic and static, failing to capture the complexity of CSR in practice. For example, Crane and Matten (2004) believe that the main limitation of the model is that it "does not adequately address the problem of what should happen when two or more responsibilities are in conflict" (p.44). In fact, Carroll reports an "interesting finding" in his original empirical study, namely that "the more economically oriented a firm is, the less emphasis it places on ethical legal, and discretionary issues" (461). However, he fails to suggest how to resolve such conflicts.

In an African context, such conflicts and contradictions tend to be the norm rather than the exception – how to reconcile job creation and environmental protection, short-term profitability and HIV/AIDS treatment costs, oppressive regimes and transparent governance, economic empowerment and social investment? And in reality, the interconnections between Carroll's four levels are so blurred as to seem artificial or even irrelevant. For example, is the issue of HIV/AIDS treatment primarily an economic responsibility (given the medium to long-term effects on the workforce and economy), or is it ethical (because HIV/AIDS sufferers have basic human rights), or is it philanthropic (HIV/AIDS is not an occupational disease, so surely treatment amounts to charity)?

De Jongh & Prinsloo (2005) concur, emphasising that the challenges facing CSR in Africa involve messy, 'on the edge of chaos' scenarios. Hence, rather than tinkering with Carroll's Pyramid, perhaps we should be looking for alternatives that better describe the reality of CSR? Indeed, in attempting to understand the CSR practices of a multinational mining company in Africa, Hamann et al. (2005) find complexity theory to be a much more useful model than Carroll's CSR Pyramid. They explain that local governance and the role of corporate citizenship within it can be described fruitfully as a complex system for the following reasons:

- The order of the system is emergent
- Relationships are non-linear
- Activities are linked through feedback loops
- The order of the system is path-dependent

McIntosh (2003) agrees and has published an entire book – *Raising a Ladder to the Moon* – which uses complexity theory as the basis for exploring corporate responsibility. Other refreshing perspectives that hold promise for providing a better understanding of CSR, especially in an African context, include holism (Visser, 1995; Visser et al., 2002), chaos theory (De Jongh et al., 2005) and spiral dynamics (Beck & Cowan, 1996; Van Marrewijk & Werre, 2002).

Conclusions and Recommendations

This chapter has sought to explore the nature of CSR in an African context, using Carroll's CSR pyramid as a framework for descriptive analysis. Evidence of how CSR is practised in an African context has also been used to challenge the accuracy and relevance of Carroll's Pyramid. Most critically, it is suggested that the relative priorities of CSR in Africa are likely to be different from the classic, American ordering. This finding remains speculative and provocative and would therefore benefit from further empirical research. However, if confirmed, this raises several important issues regarding the cross-continental CSR debate, including:

- The importance of cultural context in the determination of appropriate CSR priorities and programmes
- The desirability and appropriateness of striving for universal, standardized approaches and models for CSR
- The influence of what Fox (2004) calls the skewed CSR agenda dominated by the dogma of the North on developing countries
- The need for flexibility in approaches to CSR policy and practice by multinationals operating in Africa and globally

The normative perspective on CSR lies largely outside the scope of this chapter. The descriptive approach adopted sought to illustrate how CSR actually manifests itself in Africa, rather than presenting an aspirational view of what CSR in Africa *should* look like. For example, it is not suggested that legal and ethical responsibilities *should* get such a low priority, but rather that they do in practice.

Nevertheless, a concluding argument could be made that improved ethical responsibilities, incorporating good governance, *should* be assigned the highest priority in Africa, since this provides the key to improvements in all the other dimensions, including economic development, rule of law and voluntary action. Governance reform in Africa is what is most desperately needed to provide what Fox (2004) calls "the enabling environment for responsible business" (p.29).

Finally, this chapter suggests that Carroll's CSR Pyramid may not be the best model for understanding CSR in general, and CSR in Africa in particular. Hence, research into alternative CSR theories and frameworks is encouraged.

Bibliography

African Development Bank (2003). African Development Bank Statistics Pocket Book 2003. Abidjan: African Development Bank.

African Development Bank (2004). African Development Report 2004: Africa in the Global Trading System. Abidjan: African Development Bank.

Anglo American (2002). Good Citizenship: Our Business Principles. London: Anglo American.

Anglo American (2003). Report to Society 2003: Working for Sustainable Development. London: Anglo American.

Aupperle, K. E., Carroll, A. B. & Hatfield, J. D. (1985). An Empirical Examination of the Relationship Between Corporate Social Responsibility and Profitability. Academy of Management Journal, 28[2], p. 446-463.

Aupperle, K. E., Hatfield, J. D. & Carroll, A. B. (1983). Instrument Development and Application in Corporate Social Responsibility. Academy of Management Proceedings, p. 369-373.

Beck, D. & Cowan, C. C. (1996). Spiral Dynamics: Mastering Values, Leadership, and Change. Oxford: Blackwell.

BHP Billiton (2003). Welcome to Mozal: Together We Make A Difference. Maputo: BHP Billiton.

Burton, B. K., Farh, J.L. & Hegarty, W. H. (2000). A Cross-Cultural Comparison of Corporate Social Responsibility Orientation: Hong Kong vs. United States Students. Teaching Business Ethics, 4[2], p. 151-167.

Carroll, A. B. (1979). A Three-Dimensional Model of Corporate Performance. Academy of Management Review, 4[4], p. 497-505.

Carroll, A. B. (1983). Corporate social responsibility: Will industry respond to cut-backs in social program funding? Vital Speeches of the Day, 49, p. 604-608.

Carroll, A. B. (1991). The Pyramid of Corporate Social Responsibility: Toward the Moral Management of Organizational Stakeholders. Business Horizons, 34, p. 39-48.

Carroll, A. B. (1994). Social issues in management research: Experts' views, analysis and commentary. Business & Society, 33, p. 5-29.

Carroll, A. B. (1998). The Four Faces of Corporate Citizenship. Business and Society Review, 100[1], p. 1-7.

Carroll, A. B. (1999). Corporate social responsibility. Business and Society, 38[3], p. 268-295.

Carroll, A. B. (2000). Ethical Challenges for Business in the New Millennium: Corporate Social Responsibility and Models of Management Morality. Business Ethics Quarterly, 10[1], p. 33-42.

Carroll, A. B. (2004). Managing Ethically With Global Stakeholders: A Present and Future Challenge. Academy of Management Executive, 18[2], p. 114-120.

Christian Aid (2004). Behind the mask. The real face of corporate social responsibility. London: Christian Aid.

Commission for Africa (2005). Our Common Interest: Report of the Commission for Africa. London: Commission for Africa.

Crane, A. (2000). Corporate greening as amoralization. Organization Studies, 21[4], p. 673-696.

Crane, A. & Matten, D. (2004). Business Ethics. Oxford: Oxford University Press.

De Jongh, D. & Prinsloo, P. (2005). Why Teach Corporate Citizenship Differently? Journal of Corporate Citizenship, p. 18.

Edmondson, V. C. & Carroll, A. B. (1999). Giving Back: An Examination of the Philanthropic Motivations, Orientations and Activities of Large Black-Owned Businesses. Journal of Business Ethics, 19[2], p. 171-179.

Elkington, J. (1994). Towards the Sustainable Corporation: Win-Win-Win Strategies for Sustainable Development. California Management Review, 36[2], p. 90-100.

Elkington, J. (1997). Cannibals With Forks: The Triple Bottom Line of 21st Century Business. London: John Wiley and Sons.

Foundation Centre, T. (2004). International Grantmaking III: An Update on U.S. Foundation Trends. New York: Foundation Centre.

Fourie, A. & Eloff, T. (2005). The case for collective business action to achieve systems change: Exploring the contributions made by the private sector to South Africa's social, economic and political transformation process since the late 1980s. Journal of Corporate Citizenship, [Spring 18].

Fox, T. (2004). Corporate Social Responsibility and Development: In Quest of an Agenda. Development, 47[3].

Friedman, M. (1970). The Social Responsibility of Business Is to Increase its Profits, New York Times, p. 122-126.

Garriga, E. & Mele, D. (2003). Corporate Social Responsibility Theories: A Systematic Classification Under the AGIL Method. Paper presented at the Building Ethical Institutions for Business.

Hamann, R., Sonnenberg, D., Mackenzie, A., Kapelus, P. & Hollesen, P. (2005). Corporate citzenship, collaboration and local governance as a complex system: Lessons from mining in South Africa, Mali, and Zambia. Journal of Corporate Citizenship, [Spring 18].

IBLF (1995). Partnerships for African Development: Business and Communities Working Together in Southern Africa. London: IBLF.

IBLF (2002a.). Building a Shared Future: The Role of Business as a Partner in African Development. London: IBLF.

IBLF (2002b). Business and Poverty: Bridging the Gap. London: IBLF.

IBLF & WBCSD (2004). A Business Guide to Development Actors. London: International Business Leadership Forum.

IoD (1992). King Report on Corporate Governance in South Africa. Johannesburg: Institute of Directors in Southern Africa (IoD).

IoD (2002). King Report on Corporate Governance in South Africa. Johannesburg: Institute of Directors in Southern Africa (IoD).

KPMG (2001). Ethics Survey 2001 - Ethics in Practice. Johannesburg: KPMG, Public Service Commission & Transparency International.

KPMG (2002). Southern Africa Fraud Survey 2002. Johannesburg: KPMG.

KPMG (2004). 2004 Survey of Integrated Sustainability Reporting in South Africa. Johannesburg: KPMG.

Lundy, G. & Visser, W. (2003). South Africa: Reasons to Believe. Cape Town: Aardvark.

Madsen, H. & Ulhoi, J. P. (2001). Integrating Environmental and Stakeholder Management. Business Strategy and the Environment, 10[2], p. 77-88.

Malan, D. (2005). Corporate Citizens or Corporate Colonialists? Ethical challenges facing South African corporations in Africa. Journal of Corporate Citizenship, [Spring 18].

Matten, D. & Crane, A. (2005). Corporate Citizenship: Towards an Extended Theoretical Conceptualization. Academy of Management Review, 30[1], p. 166-179.

McIntosh, M. (2003). Raising A Ladder To The Moon: The Complexities of Corporate Responsibility. London: Palgrave Macmillan.

McIntosh, M., Thomas, R., Leipziger, D. & Coleman, G. (2002). Living Corporate Citizenship: Strategic routes to socially responsible business. London: Financial Times & Pearson.

Moon, J. (2002). Corporate Social Responsibility: An Overview. In C. Hartley (Ed.), The International Directory of Corporate Philanthropy, First ed.: 3-14. London and New York: Europa Publications.

Mwaura, K. (2004). Corporate Citizenship: The Changing Legal Perspective in Kenya. Paper presented at the Interdisciplinary CSR Research Conference, Nottingham.

Nelson, J. (2003). Economic Multipliers: Revisiting the Core Responsibility and Contribution of Business to Development. London: International Business Leaders Forum (IBLF).

Nelson, J. & Prescott, D. (2003). Business and the Millennium Development Goals: A Framework for Action. London: IBLF.

Nigeria Law Reform Commission (1987). Working Papers on the Reform of Nigerian Company Law: Volume 1 - Review and Recommendations: p. 203-204. Lagos: Nigeria Law Reform Commission.

Pakenham, T. (1992); The Scramble for Africa: White Man's Conquest of the Dark Continent from 1876 to 1912. London: Perennial.

Pinkston, T. S. & Carroll, A. B. (1994). Corporate Citizenship Perpectives and Foreign Direct Investment in the US. Journal of Business Ethics, 13[3], p. 157-169.

Pinkston, T. S. & Carroll, A. B. (1996). A Retrospective Examination of CSR Orientations: Have They Changed? Journal of Business Ethics, 15[2], p. 199-206.

Prahalad, C. K. (2004). The Fortune at the Bottom of the Pyramid: Eradicating Poverty Through Profits. London: FT Prentice Hall.

Prahalad, C. K. & Hammond, A. (2002). Serving the world's poor, profitably. Harvard Business Review, 80[9], p. 48-57.

Springett, D. (2003). Business Conceptions of Sustainable Development: A Perspective from Critical Theory. Business Strategy and the Environment, 12[2], p. 71-86.

SustainAbility (2002). Developing Value: The Business Case for Sustainability in Emerging Markets. London: SustainAbility.

Sustainability (2004). Gearing Up: From Corporate Responsibility to Good Governance and Scaleable Solutions. London: Sustainability.

Transparency International (2004a.). Corruption Perceptions Index 2004. Berlin: Transparency International.

Transparency International (2004b.). Global Corruption Barometer. Berlin: Transparency International.

Transparency International (2005). Global Corruption Report 2005. Berlin: Transparency International.

Trialogue (2004a). Corporate Social Investment Handbook.

Trialogue (2004b). The Good Corporate Citizen. Johannesburg: Trialogue.

UN Security Council (2002). Final report of the Panel of Experts on the Illegal Exploitation of Natural Resources and Other Forms of Wealth of the Democratic Republic of the Congo. Brussels: United Nations.

UNDP (2004). Human Development Report 2003. Brussels: United Nations.

Van Marrewijk, M. (2003). Concepts and Definitions of CSR and Corporate Sustainability: Between Agency and Communion. Journal of Business Ethics, 44, p. 95-105.

Van Marrewijk, M. & Werre, M. (2002). Multiple Levels of Corporate Sustainability. Unpublished.

Visser, W. (1995). Holism: A New Framework for Thinking About Business. New Perspectives, 7, p. 41-43.

Visser, W. (1999). Greening the corporates: The transition, local business and sustainable development. Development Update, 3[1], p. 65-76.

Visser, W. (2003). Corporate Responsibility in a Developing Country Context. Ethical Corporation, 20.

Visser, W. (2005a). The emergence of corporate citizenship in South Africa: A ten-year review of key influences, milestones and trends - 1994-2004. Journal of Corporate Citizenship, [Spring 18].

Visser, W. (2005b). Is South Africa World Class in Corporate Citizenship? In A. Freemantle (Ed.), The Good Corporate Citizen. Johannesburg: Trialogue.

Visser, W. & Sunter, C. (2002). Beyond Reasonable Greed: Why Sustainable Business Is A Much Better Idea! Cape Town: Tafelberg Human & Rousseau.

WBCSD (2004). Doing business with the poor: A field guide. Geneva: WBCSD.

Welford, R. (2003). Beyond systems: A vision for corporate environmental management for the future. International Journal of Environment and Sustainable Development, 2[2].

Wheeler, D., Colbert, B. & Freeman, R. E. (2003). Focusing on Value: Corporate Social Responsibility, Sustainability and a Stakeholder Approach in a Network World. Journal of General Management, 28[3], pp. 1-28.

World Bank (2004). African Development Indicators 2004. Washington, D.C.: World Bank.

World Bank (2005a). Africa's Growing Pains: The Final Development Frontier, World Bank Press Release. Washington, D.C.

World Bank (2005b). World Development Report. Washington, D.C.: World Bank.

World Economic Forum, UNAIDS, & Harvard School of Public Health (2004). Business and HIV/AIDS: Commitment and Action? Geneva: World Economic Forum.

CHAPTER 2

BUSINESS ACTION ON HUMAN RIGHTS

DOING NO HARM, GOOD WORKS, AND GOOD BUSINESS IN THE DEVELOPING WORLD

Nicky Black

Doctoral Candidate, Kevin Roberts Sustainable Enterprise Scholar.
School of Management Waikato University, Hamilton, New Zealand.

Abstract

This chapter explores the role the global private sector can potentially play in promoting a culture of human rights observance through corporate citizenship. Introducing the human rights framework itself, the chapter presents a conceptual map of business action on human rights (BAHR) which places corporate, industry and global initiatives within a framework of the rights they consider and the degree of responsibility they imply. Drawing on the Voluntary Principles on Security and Human Rights, SA8000, the OECD Guidelines for Multinational Enterprises, the UN Global Compact and corporate initiatives on HIV/AIDS, it is argued that BAHR has expanded from a focus on complicity to encompass a more positive responsibility for the enjoyment of human rights in the project of sustainable development. In asking why, when there seems to be a groundswell of support for BAHR, there is strong protest from the private sector against the Draft Norms on the Responsibilities of Transnational Corporations and Other Business Enterprises, the chapter explores the barriers to engagement by the private sector in human rights efforts and the steps needed to enable 'better standards of life in larger freedom' (UNDHR) for the world's poor majority.

Introduction

Navigating the field of corporate citizenship can be bewildering for the novice businessman, academic, civil servant or layperson. For the manager who feels they have a handle on the general field of corporate social responsibility (CSR), the world of human rights appears to be another impenetrable thicket; highly charged, contested and emotive, and increasingly high profile as a growing number of the world's largest corporations profess support for human rights and attempt to embed these principles into their business operations. Equally, the last five years have witnessed a number of industry initiatives around human rights, particularly in relation to security and child labour in the extractive and manufacturing industries respectively, and global initiatives such as the UN Global Compact for good corporate citizenship. In discussing these phenomena, the chapter explores the role the global private sector can play in promoting an international culture of human rights observance.

In attempting to map out the field of business engagement with human rights, a number of questions present themselves. Beyond supporting human rights in principle, how do corporations engage with human rights in the developing world? Do all these corporate citizens share a common understanding of their human rights responsibilities? What implications might this have for the responsibilities of corporations vis-à-vis governments and why, when over 1,200 corporations express their support for human rights through the Global Compact, is there such vociferous corporate opposition to the draft norms on the human rights responsibilities of multinational corporations? To suggest some answers to these questions, I will in the following argument look at the emerging field of business action on human rights through the human rights framework itself. Built as it is on the equal foundations of rights and responsibilities, the framework goes to the heart of the central debate of the CSR arena around the limits of the responsibility of corporations for social conditions in the communities in which they operate. Far from further complicating the field of corporate social responsibility as another set of guidelines and regulations to be gerrymandered into corporate policy, the human rights framework can give the bemused manager much needed purchase on the slippery terrain of CSR and corporate citizenship, both at the operational and conceptual level.

The chapter is written with two main aims. First, it aims to provide a conceptual framework within which to consider corporate human rights initiatives in the developing world. In the process it will introduce the human rights framework itself for those readers who may be unfamiliar with its structure and history. Second, the chapter aims to identify the points of tension and conflict in the evolving arena of corporate citizenship as it relates to human rights - particularly in the area of regulation – and, by clarifying the terms of the debate, to identify emerging trends and potential avenues to move towards corporate observance of the Universal Declaration of Human Rights.

The chapter first briefly introduces the international human rights framework; its development, focus and aims, and the types of responsibility it entails. The main body of the argument then charts the evolution of business action on human rights (BAHR) from a focus on complicity and compliance, to promotion and protection, drawing on five BAHR initiatives – the Voluntary Principles on Security and Human Rights, Social Accountability 8000, the OECD Guidelines for Multinational Enterprises, the UN Global Compact, and corporate HIV/AIDS. These initiatives are placed within a conceptual framework of broad classes or generations of rights, and against the depth of responsibility that is implicitly assumed within them. This rough model finds both negative and positive forms of responsibility for human rights reflected in these initiatives, analogous to the responsibility held by states for human rights. The third section of the chapter discusses whether this represents a significant change in the responsibility of corporations vis-à-vis states for social conditions in the developing world. Here, an attempt is made to bring some conceptual clarity to corporate opposition to greater international regulation of the human rights responsibilities of multinational companies, with an eye to suggesting what barriers need to be overcome to foster an international social and political climate that supports the full and universal enjoyment of human rights.

The International Human Rights Framework

The international human rights framework affirms the dignity and worth of the human person as the bearer of fundamental human rights which should be protected under law to guard against tyranny and oppression. The Universal Declaration of Human Rights (UNDHR), adopted by the General Assembly in 1948, serves as the central pillar of the international human rights framework. The rights listed in its 30 articles are elaborated in seven international treaties, including the International Covenant on Economic, Social and Cultural Rights and the International Covenant on Civil and Political Rights. The UNDHR and these two key covenants are collectively referred to as the International Bill of Human Rights.

Whilst all the rights contained in the International Bill of Human Rights are considered to be universal, interrelated, interdependent and indivisible, three generations of human rights grouped under the French Revolution's watchwords of *Liberté, Égalité, Fraternité* are often distinguished, and enjoy different levels of recognition and support in the international arena. First-generation rights are civil and political in nature, covered in Articles 1-21 of the UNDHR. Often referred to as negative rights, they are those rights that should not be taken from the individual by the state, and include the right to life, a fair trial, freedom of speech and religion. Second-generation rights, Articles 22-27, deal with equality and are principally social, cultural or economic in nature. Including the right to work, to social security, health and education, these are positive rights which outline the things a state should provide for its people. Third-generation rights, which include collective rights such as the right to self-determination as well as economic and social development, have yet to be incorporated into any international legally-binding framework.

The principal focus of the UNDHR is the relationship of the state to the individual, as it describes the rights held by the individual, and the responsibility of the state to protect and ensure the enjoyment of those rights. Just as the individual is the bearer of negative and positive rights, there are both negative and positive responsibilities on the part of states – i.e. to not deprive or deny a person's rights, and to promote and ensure the full enjoyment of those rights respectively. The following section considers whether, as corporations express support for the human rights framework in increasing numbers, similar 'depths' of responsibility are reflected, tacitly or explicitly, in their actions. Although ultimate responsibility for the observance and enjoyment of rights must remain with the state, the discussion traces the evolution of BAHR in countries where governments are unable or unwilling to meet their human rights responsibilities - from a focus on avoiding complicity in human rights abuses, to corporate and global initiatives that attempt to promote and ensure the enjoyment of human rights. These latter initiatives suggest a tacit acceptance of a greater depth of responsibility and an expansion of the legitimate role of business in global society - more specifically in the project of development.

The Evolution of Business Action on Human Rights

The human rights movement first turned its attention to the human rights responsibilities of the private sector during Apartheid in the 1970s, and broadened this focus to businesses operating in other countries with poor human rights records in the 1980s. The 1990s saw an explosion of human rights activism aimed at the private sector, around both labour conditions and the use of security forces in the developing world. Charges of corporate complicity in human rights abuses by the Nigerian dictatorship of General Abacha from networks of transnational non-governmental organisations (NGOs) threw oil behemoth Shell and the issue of corporate complicity in rights abuses into the international spotlight in the mid-1990s (Chandler, 2003). Broadly speaking, corporate complicity in human rights abuses means that a company knowingly or unknowingly participates in or facilitates human rights abuses committed by others, whether it is a state, a rebel group, another company or an individual (UNGC, Compact, & Rights, 2004). The perceived failure of Shell to take any action in the arbitrary execution of Ken Saro-Wiwa and eight other Ogoni tribes-people in November 1995, caused a global wave of protest around the company's complicity in this and other systematic rights abuse by the government in relations to Shell's operations. In response, the company held discussions with representatives from the Dutch and British sections of Amnesty International and Pax Christi of the Netherlands to develop a human rights policy. This led to a revision of the company's General Business Principles to include 'support for fundamental human rights in line with the legitimate role of business' (Dutch/Shell, 1997), a position quickly adopted by BP when it faced a similar scandal in Columbia the following year, resulting in its adoption of an Ethical Conduct Policy in 1998.

A number of questions can be asked of this position. First, whilst there may be a moral imperative to not directly or indirectly harm individuals in the course of doing business, does business have any legitimate role to play in supporting fundamental human rights, given that the human rights framework speaks directly to the relationship of states to individuals? Under international law such a position is legitimate, with the preamble of the UNDHR calling on 'every individual and every organ of society' to 'promote respect for these rights and freedoms and by progressive measures, national and international, to secure their universal and effective recognition and observance' (UNDHR, 1948). The concept of 'every organ of society' includes private entities such as companies. As such, the degree to which Shell - or any other company adopting this benchmark stance - may promote respect for human rights, or engage in progressive measures to secure their universal and effective recognition is governed by what it perceives to be the legitimate role of business.

From here, two further and inter-related questions can be asked: Does support for fundamental human rights include first, second and third-generation rights? Does promoting respect and ensuring recognition of fundamental human rights entail a negative and positive responsibility similar to that held by states to not only refrain from direct or complicit abuse, but to actively work for full rights enjoyment? The answer to both is the less resounding 'it depends'. It depends on what is considered to be the legitimate role of business, and it is for this reason that elaborating the role of business in society has been a key focus of the burgeoning corporate responsibility movement for the last decade.

From Preventing Complicity to Promoting Human Rights

The development of a global culture of corporate human rights responsibilities which includes a role in both actively avoiding complicity in human rights abuses (a negative responsibility) and more recently in supporting and promoting human rights (a positive responsibility) is illustrated below with a number of initiatives spanning the corporate, national and international levels. The content and development of five BAHR initiatives are first described, and then compared and contrasted with an eye to the rights they address and the degree of responsibility they entail.

Initiative A: The Voluntary Principles on Security and Human Rights

The adoption of a position supporting human rights by Shell and BP in 1996 quickly led to a sector-wide initiative involving the US and UK governments, NGOs, and companies in the extractive and petrochemical industries in the development of guidelines for managing the relationship between a company's security and state security, such as the army or police. The two governments were keen to protect the reputation of their companies and ensure the security of their citizens abroad and thus acted as convenors, using their diplomatic weight to bring the companies and NGOs together (B. Freeman, 2001). The Voluntary Principles on Security and Human Rights were developed within a year, and first released in December 2000. These guidelines set criteria to be considered by a company to assess the human rights risk in forming security agreements with state security or private armies in order to avoid complicity in abuses relating to, for example, the right to life, freedom from torture, arbitrary arrest, and freedom of assembly and speech (Leipziger, 2003; p.95-105).

Initiative B: Social Accountability 8000

Social Accountability 8000 (SA8000) is a process and performance standard that brings together a number of International Labour Organization (ILO) standards with the management systems of the International Organization for Standardization (ISO), with the aim of making workplaces more humane. An international standard developed in multi-stakeholder dialogue with trade unions, companies, NGOs and academics, it calls for social issues to be integrated into all aspects of company policy and operations, and as such is a benchmark to ensure that basic rights are respected within the direct operations of companies and down their supply chains (Leipziger, 2003; p.156). The SA8000 forbids child and forced labour, ensures basic standards of health and safety, protects freedom of association and bargaining, prevents discrimination, and outlines acceptable disciplinary practices as well as fair working hours and compensation (Leipziger & Kaufman, 2003).

Initiative C: The OECD Guidelines for Multinational Enterprises

The Organisation for Economic Cooperation and Development (OECD) was founded in 1961 and is a membership organisation for governments from 30 countries, drawn primarily from the more economically developed world. The organisation promotes policies that contribute to economic growth and development, and has crafted a number of corporate responsibility related principles, including the OECD Guidelines discussed here, the OECD Principles of Corporate Governance, and the OECD Convention on Combating Bribery of Foreign Public Officials in International Business Transactions. The OECD Guidelines were first adopted in 1976 as recommendations from the member governments to companies, particularly multinational enterprises operating on their territory. They have since been revised to incorporate sustainable development issues and the core labour standards, and form part of the OECD Declaration on International Investment and Multinational Enterprises (OECD 2000).

The ten Guidelines are remarkably comprehensive – covering all aspects of corporate behaviour, from taxation and competition through to consumer interests, science and technology, human rights, labour rights, and the environment. Voluntary and non-binding, the Guidelines aim to foster a climate of international business in which common principles of behaviour are encouraged that:

1. Ensure that corporate operations are in harmony with government policies
2. Strengthen mutual confidence between enterprises and the societies in which they operate
3. Help improve the climate for foreign investment
4. Enhance the contribution to sustainable development made by multinational enterprises. (OECD Guidelines; Preface.1. 1994)

The human rights component of the Guidelines are found in the General Policies and in section IV covering employment and industrial relations. In the former, enterprises are encouraged to 'respect the human rights of those affected by their activities consistent with the host government's international obligations and commitments' (ibid; II.2). In the latter, enterprises are asked, amongst other things, to respect the rights of their employees to representation by trade unions, to contribute to the effective abolition of child labour and the elimination of all forms of forced or compulsory labour, and to not discriminate on the basis of race, colour, sex, religion, political opinion, national extraction or social origin.

Whilst voluntary, the Guidelines have more institutional teeth than the majority of other corporate responsibility initiatives, as they engage public authorities in disputes or issues of concern arising from the Guidelines. Supporting member states are expected to appoint a National Contact Point (NCP), whose role it is to promote the Guidelines and address any issues that may arise, by assessing the problem and mediating between the parties. The NCPs then report to the OECD's Committee on International Investment and Multinational Enterprises (CIME). The strength of the Guidelines lies in their comprehensive approach to corporate responsibility. However, they have not yet been comprehensively adopted and implemented either by the member states of the OECD, or the international community more broadly. Equally, whilst the Guidelines have provided a framework to guide the development of individual corporate responsibility platforms, there have not enjoyed wide corporate buy-in. This is partly due to the nature of the Guidelines; effective as a set of principles to guide corporate behaviour, they lack management systems for implementation. It is this gap that the next global initiative attempts to fill.

Initiative D: The United Nations Global Compact

The UN Global Compact is a voluntary initiative, housed within the office of the UN Secretary-General, Kofi Annan. The Compact itself is a brief document of the 'ten commandments' of good corporate citizenship, covering human rights, labour, the environment and bribery. Similar to the OECD Guidelines, the principles are derived from the UNDHR, the International Labour Organization's Declaration on Fundamental Principles and Rights at Work, and the Rio Declaration on Environment and Development. Whilst the OECD Guidelines speak to enterprises through its member governments, the Compact attempts to directly engage corporations in the project of corporate citizenship and sustainable development. It brings together corporations, labour representatives, NGOs and development agencies in a learning network within the institutional auspices of the United Nations, exploring how corporations can mainstream the ten basic principles of corporate citizenship into their operations.

Human rights are given particular prominence in the Global Compact. The first two principles call on signatories to '1. support and respect the protection of international human rights within their sphere of influence' and '2. make sure their own corporations are not complicit in human rights abuses' (UNGC et al., 2004). In pledging support for the Compact, corporations agree to report on projects aimed at mainstreaming these principles into their operations, and to engage in collaborative projects that, for example, facilitate technology transfer and human capital development in developing countries. Since its launch in 2000, more than 1,200 companies from over 70 countries and dozens of civil society organisations and trade unions have worked together under the auspices of the Compact. For some it is primarily an ethical framework and value proposition, for others a way to acquire the skills of partnership and alliance-building in the pursuit of common goals (McIntosh, 2004; Foreword).

The relative success of the Compact in its first five years is partly the result of the growing wave of anti-globalisation protests worldwide, in which transnational corporations have received a lion's share of the blame for environmental degradation, poor labour conditions and undue or unethical economic and social influence. UN Secretary-General Kofi Annan referred to this when he introduced the Global Compact at the World Economic Forum in Davos in 1999. Warning that 'unless more serious consideration were given to social and environmental issues, the global economy would grow ever more fragile', he called on 'business leaders to join a Global Compact as a vehicle for exercising enlightened self-interest: to embrace universal principles in the area of human rights, labour and the environment and to support United Nations goals to contribute to more stable and inclusive markets' (McIntosh, Waddock, & Kell, 2004: Foreword by K. Annan). The United Nations goals he refers to are the UN Millennium Development Goals (UNMDG), an eight-point programme of specific targets undertaken by all 191 member states of the UN to address the challenges of globalisation and underdevelopment by 2015. For example, the first goal aims for the eradication of extreme poverty and hunger - reducing by half the proportion of people living on less than a dollar a day and/or who suffer from hunger. In the last of these eight goals, the international community pledged to develop a global partnership for development which explicitly calls on the private sector - specifically the pharmaceutical industry - to make available the benefits of new technologies. In this sense, the UNMDG Declaration and the Compact are sister initiatives, with the Declaration recognising the role the private sector must play in facilitating sustainable development, and the Compact providing a framework in which to explore how this can be achieved in practice.

Initiative E: Responding to the HIV/AIDS pandemic

The HIV/AIDS pandemic is staggering in its scale, with an estimated 40 million people world-wide living with HIV in 2003 (Maplecroft, 2004). Approximately 50% of new infections occur in those under 25 in the developing world, with most of these people dying within ten years, thereby decimating the ranks of carers and workers in those countries worst affected. As such, the impact of the disease is felt not only by families and societies, but also by the private sector as the disease hits profits through productivity losses, high staff turnover rates and increased absenteeism, and threatens future generations of employees and consumers.

Companies - including such well-known brands as DHL, De Beers, Anglo American, Standard Chartered Bank and Heineken International - have run education campaigns for employees, developed outreach education programmes, and provided free testing, counselling and antiretroviral treatment for employees, as well as their families on occasion. Such efforts may be made independently or in partnership with local government and NGOs. In 2000, for example, Merck & Co., the Bill & Melinda Gates Foundation and the Botswana Government developed a partnership to support the national response to HIV/AIDS in prevention, care, support and treatment (ibid).

A Human Rights Framework for BAHR
The five initiatives above represent quite different forms of corporate involvement with human rights, engaging different groups of actors through various forms and levels of organisational and institutional support, in the pursuit of a range of aims. The key issue for this discussion is what form of responsibility they imply and what this indicates for the role of the private sector in global governance and sustainable development.

The central focus of BAHR is how to avoid complicity in human rights abuse, and this is reflected in the first four initiatives described. Both the Guidelines and the Global Compact call for human rights to be respected and complicity avoided; the second principle of the Global Compact states this clearly, whilst the term 'respect the human rights of those affected by their activities consistent with the host government's international obligations and commitments' in the General Policies of the Guidelines means that whilst the host country government may ignore their international commitments to human rights, the corporation should not. Equally, both in their content and their use the Voluntary Principles and SA8000 set standards of procedure that attempt to prevent direct corporate abuse or corporate complicity in human rights abuse by state security forces, or those down the supply chain.

In taking a stance against complicity, a corporation agrees that it will not authorise, tolerate or knowingly ignore human rights abuses committed by an entity associated with it, or provide any practical assistance or encouragement that has a substantial effect on the perpetration of human rights abuse (UNGC et al., 2004; p.19). The first four initiatives therefore confer on corporations a negative responsibility for human rights analogous to that of states - to not engage, directly or indirectly, in human rights abuse.

However, these initiatives – particularly in the process systems and implementation of the Voluntary Principles and SA8000 - can also be considered to partially fulfil a positive responsibility through their general contribution to the development of a human rights culture within the developing world. In educating workforces of their rights and pushing this responsibility down the supply chain through promoting SA8000, or taking a principled rights-based stance vis-à-vis a government, companies involved in these initiatives promote human rights and the full enjoyment of those rights in a broader sense. It is this potential role the private sector can play in actively fostering a human rights culture, and thereby facilitating sustainable development, is the primary focus of the Global Compact.

That a broader, more active view of the potential role of the private sector is envisaged by the architects of the Global Compact is clear in its first principle calling on corporations to 'support and respect the protection of international human rights within their sphere of influence'. For global companies, it is difficult to establish the boundaries of one's sphere of influence geographically, politically or economically, and therefore the degree of engagement that is expected of them. In this, the Global Compact starts with the assumption that corporations should assume this more positive responsibility for human rights – to not only avoid complicity and by so doing passively foster a culture of human rights, but also to more actively encourage such a culture through processes similar to those described in SA8000. It is through these processes that corporations can not only respect the protection of human rights, but actively *support* the protection.

Two case studies from the Global Compact illustrate this more active engagement and attempt to foster a more positive sense of human rights responsibility. In joining the Global Compact, a company commits to incorporate the Compact's human rights principles into its operations, normally through the adoption of human rights standards derived from internationally proclaimed standards such as the UNDHR. It may then conduct a scoping study to establish its exposure to human rights complicity and particular rights that may be relevant to its business operations. The programmes and focus generated through this process vary considerably across industries and companies, but can result in a chain-effect of human rights attention in those the organisation works with or impacts on. Novo Nordisk, one of the world's leading producers of insulin with 18,000 employees, production in seven countries and affiliates in 68 countries, committed itself to improving human rights standards across its business when it adopted the UNDHR in 1999 and joined the Compact in 2001. Seeing ensuring and going beyond compliance with human rights standards as a way to express its core company values and to manage risk, Novo Nordisk undertook to systematically integrate human rights (and environmental) compliance throughout its mainstream supply chain of product and raw materials, covering 90% of the company's key suppliers in 2003. It did this, and continues to do this, through the use of self-evaluation questionnaires, followed by telephone discussions and audits of those suppliers who self-report as being non-compliant. Novo Nordisk has found that this has encouraged attention to human rights compliance in second and sometimes third-tier suppliers in a 'cascading effect'.

This active fostering of human rights can also take place on a project basis. In enacting its commitment to the Compact, BP plc., the world's largest integrated oil company with over 115,000 employees and operations in more than 100 countries, incorporated a commitment to respect applicable standards of human rights in a substantial infrastructure development spanning three developing countries. Drawing on standards articulated in the UNDHR, the Tripartite Declaration of Principles established by the International Labour Organization, and the OECD in the creation of core project documents, BP attempted to set a benchmark for human rights integration with the Baku-Tbiliisi-Ceyhan (BTC) oil and gas pipeline project, which will carry up to a million barrels of oil a day between the Caspian and Mediterranean Seas. These standards resulted in attempts to comprehensively engage local populations throughout the project's development, and to adopt a precedent-setting level of transparency.

In both these cases, human rights awareness was raised by the corporations and effectively 'pushed' down or along the lines of connection between organisations. It is this capacity of the private sector to influence and effect change in human rights conditions within their operations and the operations of those they work with that can be interpreted as conferring a positive responsibility for the promotion and enjoyment of human rights.

There is another way in which the private sector is increasingly engaged in human rights in the developing world that suggests the assumption of a full responsibility for the enjoyment of particular human rights. The response of a number of companies to the HIV/AIDS pandemic with education and health programmes represents a unique situation, in which the private sector ensures that particular rights – the rights to healthcare and education – are enjoyed by those within their sphere of influence. In recognising their ability to help develop and deliver a response to the pandemic within their sphere of influence, a corporation directly supports the rights of workers and their communities to health and education (see for example Lim & Cameron, 2003). This is not to suggest that the private sector should or can assume more responsibility for all human rights, or for all people living in the countries in which they operate. Rather, it indicates how the needs of the corporation - here battling lost productivity and higher human resources costs of employee replacement and training - can be met in such a way that human rights are supported in the most comprehensive way possible. In this specific instance, the response of the private sector is often broader than in-house engagement, and involves a degree of community and societal outreach through education. Considering corporate operations through this frame of human rights opens the path to consider the broader societal impact of their activities and the potential there may be for engagement. For example, the prevalence of HIV/AIDS is linked to wider societal issues related to poverty and underdevelopment, such as low income and few employment opportunities, a lack of empowerment of women and rural-urban migration in search of work. The ability of business to directly impact these factors, through choices about investment and facility location, and through employment opportunity standards, provides one example of why the private sector has been actively courted by the international community to engage in the challenges of global underdevelopment.

In the Global Compact and the example of HIV/AIDS responses above, we therefore see a broadening of the discourse around the depth of responsibility for human rights and the more active engagement of the private sector in promoting sustainable development. This is reflected in the types of rights considered by the initiatives. The Voluntary Principles clearly engage with first-generation rights of a civil and political nature, whilst SA8000, with its focus on freedom of association (Article 20; UNDHR), just and favourable conditions of work, and fair remuneration (Article 23; UNDHR), spans both first and second-generation rights. In the focus on the role of corporations in promoting sustainable development, both the Guidelines and the Global Compact span the entire framework, with their overall focus on the third-generation rights to economic and social development.

In summary, the evolution of corporate responsibility for human rights from a focus primarily on the negative responsibility to avoid direct abuse or complicity in human rights abuses, to the ability of corporations to shoulder and enact a positive responsibility for human rights observance reflects a broadening of the discourse around the role of the private sector in sustainable development, through working in partnership with NGOs, labour unions and inter-governmental agencies to help achieve the Millennium Development Goals of the United Nations. The initiatives described above suggest different degrees of corporate engagement with social and economic conditions in the developing world, from doing no harm, to doing what may be termed good works. The following model and its accompanying key illustrate this discussion.

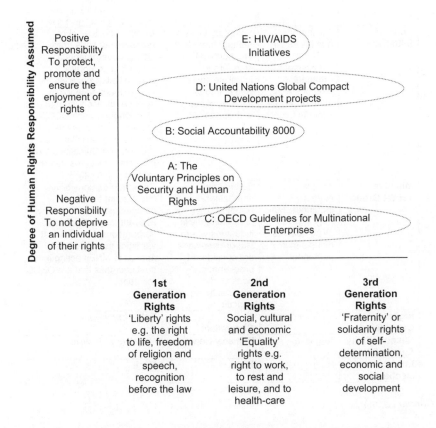

Figure 2:1 A Conceptual Map of Business Action on Human Rights

	Initiative A: The Voluntary Principles on Security and Human Rights	Initiative B: SA8000	Initiative C: OECD Guidelines for Multinational Enterprises
Level of Initiative	Industry	Industry, Global	National, Global
Aim of Initiative	To prevent complicity in rights abuses by hired security forces.	To create more humane work-places.	To provide guidelines for corporate behaviour that encourage the positive contributions MNEs can make to economic, environmental and social progress and minimise the difficulties to which their operations may give rise.
Form of Initiative	Voluntary guidelines for - HR risk assessment - managing relations with state or private security forces.	Voluntary process management tool and certification standard to integrate social issues into all aspects of policy and operations.	Comprehensive set of recommendations from OECD governments promoting corporate responsibility, covering the environment, technology, science, taxation, human and labour rights. Each OECD member state appoints a National Contact Point to promote the Guidelines, and mediate in disputes, referring reports to the CIME.
Initiative Target Group	Adopted by extractive industries, but may apply to all companies hiring security personnel.	Suited to all companies. Adopted predominantly in industries where labour conditions are considered problematic, particularly manufacturing and agriculture.	Corporate responsibility check-point for all companies, but particularly relevant for multinational corporations. International yardstick that specifically applies to MNEs acting in host countries that are OECD members.
Rights Considered	1st Generation	1st & 2nd Generations	Entire framework
Responsibility Entailed	Negative	Primarily Negative	Negative & Positive
Enforcement Mechanism:	None	None	None

Continued on next page

	Initiative D: The UN Global Compact	Initiative E: HIV/AIDS Response
Level of Initiative	Global	Company
Aim of Initiative	To harness the power of business to address underdevelopment through corporate citizenship.	To respond to the impact of HIV/AIDS within business and countries of operation.
Form of Initiative	Voluntary learning network of global companies, NGOs, labour unions, UN agencies. Companies report on efforts to mainstream ten Compact principles on human rights, labour, the environment and corruption, and engage in joint projects to further the Millennium Development Goals.	Multiple, including national engagement in education and health campaigns, and employee education, free testing, counselling and ARV treatment.
Initiative Target Group	To all signatory companies>1200.	Undertaken by a growing number of companies in the worst affected countries.
Rights Considered	Entire framework	2nd Generation
Responsibility Entailed	Negative & Positive	Positive
Enforcement Mechanism:	None	None

Table 2:1 Key to Initiatives Featured in the Conceptual Map of Business Action on Human Rights

It would seem that in eight short years, BAHR has moved beyond a single focus on complicity to encompass human rights promotion, gaining international prominence and private sector support. In this context, the vociferous corporate objection to the development of the Draft Norms on the Responsibilities of Transnational Corporations and Other Business Enterprises (hereafter the Draft Norms) by a working group within the United Nations Commission for Human Rights is puzzling. Exploring the reasons for this opposition to the Draft Norms, in themselves non-binding and not currently legally enforceable, leads us to our third and final question: What implications does this movement have for the responsibilities of corporations vis-à-vis governments. Answering this question exposes the central division in the arena of CSR around the role the private sector should play in an economically, and increasingly socially, integrated world. It is to this puzzle – private sector support for human rights as seen in principle and practice in the initiatives above, yet open opposition to the Draft Norms - that we now turn.

Corporate Citizenship – Laws versus Norms

The Draft Norms were developed by the UN Working Group on the Working Methods and Activities of Transnational Corporations, and adopted by the UN Sub-Commission for the Promotion and Protection of Human Rights, cited within the United Nations Commission for Human Rights (UNCHR) on 13 August 2003. Unlike the UNCHR, which brings together member states of the United Nations, the Sub-Commission is comprised of experts, who endorsed the Draft Norms and forwarded them to the 53-nation Human Rights Commission. In April of 2004, the Commission effectively sent the issue back to the Office of the High Commissioner for Human Rights, asking for a report of the 'scope and legal status of existing initiatives and standards relating to the responsibility of transnational corporations and related business enterprises with regard to human rights' (OHCHR, 2004). The private sector declared the issue dead, with the report-writing at most a stay of execution, whilst those in support of the Draft Norms saw this as a life-line, allowing the issue to return later in a more conducive climate.

Given the corporate support of human rights in principle and increasingly in practice as seen in the initiatives above, this corporate opposition to the Draft Norms is puzzling. Titled 'Norms', as they bring together and restate already developed expectations in international law for the behaviour of global corporations, '[the Norms] present the most comprehensive, action-oriented restatement to date of existing human rights laws applicable to global business. Taken as a whole, they confirm in fundamentally new ways (i) the many laws that do indeed apply, and (ii) how they apply and can be implemented with respect to business conduct.' (LCHR, 2002). Whilst there is as yet no mechanism for enforcing these expectations, in pulling together existing international law, the Draft Norms pave the way for such initiatives and are an authoritative voice. Those who support the Draft Norms argue that corporate opposition reveals the insincerity and rhetorical nature of corporate citizenship such as that found in the Global Compact. For these advocates, it appears that corporations want to look good without being held accountable.

Representatives of the private sector respond that the issue is indeed one of accountability, but more specifically about blurring the lines of accountability in a dangerous or imperial manner. Those opposed to the Draft Norms argue that governments, as the representatives of the people, should be the final guardian and sole arbitrator of human rights. As such, companies should not be expected to, for example, force their suppliers to undertake a particular course of action, as corporations do not possess the accountability or regulatory mechanisms to take responsibility for what is essentially a political action. Moreover, this introduces an unknown and illegitimate element into the business relationship that will conversely usurp good business practice, introducing an unwelcome and unlegislated element into contractual negotiations and conduct. In this light, the actions of Novo Nordisk and BP described earlier are unacceptable - taking corporations beyond their legitimate role. Equally, these advocates point to the different weights given to human rights in the developing world compared to the affluent North, with greater priority given to stability and economic progress than human rights and environmental protection (C.A.J. Herkstoter, CEO of Shell (1996), quoted in van der Putten, 2004) and argue that the requirement to recognise and enforce human rights is another form of imperialism. They object that the problem is not a lack of international law, as there are already laws sufficient to govern corporate behaviour, but rather the lack of political will or capability to enforce these laws on the part of national governments. Instead of attempting to shift responsibility to corporations and thereby absolving states of this responsibility, they argue that the international community should work together to strengthen the capacity of governments.[17] As Unilever NV Chairman, M. Tabasksblat stated in 1997, "companies must not be entrusted with the job of protecting general social standards and values. Companies are not equipped to determine what those standards and values ought to be. Nor are the control mechanisms within business appropriate for that purpose" (ibid).

For human rights, environmental and labour NGOs, this argument misreads the Draft Norms and does not recognise the power of global business to both improve and harm conditions in the developing world. First, the Draft Norms maintain the primary role of states in the promotion of human rights, yet argue that corporations bear a responsibility to 'inform themselves of the human rights impact of

---

[17] Comments taken from a speech by Adam Greene, Vice President, Labor Affairs and Corporate Responsibility, US Council for International Business at the Ethical Corporation Conference on Business Action on Human Rights, London, October 26, 2004.

their principal activities and major proposed activities' (Norms on the Responsibilities of Transnational Corporations: A. General Obligations). Second, they argue that the private sector's stance does not acknowledge that the factors which led to the rise of global corporations have diminished the abilities of governments to act independently in the public interest (Muchlinski, 2003). Through direct investment, customer and supplier bases and presence in at least one international capital market, transnational corporations often have substantially greater influence over the economic performance of emerging markets than national governments or inter-governmental bodies. Debate continues to rage over whether global economic integration encourages a 'race to the bottom', where developing nations lower social standards, including human rights observance, to attract trade and investment, or a 'race to the top', where trade and investment brings with it higher social standards as companies seek out the most productive workforce and stable political and social climates.[18]

The argument put by advocates of the Norms is that they have the potential to serve as a means to strengthen and facilitate governmental and inter-governmental control of multinational corporations. Rather than putting the private sector in the driving seat of enforcement, the Norms are a form of protection for weaker governments, and clearly articulate a central pillar of the environment needed for sustainable development. Some of these advocates in fact condemn the Global Compact for allowing business to set the human rights agenda for corporations without any means to monitor signatories or hold them to their commitment. They argue that the Global Compact 'blue-washes' and legitimates social or environmentally damaging companies and represents a dangerous expansion and legitimation of corporate-led development. As an international NGO Alliance for a Corporate-Free UN protests, without any mechanisms for monitoring or expelling its signatories, the Compact 'distracts Governments and the UN from the necessary steps to establish an effective inter-governmental framework on corporate accountability'; they call on the UN to 'play the more appropriate role of counter-balancing corporate-led globalization' (CorpWatch, 2001).

The debate for all parties therefore centres around the key issue in the CSR movement: What is the legitimate role of business in an economically, and increasingly socially, integrated world? Since

---

[18] For an overview, see (Held & McGrew, 2002) and (Lechner & Boli, 2000).

Shell's first declaration of support for human rights in line with the legitimate role of business, the CSR movement has attempted to incorporate, at the very least, an explicit role for business in promoting human rights observance within a corporation's own operations and its dealings with others, especially states. More recently, there has been a shift in the dialogue to incorporate a more positive, active promotion of human rights through tools such as SA8000 and within the auspices of the Global Compact. Whilst there has been some success in this attempt to broaden understandings of the legitimate role of business in society, the effort is hampered by the dominance of the more traditional views of the role business should play.

In business there are three dominant views of the role of business in society. The first two regard the ultimate purpose of the firm as wealth creation, and the return of value to the shareholder. Human rights engagement in these frames – the traditional Milton approach and the approach suggested by corporate philanthropists (e.g. Porter & Kramer, 2002) - would meet the letter of the law and go no further. Whilst the latter recognise that there are activities that can produce both economic and social outcomes, a company should only engage in them to increase its revenue, through advantages in reputation, social capital and business development. The third view of the role of business in society is put forward by corporate social responsibility advocates. This position sees the central role of the company as the enhancement of social welfare, with economic performance a necessary condition of that role (Donaldson & Preston, 1995). The overall aim of CSR is therefore to achieve full integration of social and environmental concerns into business operations, as that is the means by which social and economic development in a sustainable sense is achieved. Maurizio Zollo, Associate Professor of Strategy and Management at Insead, captures these competing views on the legitimate role of business in society in the following table (Zollo, 2004).

	Trade-off Model	Corporate Philanthropy	Social Responsibility
Ultimate purpose of firm	Wealth creation	Wealth creation	Social and economic development
Financial v Social performance	Trade-off Correlation <0	Jointly achievable Social => Financial	Jointly achievable Social => Financial
Governance mode	Shareholders' rule	Shareholders' rule	Shareholders' mode
Resource allocation criterion	Shareholders' value max. (SVM)	SVM long-term + ST social impact	LT social impact ST financial impact
Type of social impact activities	None, unless necessary	Add-on to normal (special projects)	Embedded in all normal activities
Economic logic of social actions	Risk protection	Revenue growth opportunities	Fully integrated

Table 2:2 Comparing Three 'Business & Society' Models (Zollo, 2004)

The Global Compact clearly builds on the social responsibility model of business in society. In the Global Compact, Kofi Annan is attempting to establish this model as a global norm for business (J. Bhagwati, cited in Mackenzie, 2001). The logic runs that if the estimated 65,000 transnational corporations, with more than 850,000 foreign subsidiaries and millions of suppliers (UNCTAD, 2001) operating world-wide, were moved to support human rights in their business operations, at least a floor will be established below which a race to the bottom cannot go, particularly in those countries whose leaders repress or abuse their people's rights.[19] In this sense, the global project of corporate citizenship is unashamedly political, attempting to establish some form of governance of global corporate actors, when the traditional mechanisms of government are still nation-bound. In a globalised world, global corporations become 'necessary partners to national governments and international governmental organisations in the formulation and implementation of global public policies' (Amnesty International and Pax Christi, 2000[20]).

That only 1,200 of these estimated 64,000 transnational corporations have signed on to the Global Compact indicates how much work needs to be done for CSR to become established, and how nascent this 'partnership' is. It remains the case that the most active corporate citizens on human rights issues are either those with valuable brands or

---

[19] This is, however, debated by those who see human rights as a particularly Western tool used to lever open markets and construct them in a similar fashion, and so question whether companies *should* do this (e.g. Mutua, 2002), whilst others question whether global corporations in fact *can* do this (e.g. van der Putten, Crijins, & Hummels, 2004).

[20] As quoted in van der Putten et al., 2004

those in industries where human rights advocates have focused their attention – the extractive industries; the manufacture of apparel, carpets, footwear, sporting goods and toys; the pharmaceutical and other high technology industries; and most recently, agricultural and investment firms. Without the 'stick' of some form of transnational regulation, it would appear that corporate citizenship might remain the preserve of the targeted or the particularly values-driven organisation.

This may not remain the case if a new movement in corporate citizenship – sustainable enterprise - takes hold. Sustainable enterprise is the private sector component of sustainable development, defined by the Centre for Sustainable Enterprise at UNC's Kenan-Flagler Business School as the employment of 'profitable strategies that approach social and environmental challenges as business opportunities and minimise harmful social and environmental impacts' and by The Sustainable Enterprise Project of the World Resources Institute as attempts to 'harness the power of business to create profitable solutions to environment and development challenges'. For proponents of sustainable enterprise, the term gathers together initiatives from across a broad spectrum of business activity – global business to community initiatives – that focus on sustainability, understood as the infusion of social engagement and environmental thinking throughout the processes and systems of the business. Taken together, these initiatives represent an approach that sees business activity as 'a vehicle for growth creation, social development and environmental enhancement...[which] becomes a competitive advantage' (Mike Pratt, Sustainable Enterprise Forum, WMS, November 2003).

This philosophy is captured and supported in an approach to business that is gaining purchase in the international management and development arenas, and is being championed by the Global Compact itself. C.K. Prahalad (2004; 2002; 1998), Allen Hammond (2004)), and Stuart Hart (2002; 2005) are the main proponents of a management approach termed 'Bottom of the Pyramid' (BoP), which takes the Donaldson and Preston (1995) socially responsible business and society model as their starting point, i.e. that the central role of the company is the enhancement of social welfare, with economic performance a necessary condition of that role.

Prahalad and Hammond thrust BoP into the international spotlight in their 2002 Harvard Business Review article, 'Serving the World's Poor, *Profitably'*. In this article they argue that global companies can build their profits and secure their future through serving the neglected four billion poor who live on less than two dollars a day and generate new markets in the process. Through developing new products or business models, and through innovation in meeting the challenges associated with marketing and distributing to the urban and rural poor of the developing world, business can 'enable dignity and choice through markets' and through 'converting poverty into an opportunity for all concerned' (Prahalad, 2004; p.xiii). In the process, through stimulating commerce and development at the bottom of the economic pyramid, multinational companies can 'help bring into being a more stable, less dangerous world' (Prahalad, 2002; p.48). Sustainable enterprise and BoP can be positioned at the top right-hand segment of the conceptual map of business action on human rights above, with a strong emphasis on the third-generation rights of social and economic development, and a positive ability and tacit responsibility of global corporations to engage in the promotion of these rights through their unique position in the developing world (C K Prahalad & Hammond, 2002).

As a philosophy to encourage a partnership between business, governments and inter-governmental agencies, BoP has the potential to get strong corporate buy-in through its seemingly happy marriage of profit and poverty eradication. The approach is meeting a warm reception in corporate and economic development spheres. The face of BoP - Professor C. K. Prahalad - was the plenary speaker at the second academic conference of the Global Compact's Learning Forum last year (Lifeworth, 2004), whilst the theme and title of a recent report from the Commission on the Private Sector & Development to the Secretary-General of the UN – *Unleashing Entrepreneurship; Making Business Work for the Poor* (CPSD, 2004) re-articulated and promoted his core ideas. Beyond the UN framework, the leaders of the G-8 embraced BoP in an action plan entitled *Applying the Power of Entrepreneurship to the Eradication of Poverty* at their 2004 summit in Georgia, and BoP strategies were a theme at the World Economic Forum's latest meeting in Davos, Switzerland. It is also likely to generate a large amount of opposition from those in opposition to globalisation, with a critical perspective on the historical and current role of TNCs in colonialism and the creation of the current, and growing disparities in wealth between the rich and poor in the Global South.

Whilst there are large, possibly insurmountable obstacles to BoP engagement by the majority of TNCs, given that this 'under-served' market has been valued by US$13 trillion (Economist, 2004), it is likely to remain the subject of intense interest. As such, corporate citizenship may become increasingly re-defined as not only the management of an organisation's relationships with its stakeholders through human rights observance and stakeholder dialogue (R. E. Freeman, 1984), but also the direct active engagement with the problems of under-development, through re-framing them as business opportunities *and* a chance to do good. That BoP can be made to work for companies is still unclear (Gateway, 2005) and whether it will ultimately meet the needs of the world's poor majority in a sustainable fashion – without replicating the devastating ecological footprint of the North - remains to be seen. The attempt to create social and financial value concurrently may not be a straight-forward exercise. TNCs are not necessarily designed to be 'development-agents' in the quite comprehensive ways suggested by advocates of BoP (Prahalad, 2004). Exploring the practical and conceptual limitations to this approach is the focus of my doctoral studies, and may yield some very interesting insights into how the legitimate role of global business is evolving, and what potential this particular approach holds for addressing the disparities in social and economic development. What is clear is that for the overall aim of sustainable development to be realised, corporations who attempt to access the market – and the fortune – at the bottom of the pyramid need to observe the broader guidelines for social and environmental responsibility. The rights-based approach is a central tool in development practise and, to live up to their billing as corporate citizens, companies would do well to be clear about their responsibilities and stance in dealing with the traditionally powerless poor, to avoid charges of exploitation and complicity.

Conclusion

In a globalised world, the actions of a transnational private sector are intimately linked with the development prospects of poorer countries, and poorer communities within more prosperous nations. In mapping the range of human rights initiatives that transnational companies are engaged in, and situating these within the context of the human rights framework itself, we can draw a number of conclusions. Whilst the human rights impact of the private sector was originally raised in the international arena under the cloud of complicity, and the main thrust of CSR efforts on human rights continues to focus on ensuring that corporations fulfil a negative responsibility to do no harm, this has broadened into a focus on the transformative potential of rights-aware companies that take on a deeper, positive sense of responsibility for human rights enjoyment, spearheaded by the UN Global Compact. In protecting against complicity, corporations fulfil a negative responsibility to do no harm, and through the associated promotion of a global rights-culture fulfil a 'shallow' positive responsibility, promote and encourage the conditions for rights observance. Whilst the distinction is fine, I have argued that on this sliding scale of responsibility corporations that meet a rights-shortfall – by providing HIV education or treatment for example – or who engage in specific development-focused projects, display a deeper sense of positive rights responsibility. At this end of the continuum, this responsibility is one of promoting or fulfilling rights within their sphere of influence and capacity.

Out of the inter-related and indivisible framework of rights, the private sector has typically focused on a number of rights pertinent to their sphere of influence, namely those civil and political rights likely to be abused by hired security, and labour rights - particularly those relating to children and working conditions. The HIV/AIDS pandemic has drawn multinational companies in the developing world into a new role in providing education and antiretroviral (ARV) drugs to employees and on occasion their families, and in engaging in educating the wider community in which they operate. In these actions the private sector can be seen to fulfil a positive responsibility for ensuring the right to health and education are enjoyed. More broadly, the call for an active and conscious engagement of business in sustainable development – in observing human rights standards within their normal operations, as in the Global Compact, or in seeing poverty and underdevelopment as a strategic opportunity to do well and do good, as in sustainable enterprise - straddles all three generations of human rights, falling within the third-generation right to social and economic development.

Whilst these actions do not usurp the traditional and legitimate role of states, they do stretch ideas about the role of business in society beyond Milton traditionalist and even corporate philanthropy models to create the possibility for partnership with governments and intergovernmental agencies in the pursuit of corporate profit and societal development. The Global Compact itself strengthens the emergent social responsibility frame in which the firm has as its ultimate purpose social and economic development rather than wealth creation. Support for human rights follows as the normative framework within which this development is most likely to be sustainable. Protest against the Draft Norms with its potential for regulatory strength can be interpreted as a reflection of the dominance of the more traditional models of the legitimate role of business.

In order to meet the goal of sustainable development, current CSR efforts are woefully inadequate; described by one commentator as being as 'effective as placing a band aid on the foot of someone who is haemorrhaging from a head wound' (Moon, 2004; p.3). Corporate citizenship represents a path in which the global private sector can join in finding and then delivering solutions to the challenges of globalisation, specifically the problem of underdevelopment and unsustainable development. Whilst corporate citizenship may currently have a small following, a combination of the profit and public good incentives in sustainable enterprise approaches such as BoP, and continued public and political pressure may rapidly swell the ranks of the converted. Human Rights will remain a central pillar of corporate citizenship, recognised in the OECD Guidelines and the Global Compact as a necessary element of the framework in which global business can work for everyone. However, to meet the broader challenge of sustainable development, work must be done for systemic change at an international and national level on the key issues of tax avoidance, executive accountability, currency flows, competition, and property rights (Moon, 2004). Time will tell if the current breed of corporate citizens has the appetite to engage with these issues, and if the structure of a globalised world with 'partnerships' as the key mechanism of global governance will allow such structural change. Exploring the ability of the global private sector to promote human rights – to do no harm, to encourage others to do no harm, and to do well by doing good – will remain a fascinating and crucial piece in the puzzle of how to make globalisation work for the majority of the world's poor. It is my sincere hope that corporate citizenship will be part of the effort to bring us closer to a seldom mentioned article of the Universal Declaration, that 'Everyone is entitled to a social and international order in which the rights and freedoms set forth in this Declaration can be fully realized' (Article 28; UNDHR).

Bibliography

Chandler, G. (2003). The Evolution of the Business and Human Rights Debate. In R. Sullivan (Ed.), Business and Human Rights. Sheffield, UK: Greenleaf Publishing Ltd.

CorpWatch (2001). CorpWatch Campaign Profile: Alliance for a Corporate Free UN. San Fransisco: CorpWatch.

CPSD (2004). Unleashing Entrepreneurship: Making Business Work for the Poor. New York: Commission on the Private Sector & Development. United Nations.

Donaldson, T. & Preston, L. E. (1995). The stake-holder theory of the corporation: Concepts, evidence and implications. Academy of Management Review, 20[1], p. 65-91.

Dutch/Shell, R. (1997). Revised Statement of General Business Principles. The Hague: Royal Dutch/Shell.

Economist, The (2004, Aug 21). Business: Profits and poverty; Face value: The Economist, p. 62.

Freeman, B. (2001). Corporate Responsibility and Human Rights.

Freeman, B. (1984). Strategic Management: A Stakeholder Approach. Boston: Pitman.

Gateway, D. (2005). Corporate Social Opportunity? World Business Council for Sustainable Development. http://www.wbcsd.ch/plugins/DocSearch/details.asp?type=DocDet&ObjectId=MTMyNTg:

Hammond, A. L. & Prahalad, C. K. (2004). Selling to the Poor. Foreign Policy, 142[30].

Hart, S. L. (2005). Capitalism at the Crossroads: The Unlimited Business Opportunities in Solving The World's Most Difficult Problems. Philadelphia, USA: Wharton School Publishing.

Hart, S. L. & Christensen, C. M. (2002). The great leap: Driving innovation from the base of the pyramid. MIT Sloan Management Review, 44[1], p. 51.

Held, D. & McGrew, A. (Eds.) (2002). The Global Transformations Reader (2nd ed.). Cambridge, UK: Polity Press.

LCHR (2002). Statement to the UN Sub-Commission on the Protection and Promotion of Human Rights: Lawyer's Committee for Human Rights.

Lechner, F. J. & Boli, J. (Eds.) (2000). The Globalization Reader. Malden, Massachusetts, USA: Blackwell Publishers Inc.

Leipziger, D. (2003). The Corporate Responsibility Code Book. Sheffield, UK: Greenleaf Publishing Ltd.

Leipziger, D. & Kaufman, E. (2003). SA8000: Human Rights in the Workplace. In R. Sullivan (Ed.), Business and Human Rights. Sheffield: Greenleaf Publishing Ltd.

Lifeworth (2004). 2004 Lifeworth Annual Review of Corporate Responsibility. Sheffield.

Lim, S. & Cameron, M. (2003). The Contribution of Multinationals to the Fight against HIV/AIDS. In R. Sullivan (Ed.), Business and Human Rights: Greenleaf Publishing Ltd.

Mackenzie, K. (2001) Part of a Tapestry of Actions. International Herald Tribune, [25 January 2001], p. 13.

Maplecroft (2004). Global Map of HIV/AIDS Prevalence, prevention & protection. Bradford on Avon, UK: Maplecroft.

McIntosh, M., Waddock, S. & Kell, G. (Eds.) (2004). Learning to Talk: Corporate Citizenship and the Development of the UN Global Compact. Sheffield: Greenleaf Publishing Ltd.

Moon, J. (2004). Introduction: From Review to Preview - An Agenda for the Future of CSR. Sheffield.

Muchlinski, P. (2003). The Development of Human Rights Responsibilities for Multinational Enterprises. In R. Sullivan (Ed.), Business and Human Rights. Sheffield, UK: Greenleaf Publishing Ltd.

Mutua, M. (2002). Human Rights: A Political and Cultural Critique. Philadelphia, Pennsylvania: University of Pennsylvania.

OHCHR (2004). Office of the High Commissioner for Human Rights. 2004/116. Responsibilities of transnational corporations and related business enterprises with regard to human rights.: United Nations Office of the High Commissioner for Human Rights.

Porter, M. & Kramer, M. (2002). Challenging Assumptions. London: European Business Forum Ltd.

Prahalad, C. K. (2004). The Fortune at the Bottom of the Pyramid. Eradicating Poverty Through Profits. Upper Saddle River, New Jersey: Wharton School Publishing.

Prahalad, C. K. & Hammond, A. (2002). Serving the world's poor, profitably. Harvard Business Review, 80[9], p. 48.

Prahalad, C. K. & Hart, S. L. (2002). The Fortune at the Bottom of the Pyramid. Strategy + Business, First Quarter, [First Quarter, 2002].

Prahalad, C. K. & Lieberthal, K. (1998). The End of Corporate Imperialism. Harvard Business Review, 76 [July-August, 4].

UNCTAD (2001). "Overview" World Investment Report 2002: Transnational Corporations and Export Competitiveness 1: UNCTAD.

UNGC Compact, U. N. G. & Rights, O. o. t. U. N. H. C. f. H. (2004). Embedding Human Rights in Business Practice. New York: United Nations.

Van der Putten, F. P., Crijins, G. & Hummels, H. (2004). The ability of corporations to protect human rights in developing countries. In R. Sullivan (Ed.), Business and Human Rights. Sheffield: Greenleaf Publishing Ltd.

Zollo, M. (2004). Philanthropy or CSR: a strategic choice. London: European Business Forum.

CHAPTER 3

STRENGTHENING CORPORATE SOCIAL AND ENVIRONMENTAL RESPONSIBILITIES IN SMEs

STRENGTHENING DEVELOPING COUNTRIES?

Søren Jeppesen

Assistant Professor, Department of Intercultural Communication and
Management, Copenhagen Business School, Denmark

Abstract

International and national institutions have targeted the small and
medium-sized enterprises (SMEs) with efforts to engage these firms in
corporate social and environmental responsibility (CSER) issues.
However, as experiences are limited and, as claimed by some, the
results poor, the key issue is whether the anticipated development
potential of SMEs can be realised. The author makes a critical
assessment of the potentials, arguing that they exist, but are dependent
on a number of factors, including context, approach and perception of
the involved agencies. The chapter then discusses the present practical
and conceptual/theoretical limitations of many approaches and
concludes with an illustration of how to overcome this by emphasising
the context and focusing on the situation of the SMEs, the role of
involved actors and different firm-level conditions.

The frame: Introduction

In the wake of neo-liberal policies and the focus on private sector development, the often overlooked, major segment of companies - the small and medium-sized enterprises (SMEs)[21] - has to an increasing extent entered the debate. Many institutions, including bilateral and multilateral donor agencies and national governments in developing countries have targeted SMEs in their aim to promote industrial development, environmental management and corporate responsibility. Notwithstanding such effort to engage SMEs in issues concerning corporate social and environmental responsibility (CSER)[22], the experiences so far are limited (see e.g. Luetkenhorst 2004, Fig 2004 and Jeppesen & Granerud 2004). Not only have the experiences been few, but some authors also state that the results of seeking to engage SMEs in CSER initiatives as a part of private sector development and industrial programmes have been meagre (EC 2002:15). With few positive examples identified, one might argue that little empirical support so far is available to substantiate the aspirations of the above-mentioned agencies. And maybe, the expected development potential of SMEs is not even there?!

I will argue that the potential is there, but the extent to which it can be realised depends on a set of related conditions, and in some situations it is difficult or simply impossible, at least in the short term, to achieve the objectives. I adhere to the point that the results so far of engaging SMEs in CSER activities have been limited, but the difficulties in realising the potentials are as much about the approaches and perceptions of the agencies as that of the SMEs. The difficulties seem to be based on a series of related factors of practical and conceptual/theoretical character. The practical problems include,

---

[21] As no universal definition of SMEs exist, the term here denotes companies of a relative size, typically with less than 200 or 250 employees. The EU official definition sets 250 persons as the threshold plus specifications of total assets and output. The South African definition is less than 200 employees and the US definition is yet again different.

[22] CSER is defined in many ways, in most cases associated with: 'voluntary' and/or 'beyond compliance' behaviour; sustainable development; and being about how business are managed (see e.g. the EU understanding in EC 2002:7). Other definitions refer to standardized or specified management systems or codes of conduct. In this chapter, the term refers to the two latter parts of the EU understanding and, more specifically, to a set of practices concerning labour standards, safety and health conditions and environmental conditions, which affect workers, local communities, consumers and the environment. See also Blowfield and Frynas (2005).

among others, a poor understanding of the particularities of SMEs, flaws about what SMEs do and do not do, and poor outreach from and limited capacity to deal with SMEs among donors and national government institutions. The theoretical flaws include among others failure to address SMEs in their own rights, the application of generalised and some times universal approaches combined with insufficient and biased analytical frameworks (Jeppesen 2004, chapter 2).

An important element is that donor agencies in many cases implement programmes that are (very) uniform in terms of aim, underlying assumptions, content, requirements of participants etc, and accordingly tend to promote ethno-centric views on development, such as Schulpen and Gibbon do concerning private sector development programmes (2001). It is relevant to promote CSER in the South, but as the history and contexts in the North among the more developed countries vary immensely compared to the history and contexts in the South among the developing countries, the approach needs to be adjusted accordingly. In the North, the general picture is a history of widespread regulation of firms in many areas where CSER for a number of reasons has been promoted as a way of moving towards (more) self-regulation, introducing voluntary approaches etc. In the South, the general picture – obviously a very crude one – is that little or no regulation of firms has taken place (see Fox 2004 for an elaboration). The state has had a much more limited and different role. To talk about CSER as self-regulation and voluntary approaches is more or less equivalent to 'business-as-usual', and whatever problems encountered, should one hope to be remedied on that note? As the World Bank states in a recent report on CSR, the developing government initiatives are very important (World Bank 2003:3).

So, obviously there is potential in involving the vast majority of all firms in particular programmes. However, the question is more how to unleash this potential and at the same time not be blind to the limitations of engaging SMEs. In this article, I first attempt to take stock of the potential (and limitations) of engaging SMEs in CSER activities in developing countries. I discuss the existing experiences of addressing SMEs, drawn from studies of SMEs & environment, SMEs & occupational health and safety, and SMEs & CSER. Based on the discussion, I identify a number of problems in the existing literature, and finally, I suggest how some of the identified difficulties could be encountered and turned into more productive initiatives.

The potential: What SMEs are hoped to and could do

Large firms, including state-owned enterprises (SOEs) and transnational corporations (TNCs), have received the majority of attention from politicians, governments and researchers alike until recently (Acs (ed.) 1999:4). As our knowledge on the private sector has deepened, it has dawned on policy-makers and researchers that SMEs in fact constitute by far the largest number of firms in the private sector, accounting for up to 90% of all registered firms in an economy, and even more if the informal sector is included. In addition, SMEs are important providers of employment and producers of a large share of total industrial output (UNEP 2003:2, Luetkenhorst 2004:158). These factors, together with examples of SMEs being contributors to innovation (Tidd, Bessant & Pavitt 2001:130-132) and more broadly to growth and development (see e.g. Acs (ed.) 1999, Karnoe et al. 1999 and Spence et al. 2004), have turned the tables and SMEs are now promoted as (the most) important contributors of development.

Many private sector programmes formulated by third world governments, international donor agencies, or by the two together, include a focus on SMEs (see Schulpen & Gibbon 2001, chapter 3 for an overview of several such programmes). Often high expectations to the outcome of developing the group of SMEs are an important of the rationale behind such programmes. As one example, the South African government has formulated these expectations:

> "With their generally lower capital/labour ratio, SMEs have the capacity to make a particular contribution to employment creation and with their flexibility to make a particular contribution to innovation. They also enhance competition. Of particular importance in the South African context, SME development is a principal mechanism for the enhancement of black entrepreneurs." (DTI 2001:13. See also Government of South Africa 1996).

While the already mentioned points regarding employment, production and output, and innovation are repeated here, the South African government also brings issues concerning assets and ownership in the economy to the table ('enhancement of black entrepreneurs'). Luetkenhorst argues that SMEs have a role concerning reduction of disparities by distributing gains of economic growth (op.cit 2004:159). These are arguments which others have extended by stating that SMEs also are or tend to be less hierarchical compared to large firms and hence secure a higher level of democratisation in firms, not only in the private sector, but also in societies in general (Fig 2004, Hamann 2004, www.ifc.org/ and www.ilo.org/seed).

It has also been argued that SMEs have an important or even crucial role to play in the field of CSER. On the environmental front, improved environmental management in SMEs could have a high impact on pollution levels, as SMEs have been said to account for up to 70% of total industrial pollution (Hillary (ed.) 2000:11). Similarly, improving the working environment as well as safety and health conditions could change the conditions of the workers significantly as, for example, lack of unionisation and poor working conditions are said to be important contributing factors behind long working hours, poor wages, dangerous and unhealthy work of many employees in SMEs (see e.g. www.ilo.org/seed). Furthermore, improved CSER practices focusing on prevention of HIV/AIDS, securing job guarantees and pensions would help in fighting spread of fatal diseases like HIV/AIDS and establishing social safety nets in vulnerable and unstable socio-economic situations.

Clearly, any government, bilateral donor agency or international organisation would be seriously mistaken not to seek to exploit such potentials. Obviously, along these lines, strengthening CSER in SMEs would strengthen corporate citizenship in developing countries. However, in spite of the potential, the experiences to date do not quite live up to the expectations. Firstly, SMEs are a very heterogeneous group of firms in terms of size (from one-person operations to 100-200 or more people), age (newly started to established/old firms being in existence for 10, 20 or more years) and sector (from agro-industry, manufacturing to a wide range of services). These differences in themselves indicate that the CSER practices also are very different (see Jeppesen op.cit 2004, chapter 12). Secondly, the differences also mean that apart from the 'innovative', 'dynamic' SMEs, there is a proportion of SMEs that will be conservative, show weak dynamics, have limited growth and hence limited employment potential (Katrak & Strange 2002:3). There will be SMEs that are low-tech oriented and without ambitions of technological development. Thirdly, there will be a section of SMEs – as with larger firms - which neglect their responsibility in terms of employee conditions and environmental regulation (Fig op.cit:9). So, there is a potential of engaging SMEs in CSER activities and there are high expectations to the outcome – although there are more cautious voices too. But apart from these positions, what do we already know?

The reality: What SMEs do and do not do concerning CSER

There are three important and related issues to highlight concerning SMEs and CSER in developing countries. Firstly, the numbers of experiences are limited in spite of all the attention given to SMEs and CSER (Luetkenhorst op.cit:158, Fig op.cit:18, Jeppesen & Granerud op.cit:6 and Luken & Stares 2005:39-40). However, it should be noted that some studies have been conducted before the CSER term gained prominence and hence, experiences concerning environmental, safety and health, as well as employment and working conditions are found (see below). Secondly, and related to the first, only a limited number of aspects of SMEs and CSER have been investigated. A main focus has been on the TNC-SME relations, as an element of production or supply chains and how demands from the chain, directly or indirectly, from the foreign TNCs, impacts, pressures or forces SMEs to implement certain standards or systems, including to adopt CSER practices in order to maintain their position as suppliers. The policy implications concerning growth and development for developing country governments are discussed (see e.g. Altenburg 2002, Humphrey 2002 and Kaplinsky & Readman 2001), as well as the more specific CSER issues (Jenkins et al. 2002, Jenkins 2004, World Bank 2003, Luetkenhorst op.cit and Luken & Stares op.cit). Studies of SMEs producing for and servicing domestic markets and/or supplying large domestic firms are almost non-existing, and, as Jeppesen & Granerud point out, little emphasis has been given to firm-internal conditions (op.cit). Thirdly, and in spite of these shortcomings, often still quite firm conclusions have been drawn about the motives, willingness, resources and capabilities of SMEs to engage or especially not to engage in CSER activities. This asks the question of why, which I return to in the next section.

Even though studies on various aspects of SME practices have been conducted, the bulk on SMEs & environment, for example, has been conducted in the developed part of the world, while fewer studies have been carried out in the developing world, as highlighted by Jeppesen (op.cit 2004).[23] The studies conducted fall into three broad groups: one group investigating government programmes and initiatives (see e.g. World Bank 2000); one (and major) group looking at cross-border activities of TNCs engaging with SMEs, also termed supply-chain

---

[23] Luken & Stares make a similar observation concerning SMEs and CSR (Luken & Stares op.cit:39-40).

management and TNC-SME linkages (see e.g. World Bank op.cit 2003, Luetkenhorst op.cit and Luken & Stares op.cit)[24]; and one group examining the practices and performance of SMEs (see e.g. Scott 2000 and Frijns & Van Vliet 1999).

Concerning SMEs and working environment or occupational health and safety, the International Labour Organization (ILO) has conducted a number of studies (see e.g. Norton 2004).[25] Nevertheless, not so much on SMEs directly as the main focus has been on governments, particularly third world governments; policy and service development and issues concerning larger firms; and the interaction between foreign and local firms. Also other international organisations like UNRISD and the World Bank have been active in the field, but while these studies have investigated issues concerning working environment, safety and health, and CSR, particularly in the field of codes of conduct (see Jenkins et al. 2002, Jenkins 2004, Mamic 2004 and World Bank 2003), none of these studies have focused on SMEs.

The number of studies directly dealing with issues concerning SMEs and CSER is, as mentioned, limited. The works of Luetkenhorst and Luken & Stares discuss issues relating to global supply chains.[26] Luetkenhorst takes the point of departure in the above-mentioned situation concerning the potential of SMEs for growth and development, and discusses how to establish and promote the 'business case for CSR among SMEs'. He argues that for CSER to matter, such practices need to be integrated in the practices of SMEs (op.cit:166). However, we are yet again to find few experiences and perspectives of SMEs. Instead, the article stays at the normative level, arguing the importance of recognising that 'CSR practices are part and parcel' of a section of SMEs; that size matters, that 'dynamism' matters and that context matters (op.cit:164-165). Furthermore, business associations, public action and the public sector/government should be involved or involved more in promoting CSER in SMEs (op.cit:166).

Luken & Stares focus on the practical side of SMEs engaging in CSR practices. They present findings from a UNIDO study targeted at

---

[24] See Hansen (ed.) 2002 for a broader discussion of TNCs and their cross-border environmental practices.

[25] For an overview, see: www.ilo.org under the INFOCUS Small Enterprise Development (SEED) programme.

[26] Fig highlights with a reference to the South African food and beverages sector that little attention has so far been placed on CSR in SMEs in general, apart from the exception which seems to be the SMEs that are linked to foreign TNCs in global supply or value chains (Fig op.cit:18).

promoting CSR-oriented business support termed Triple-Bottom-Line (TBL) to 22 Asian firms, 16 of which participating in supply chains (op.cit:43-44). They find that substantial improvements have taken place on the environmental and social side, though mostly on improved resource efficiency, while the social – particularly human resource – improvements are fewer (op.cit:51). However, as the main focus is on the TBL programme - elements and implementation, ending with policy recommendations on what business associations, governments etc should do - once again little insight is provided into the SMEs and the motives for engaging in CSER practices. The point of departure was the potential problems for SMEs if they did not engage in CSER practices (op.cit:39). However, the conclusion ends up being yet a promotion of the business case for CSER – i.e. that substantial benefits can be achieved (op.cit:51).

The tendency to focus on external conditions is the point of departure for Jeppesen & Granerud, who argue, with reference to African SMEs in general and South African in particular, that the existing literature is flawed by the tendency to use an external view on SMEs and hence are missing the internal (firm) dynamics. They argue that by understanding the processes in the SMEs, one can also understand why CSER practices spread or do not spread – and this also without necessarily being confined to TNC-SME relations in supply chains. Drawing on different cases from South Africa, Jeppesen & Granerud illustrate how the level of CSER practices is linked to different conditions such as the history of the firm, the (patriarchical) management style, the emphasis on resource efficiency, and the relationship between management and employees (Jeppesen & Granerud op.cit:19-20). Hence, they further argue that the level of engagement has got little to do with lack of understanding of the CSER concept or willingness to engage. Such an approach further opens up for assessment of how government or donor initiatives should be framed (op.cit:19ff).

In sum, our knowledge about SMEs & CSER practices is still limited. The main bulk of the knowledge stems from investigations of TNC-SME supply chain relations, while literature on government initiatives is more modest and on SMEs & CSER quite limited. This focus can partly be explained by the Northern interest in investigating situations with 'less government', self-regulation and voluntary approaches and what drives CSER. When this is combined with a political agenda, where the government is either 'invisible' or at least has a diminishing role, it naturally places considerable emphasis on

TNC-SME supply chains. However, a second part of the explanation stems from an underlying assumption that SMEs are passive. The focus on conditions external to SMEs and without investigating what drives or motivates SMEs leaves the SMEs as if with no agency. When the firm perspective is left out, the studies black-box the SMEs, with the result that SMEs are understood as not taking action concerning CSER. I discuss these perceptions of SMEs in the next section.

The flaws: Perceptions of SMEs

The majority of literature on SMEs and CSER can be characterised by a number of practical and theoretical problems, albeit interlinked. On the practical front, the problems include three dimensions: lack of understanding of the particularities of SMEs (EC op.cit:15), flawed perceptions about what SMEs do and do not do, and poor outreach from donors and national governments, including limited capacity to deal with SMEs. In my view, these problematic features are to some extent related. The notion of SMEs as 'passive', or at least not forthcoming, and difficult to engage with etc is in vast parts of the literature taken as lack of resources and capability to deal with CSER or lack of finances, and/or not caring about the CSER issues and/or society. In my opinion, it seems more an issue of investigations often being framed in way which is uninteresting for SMEs to participate in, combined with lack of outreach and capacity from regulators to deal with SMEs.

A first feature is the lack of understanding of the particularities of SMEs[27], which is due to the focus on large firms in vast parts of the literature, where these firms (e.g. 3M, Shell, Monsanto, Novo Nordisk, Volkswagen) have acted as the 'cases' of many investigations concerning CSER.[28] Consequently, the models and constructs of what CSER is or should be to a high extent stem from those investigations. In many cases, this has led to the formulation of 'hard', tangible indictors of SMEs & CSER activities, such as implementing a code of

---

[27] An attempt to take the particularities of SMEs into consideration is made by Kuhndt et al. (2004).

[28] The focus on large firms is understandable, in the sense that these firms are much more visible than the SMEs, making them therefore an 'easier' target for NGOs, community movements, regulators and researchers. In terms of spending scarce resources, it makes sense to engage with large firms. However, it also leads (or should lead) to a restricted focus regarding sector, practices and the possibilities for generalization.

conduct, an environmental management system, employing a CSER officer, producing a CSER account etc. If such an 'indicator' is not found, it is equal to not doing or caring about CSER in the investigated firms - in this case, the SMEs.[29]

Another flawed perception is, as mentioned above, that SMEs are responsible for up to 70% of total industrial pollution (Hillary op.cit and Gerrans & Hutichson 2000:75). The first problem is obviously how to make such an 'estimate' given the insecurity of figures and not least the lack of or limited number of investigations. Here, different sources seem to apply a more solid approach. Scott & Dasgupta et al. argue that the level of pollution can only be estimated if a) an overview of the composition of industries according to sub-sector in a geographical area is established, along with recognition of their relative level of pollution, b) if the number of SMEs is known, and c) the level of regulation is known (Scott 2000:279-280 and Dasgupta et al. 1998:1-4). If we follow the example of a World Bank investigation, the advice is to focus on large firms as a visible and 'quick' means of reducing pollution. In collaboration with the Brazilian authorities in the San Paolo area, the targeting of the 50 major firms in the area helped reduce levels of pollution by 60% (World Bank 2000:49).

Finally, the limited outreach from developing government and donor agencies and the limited capacity to deal with SMEs have an impact. As highlighted above and repeated below, it is essential to have appropriate and solid information on the number and distribution of SMEs if one wants to set up targeted programmes. As this sector is often much bigger, more fragmented, less visible and less organised (in terms of industrial associations) compared to the large firms, it is a major task to establish the data foundation. It has been assumed difficult or cumbersome to address SMEs which, combined with lack of experience, lack of capabilities – or again time[30] – have often meant that government and donor officials have not invested the time it takes to engage with and gain an overview of the SME sector, resulting in a poor data foundation.[31] These reasons combined with the often limited

---

[29] This has in turn been spurred by somewhat slack research designs and poorly conducted research which has established a set of myths about SMEs & CSER.

[30] Furthermore, political, economic and socio-cultural reasons also have a part to play.

[31] Even a relatively resourceful government like the South African is a case in point here. In the national small business white paper (Govt. of South Africa 1996), it was stated that the poor data foundation was a critical issue to deal with. However, little has happened over the years. Indeed, the quality of the data in the annual reports on the 'State of Small Business in South Africa' deteriorated over time.

resources, have meant that particularly manpower of third world governments – and to some extent donor agencies – have tended to mainly include the more visible and better connected large firms in activities like industrial development programmes and PSD programmes. While the number of programmes targeting SMEs clearly has expanded during the last ten years, the content has left much to say and the impact has been limited. When initiatives then are taken, the channels used are often inappropriate, the message and the substance not sufficiently targeted towards the situation and needs of the SMEs, and the follow-up limited. As the response rate from SMEs is – naturally - poor, governments, consultants, donors and, to some extent, researchers conclude that the SMEs are unwilling or lack the resources etc – not that the programme and its implementation was flawed (see e.g. Hunt 2000 and Whalley 2000).[32]

While the practical problems to some extent can be explained by limited experience and resources, habits and traditions, they are also to some extent linked to different theoretical and maybe conceptual flaws. The theoretical flaws include: failure to address SMEs in their own rights (as discussed above); application of rational, normative approaches; and slack analytical and methodological frameworks. I will not go into depth with these issues, as they are discussed at length in Jeppesen op.cit, 2004, but I would like to illustrate the point with one example.

Many investigations on sustainable development, environmental management and now CSER take their point of departure in the assumption that enhancing CSER practices also means enhancing the economic foundation of a company. For example, investing in cleaner production technology will cut spending on resource input, which is good for the environment and good for company profits. Similar adhering to certain social responsible standards (e.g. paying minimum wages, securing good working environment and upholding labour rights) will improve the motivation of the employees, enhance the image of the company and hence lead to increased productivity and sales, which in turn will lead to improved profits. However, while the countless case stories of companies experiencing such situations probably are correct, and that such 'win-win situations' might exists, it is important to remember that win-win situations might NOT exist. If the competition in the industry is fierce and no extra premium is given

---

[32] The input coming from consultants, service providers or academics is some times not of more value. In fact, the laws in many analytical perspectives tend to reinforce the practical problems just mentioned.

either by larger firms or by the end-consumer the likelihood of getting a return from implementing in an environmental management system like ISO14001, or in guidelines for codes of conduct are very slim – probably non-existing. While it is true that in supply chains, many SMEs are then pressured to make such investments as they would otherwise lose the contracts, the economic gain is absent. One of the reasons for the little uptake of CSER practices among SMEs producing for the domestic market – and NOT part of a global supply chain – is that there are no reputational issues at stake, no extra premium, no willingness among local consumers and hence no win-win situations to be exploited. Obviously, in such situations SMEs are – and will continue to be – reluctant to invest in such activities. It is not because of lack of understanding of the concept, or not wanting to pay minimum salaries, or a question of lagging behind the greening processes in society, but rather a straightforward assessment of the difficulties in making (business) sense of engaging in these activities and getting some return on the 'investment'.

The key question is then, keeping in mind the assumption that it is possible to make SMEs engage in CSER practices and doing so will strengthen developing countries: How is it possible to overcome the mentioned obstacles and maybe realise the potential?

The way forward: Means to strengthening CSER in SMEs – and developing countries?

I will focus on the same two conditions as mentioned above in my critique of the existing perceptions of SMEs, namely the practical and the theoretical. I intend to extend the discussion to all SMEs in principle and hence beyond the present focus on SMEs engaged in global supply chains. As the possibilities relate to the context, it is not possible to present any universal 'one-fits-all' approach. Instead, I will highlight some key elements of the process which needs to be undertaken.

The first and highly important 'practical' element is to establish a better (or 'real', as Schulpen & Gibbon 2001 argue) picture of the importance of SMEs to the economy, to the industrial development and to the issues concerning CSER. A 'real' overview guides which sectors of firms to target, while an appropriate understanding of what drives and motivates SMEs and a political process decide which (CSER) issues to address. Looking at the reality that many developing country governments are facing, this is easier said then done. Budget constraints, the fight against poverty, politics in general, and lack of traditions and experiences in dealing with SMEs are among the key factors making such a situation more of an ideal. However, following for example Scott (op.cit) and the World Bank (op.cit 2000), such investment is necessary in order to establish the data foundation, which in turn can direct the course of action.

The actual approach needs to be pragmatic and adjusted to the mentioned reality in the specific context. This will often imply that a gradual process is needed that a) takes stock of the present (poor) data foundation, b) involves many stakeholders, and c) identifies how to enlarge the data foundation and engage with SMEs. Then, over a number of years, it is possible to build up a (more) thorough database and, perhaps even more important, to institutionalise approaches engaging with SMEs.[33] In previous research I established such a foundation for an investigation of all manufacturing SMEs in a major urban area in South Africa. The key was to draw on various levels of government, donor agencies, consultants, universities and business associations (see Jeppesen op.cit 2004, chapter 7). Similarly, such types of partnerships which pool resources and contribute to the process with their particular competencies, seem like one possible way of seeking to overcome the constraints (see Jeppesen & Lehmann 2005).

A second element, also on the practical front, is to get the view of the SMEs embedded in the way the programmes and initiatives are formulated and implemented. As Castka & Sharp show, based on UK experience, if we then evaluate the SMEs based on implementation of certain known, visible or fixed CSER practices and standards, we will overlook a number of 'informal' practices. Many SMEs are carrying out various CSER practices, which are often of 'internal nature'. However, the drivers, due to personal motivation, do not conceptualise the practices as 'CSER practices'. If the appropriate support structures, like intermediaries, were established and 'simple, transparent and local' programmes initiated, SMEs are engaging or will be willing to engage in CSER activities (Castka & Sharp 2004:4-5). Presently, there seems to be some – or a long – way to go before we will see such understanding embedded in private sector development programmes, due to the discussed problem of large firms being the 'models' for such programmes.

---

[33] The work of the Manufacturing Advisory Centres in South Africa and the process involved is one example of this.

This is finally linked to the theoretical element and the need for changes in the analytical and conceptual understanding of what drives private sector development, including SMEs. First of all, this entails overcoming the normative, rational emphasis in much of the literature in order to avoid the universal, 'one-fits-all' approaches – i.e. context needs to taken seriously. Secondly, we need to overcome the static picture that many approaches depict and instead ensure that dynamics and processes are emphasised – i.e. relations and changes have to be emphasised. Thirdly, we need to move beyond the uniform emphasis on firm-external conditions and focus on seeing firm-internal and firm-external conditions in relation. An example of such framework can be found in Jeppesen (op.cit 2004: chapters 3-5).

With reference to the mentioned framework in Jeppesen (op.cit 2004), I will sketch three key elements of an initiative aimed at strengthening CSER practices in SMEs and then illustrate it with an example of SMEs in South Africa. Firstly, it should be pointed out that no uniform approach exists, but has to be established based on factors like the particular context: the history, size and CSER issues of the particular industry, including distribution of SMEs according to size and the actual importance of SMEs in CSER activities vis-à-vis larger firms; and the important firm-external and internal conditions. This aligns with the mentioned authors that argue the importance of a 'real' picture of the private sector – and of the SMEs. Table 3:1 below illustrates these aspects and their relations.

Context:	History Political, economic and social conditions Environmental conditions National legislative framework
Industry characteristics:	History and size of industry (output, employment) Industry structure (no. of SMEs and large firms) Distribution of SMEs (micro, small and medium-sized firms) Kind of production and CSER issues Industry associations Level of (industry) regulation and enforcement
Firm-external elements:	Relations to and importance of: - suppliers - customers - local government structures - consultants - research institutions - local communities and NGOs - banks and financial institutions
Firm-internal elements:	Ownership Size of SME Willingness and motivation Capabilities Business strategy History/previous experiences Organisational culture Level of CSER practices

Table 3:1 Factors Influencing CSER Practices in SMEs
Source: Adapted from Jeppesen op.cit 2004:80

Secondly, the aim and focus of the intervention need to be decided. SMEs should be engaged in enhancing CSER issues in developing countries to a higher extent than at present. However, as SMEs cannot solve all issues and cannot do everything in one, the key issue is what aspects of CSER to address. If it is employment, then certain aspects are in focus; if it is safety and health, then other aspects are in focus; and if it is community development, then yet other aspects are in focus. Thirdly, it is important to assess the resources needed to motivate SMEs to take up CSER activities and the actors/institutions to be involved, because it will have to be a partnership in order to overcome the present constraints and make changes and improvements happen, as highlighted above with reference to Castka & Sharp.

The example concerns how SMEs in the metal-finishing industry in South Africa can be engaged in CSER practices regarding improved working conditions for employees (see Jeppesen 2005). With reference to Table 3:1 above, we consider the particular South African context, the implications of the former Apartheid regime and the economic, political and environmental situation. Next, we look at the metal-finishing industry, which is characterised by highly toxic waste products, intensive price competition and low profit margins, if any at all. The industry is dominated by SMEs and is to a large extent also characterised by low-level skills among managers and employees. From this perspective, we have an industry and a number of SMEs which seem to fit the perception in the international literature, lacking resources and capabilities to do anything about CSER issues, including working conditions. However, if we take the third step and apply a firm perspective on the important firm-external and internal conditions, a slightly more nuanced picture emerges.

First of all, the SMEs are predominantly white-owned and have an average workforce of 20 employees, with key external contacts primarily being their suppliers – and to some extent their customers. Secondly, in terms of knowledge of relevant legislation, 90% of SMEs are familiar with the Occupational Safety and Health Act (OSHA) of 1989, and 90% of these firms, equivalent to roughly 80% of all SMEs, regard OSHA a 'very important law in their daily work'. Thirdly, when we identify what are the practices and the driving forces of greening (here to improve safety and health and improve waste management practices, as this is closely related to the quality of the working conditions), it turns out that a section of the SMEs do something in the field and are sympathetic to suggestions of doing more. However, a main reason for not going further is that some SMEs cannot afford to implement the needed changes, including systems like ISO14001 or OHS18000 or NOSA (a South African system).[34] Some have tried implementing quality management systems, but did not experience any changes in their market situation. Furthermore, some firms are reluctant to move further if they are not assured that this will apply to the others in the industry. They argue for what is termed 'levelling the playing field' by interventions of the government. All in all, instead of just anticipating that no CSER practices take place, an assessment of both qualitative and quantitative data shows that 25-30% of the firms could in fact be engaged in various ways (Jeppesen op.cit 2004:243).

Concerning the aim and focus of the intervention, I defined the key CSER issue above as improving the working environment, due to the detrimental effects on the workers' health, which includes enhancing

---

[34] National Occupational Safety Accreditation.

the waste management practices due to the toxic nature of the waste products. Although other issues could have been included[35], I chose to concentrate on only one. With this in mind, the third and final element is to assess the resources needed and the actors to be involved. Concerning the resources, the industry is a major sub-industry in the local area due to the presence of a number of automotive assemblers and automotive first-tier suppliers. This in turn underlines the importance of the key issue – i.e. many are employed in SMEs and affected by the working conditions. The actors to be involved can first be provincial and local government, as the issue of regulation is important. A critical issue is lack of enforcement, mainly due to lack of personnel, but also due to lack of overview of the industry and the location of SMEs. The importance of enforcement concerns on the one hand primarily the OSHA, which the vast majority of SMEs are aware of, and a number of relevant by-laws concerning the waste management practices. On the other hand, it is, as mentioned, also an issue of 'levelling the playing field' that the target SMEs develop a sense of initiative, which in turn will spur their forthcomingness to engage in CSER activities. Secondly, different industry actors need to involved. The local branch of what is called the Manufacturing Advisory Centre (MAC) Programme is important to extend various services, which might help companies enhance their general management and promote different schemes, including the ones which enable subsidies to use new cleaner technology. The local MAC is important, as it has established a comprehensive database of the manufacturing SMEs in the local area. The local business association is important in terms of distributing information to its members, providing information (addresses) on their members, for example in the service sector, and arguing the relevance of engaging in such activities. Finally, consultants with local expertise as well as researchers should be involved due to their knowledge of working with SMEs on these issues and being important knowledge brokers between these firms and local government.

With such a set-up and a skilful roll-out and implementation, future programmes will be more likely to reach SMEs and hence bring about the much discussed potential of these firms concerning CSER. SMEs have different reasons for engaging in CSER: *personal* (e.g. the views of the owners), *economic* (e.g. making the firm operate more

---

[35] See e.g. Granerud (2003) concerning the importance of learning and organisational culture.

efficiently and securing financial benefits from sales of waste products), *management* (e.g. ensuring a conducive relationship between management and employees, and emphasising safe and health working conditions), and *outside pressure* (e.g. through supply chains or from local communities). The key point is to activate the positive elements.

At the same time, we should not forget the limitations. In the mentioned example, even with a successful outcome there will still be up to 70-75% of the metal-finishing SMEs not engaging in CSER activities. Consequently, what kind of approaches can be employed in order to change their behaviour in this field? Furthermore, the outlined approach is based on the willingness and ability of the mentioned parties to collaborate, which is far from certain. The number of existing 'green' public-private partnerships is limited, not only because the concept is new, but also because of the difficulties in getting all actors to work together. Clearly, the outlined approach can be carried out, for example, by local governments and is not limited to only being implemented by a partnership. However, the different requirements make the chances slim.

While I have argued in favour of including (government) regulation in enhancing CSER practices in SMEs, the role of self-regulation still needs to be remembered. However, while TNC-SME supply chain linkages might hold promise in furthering CSER in SMEs, it also has its limitations. There are indications that TNCs tend to exclude SMEs when they implement CSER programmes (code of conducts etc), because TNCs raise demands on their suppliers which a number of SMEs fail to meet and hence experience their contracts being terminated. Some TNCs simply cut down on the number of suppliers to handle the work of fulfilling the codes of conduct (see e.g. Raworth 2004, Andersen 2005 and Castka & Sharp op.cit:10). Here, the discussion comes full circle, as one critical issue is the involvement of developing country governments and donor agencies in trying to circumvent such development by assisting SMEs to upgrade their CSER practices and stay included in supply chains. The potentials are numerous – so are the challenges.

Bibliography

Acs, Z. (ed.) (1999). Are Small Firms Important? Their Role and Impact. Boston: Kluwer Academic Publishers.

Altenburg, T. (2002). Transnational Corporations and the Development of Local Firms. p. 43-76, In: Proceedings from the FAU Conference 2002 Partners in Development? Djursvold, The Association of Development Researchers in Denmark, Copenhagen, 7-9 March.

Andersen, M. (2005). Corporate Social Responsibility in Global Supply Chains. Understanding the uniqueness of firm behaviour. PhD School of Technologies of Managing. PhD Series 15.2005. Copenhagen: Copenhagen Business School.

Blowfield, M. & Frynas, J.G. (2005). Setting new agendas: critical perspectives on corporate social responsibility in the developing world. International Affairs 81[3], p. 499-514.

Castka, P. & Sharp, J. M. (2004). Bridging the gap between quality management and CSR. A multiple case study view on how UK SME companies embed CSR practices into the ISO management systems. Paper presented at the Interdisciplinary CSR Research Conference, University of Nottingham, UK, 22-23 October.

Dasgupta, S., Lucas, R.E.B. & Wheeler, D. (1998). Small Manufacturing Plants, Pollution, and Poverty. New Evidence from Brazil and Mexico. Policy Research Working Paper 2029, Infrastructure and Environment, Development Research Group. Washington: World Bank.

DTI (Department of Trade and Industry) (2001). Driving Competitiveness: An integrated industrial strategy for sustainable development and growth. Republic of South Africa: Johannesburg.

EC (European Commission) (2002). Corporate social responsibility. A business contribution to sustainable development. Employment & social affairs. Industrial relations and industrial change. Directorate-General for Employment and Social Affairs, Unit D.1. Luxembourg.

Fig, D. (2004). Corporate Social and Environmental Responsibility in the South African Food and Drink Industries. Paper presented at 'CSR in the Third World – Towards a Critical Agenda' workshop, Copenhagen Business School, Copenhagen: Denmark, 18-20 August (http://web.cbs.dk/centres/cvr/critical.shtml)

Fox, T. (2004). Corporate Social Responsibility and Development: In the quest of an agenda. Development, 47[3], p. 29-36.

Frijns, J. & van Vliet, B. (1999). Small-Scale Industry and Cleaner Production Strategies. World Development, 27[6], p. 967-983.

Government of South Africa (1996). National Small Business Promotion Act. Government Gazette, Cape Town.

Granerud, L. (2003). Exploring Learning. Inside the technological learning in small manufacturers in South Africa. Draft PhD Thesis. Department of Intercultural Communication and Management, Copenhagen Business School, Copenhagen.

Hamann, R. (2004). Corporate Social Responsibility in Mining in South Africa. PhD Thesis, School of Environmental Studies, University of East Anglia, UK.

Hansen, M. W. (ed.) (2002). Managing the Environment Across Borders. A study of TNC affiliates' environmental practices in China, Malaysia and India. Copenhagen: Samfundslitteratur.

Hillary, R. (ed.) (2000). Small and Medium-Sized Enterprises and the Environment. Business Imperatives. Sheffield, UK: Greenleaf Publishing Limited.

Hunt, J. (2000). Environment, information and networks: how does information reach small and medium-sized enterprises. In: Hillary, R. (ed.), Small and Medium-Sized Enterprises and the Environment. Business Imperatives. Sheffield, UK: Greenleaf Publishing Limited.

Humphrey, J. (2002). Opportunities for SMEs in Developing Countries to Upgrade in a Global Economy. SEED Working Paper no. 43, Series on Upgrading in Small Enterprise Clusters and Global Value Chains, Geneva: ILO.

Jenkins, R., Pearson, R. & Seyfang, G. (eds.) (2002). Corporate Responsibility and Labour Rights: Codes of Conduct in the Global Economy. London: Earthscan Publications Ltd.

Jenkins, R. (2004). Globalisation, Corporate Responsibility and Poverty. Paper presented at the 'CSR in the Third World – Towards a Critical Agenda' workshop, Copenhagen Business School, Copenhagen: Denmark, 18-20 August. (http://web.cbs.dk/centres/cvr/critical.shtml)

Jeppesen, S. (2005). Small manufacturers – How much do resources and capabilities matter in the greening process? A case study from South Africa. Pp. 77-116, in L. Füssel (ed.), Corporate Environmental Governance. Perspectives on Organizing and Communication. Lund: Studentlitteratur.

Jeppesen, S. (2004). Environmental Practices and Greening Strategies in Small Manufacturing Enterprises in South Africa. A Critical Realist Approach. PhD Series 11.2004. Copenhagen: Copenhagen Business School.

Jeppesen, S. & Granerud, L. (2004). Does corporate social responsibility matter to SMEs? The case of South Africa. Paper presented at the Interdisciplinary CSR Research Conference, University of Nottingham, UK, 22-23 October.

Jeppesen, S. & Lehmann, M. (2005). Public-Private Partnerships as facilitators of environmental improvement. Green Networks in Thailand. In: Welford, R. and Hills, P. (eds.): Partnerships for Sustainable Development: Perspectives from the Asia-Pacific Region. Forthcoming, London: Earthscan Publications Ltd.

Kaplinsky, R. & Readman, J. (2001). How Can SME Producers Serve Global Markets and Sustain Income Growth? University of Sussex and University of Brighton.

Karnoe, P., Hull Kristensen, P. & Andersen, P. H. (eds.) (1999). Mobilizing Resources and Generating Competencies. The Remarkable Success of Small and Medium-sized Enterprises in the Danish Business System. Copenhagen: Copenhagen Business School Press.

Katrak, H. & Strange, R. (2002). Introduction and Overview, p. 1-8, in: H. Katrak and R. Strange (eds.), Small-scale enterprises in developing and transitional economies. New York: Palgrave.

Kuhndt, M., Türk, V. & Herrndorf, M. (2004). Stakeholder engagement: an opportunity for SMEs? Industry and Environment. UNEP [October-December 2004], p. 40-43.

Luetkenhorst, W. (2004). Corporate Social Responsibility and the Development Agenda. The Case for Actively Involving Small and Medium-sized Enterprises. Vienna: UNIDO. Intereconomics, [May-June 2004], p. 157-166.

Luken, R. & Stares, R. (2005). Small Business Responsibility in Developing Countries. A Threat or an Opportunity? Business Strategy and the Environment, 14, p. 38-53

Mamic, I. (2004). Implementing Codes of Conduct – How Business Manage Social Performance in Global Supply Chains. Sheffield, UK: Greenleaf Publishing.

Norton, P. (2004). Job Quality in Micro and Small Enterprises in Ghana: Field Research Results. SEED Working Paper no. 68. Geneva: ILO.

Raworth, K. (2004). Trading Away Our Rights. Women working in global supply chains. Make Trade Fair. Oxford: Oxfam International.

Scott, A. (2000). Small-scale enterprises and the environment in developing countries, in R. Hillary (ed.), Small and Medium-Sized Enterprises and the Environment. Business Imperatives. Sheffield, UK: Greenleaf Publishing Limited.

Schulpen, L. & Gibbon, P. (2001). Private Sector Development. Policies, Practices and Problems. CDR Policy Paper. Copenhagen: Centre for Development Research.

Spence, L. J., Habisch, A. & Schmidpeter, R. (2004). Responsibility and Social Capital – the World of Small and Medium-sized Enterprises. London, UK: Palgrave-Macmillan.

Tidd, J., Bessant, J. & Pavitt, K. (2001). Managing Innovation. Integrated Technological, Market and Organizational Change. Chichester, UK: Wiley.

UNEP (2003). Big challenge for small business: sustainability and SMEs. Industry and Environment, October-December 2003, 26[4].

Whalley, S. (2000). What are 'appropriate' systems for assessing environmental risks and performance in small businesses? In R. Hillary (ed.), Small and Medium-Sized Enterprises and the Environment. Business Imperatives. Sheffield, UK: Greenleaf Publishing Limited.

World Bank (2003). Strengthening Implementation of Corporate Social Responsibility in Global Supply Chains. World Bank, [October].

World Bank (2000). Greening Industry. New Roles for Government, NGO's and Local Communities' New York & London: Oxford University Press.

CHAPTER 4

CORPORATE SOCIAL RESPONSIBILITY AND SUSTAINABILITY OF DONOR-FINANCED INTERVENTIONS IN THE SOUTH

THE CASE OF PAKISTAN

Peter Lund-Thomsen

Center for Corporate Values and Responsibility,
Copenhagen Business School, Denmark

Aisha Mansur

Young Professional Officer (CSR), LEAD Pakistan

Hina Lotia

Manager, Corporate Social Responsibility, LEAD Pakistan

Introduction

Corporate social and environmental responsibility (CSER) in the South is a new research field emerging as international companies and small and medium-sized enterprises[36] (SMEs) are increasingly concerned with the social and environmental impact of their operations. The purpose of the article is to investigate whether CSER initiatives

---

[36] An SME is here defined as an enterprise with less than 250 employees.

improve or worsen the conditions of workers and households in the South. The article will use Pakistan as a challenging case in order to investigate this question. Focus is on the export-oriented leather tanning industry, which has a high degree of child labour, is the country's most polluting industry, and has a history of conflict between producers and local communities.

The significance of the CSER debate is linked to the gradual migration of a number of pollution-intensive industries[37] from the industrialised North to countries in the South where labour costs are lower, environmental regulations more difficult to enforce, and workers/communities more directly exposed to hazardous substances and health problems arising from industrial pollution (Bryant & Bailey 1997). The significance of the CSER debate is also related to the integration of these industries into global supply chains, where Northern buyers require Southern SMEs to demonstrate that they abide by social and environmental standards if they wish to sell their products in the North (Klein 2000).

The paper argues that academic and policy debates on corporate social and environmental responsibility (CSER) in developing countries frequently focus on the social, environmental and human rights performance of multinational companies. Less attention has been paid to the role that international donor agencies play in mediating conflicts between local export industries and workers/communities in the South. Since Southern governments often lack capacity (and sometimes political will) to monitor the CSER performance of their own export industries, international donor projects become an instrument that has the potential to transform conflicts between local stakeholders by improving workers' conditions and preventing environmental disasters arising from industrial production. However, the question is whether such CSER projects are sustainable. What happens when donor support is withdrawn? Using evidence from Pakistan's leather tanning industries, the paper explores the potentials and limitations of donor aid in bringing about sustained improvements in the social and environmental performance of Southern industries that produce for global markets.

The article will seek to answer three interrelated research questions:

---

[37] Such as the textile, leather tanning, footwear and chemical industries.

- Why do companies in the Pakistani leather tanning industry engage in CSER[38] initiatives?

- How does the adoption and implementation of donor-funded CSER initiatives in the Pakistani leather tanning industry affect the conditions of workers and households residing near production sites?

- Do the benefits associated with CSER initiatives continue once donor funding has expired?

Theoretical Considerations

The academic literature on CSER in the South is still in its early phases of development.[39] We will first briefly outline some of the main approaches in the CSER literature. We then critique their ability to explain the kinds of change that CSER initiatives can/cannot bring about in the conditions of workers and households residing adjacent to production sites. Finally, we argue that this calls for an alternative framework for understanding the role of CSER initiatives in the South, which I call a critical framework on CSER.

A dominant theme in the CSER literature is related to what constitutes the proper role of business in relation to society. The question is whether business should have any social responsibilities or whether their only social responsibility is profit-making (The Economist 2005). Much attention is paid to whether it is financially profitable for companies to engage in CSER practices, and how management tools can be devised to help corporate managers solve CSER problems (see e.g., Hopkins 2003, Harvard Business Review 2003). The potential drivers behind business engaging in CSER

---

[38] We use Blowfield & Frynas' (2005) definition of CSER as "an umbrella term for a variety of theories and practices that each recognise the following: (a) the companies have a responsibility for their impact on society and the natural environment; sometimes beyond legal compliance and the liability of individuals; (b) that companies have a responsibility for the behavior of others with whom they do business (e.g. within supply chains); and (c) that business needs to manage its relationship with wider society, be that for reasons of commercial viability or to add value to society".

[39] There is, however, a large 'grey literature' on the subject. Several national and international human rights organizations, trade unions, environmental NGOs and consumer groups have produced policy reports documenting corporate human rights abuses, exploitative working conditions, and pollution from factories that posed a health threat to local communities living adjacent to production sites (see e.g. ICFTU 2003, Oxfam 2004, Christian Aid 2004).

practices is related to the possibility for reducing production costs (Porter & Van der Linde 1996), public relations benefits (O'Brady 2003 & Middlemiss 2003), organisational politics (Prakash 2000, 2001) and managers' personal motives for making a difference (Hemingway & MacLagan 2003). In addition, public-private partnerships are seen as adding value to the implementation of sustainable development[40] by promoting collaboration amongst actors who share skills, resources, expertise, and work together to develop innovative solutions to pressing problems (Utting 2000, p. 32).

Whereas the management-oriented literature has been able to demonstrate the potential financial gains for companies engaging in CSER, it is being criticised for turning questions of social, environmental and economic justice into technical problems that can be solved through a managerial problem-solving approach (Blowfield forthcoming 2005). If the incorporation of social, economic or environmental considerations into business decision-making depends on their financial profitability, "what happens to those issues where such a case cannot be made?" (Frynas & Blowfield 2005). Similarly, the public-private partnership literature emphasises the role of cooperation between stakeholders, assuming commonality of interests and purpose in solving CSER problems. What is missing from such discussions is a willingness to consider the complexity of multi-layered, structurally rooted problems, the potential for conflict between actors, and the unequal power relations that exist between them. It is exactly at this point that the limitations of the management-oriented literature become obvious. It ignores that CSER problems are not simply an outcome of management failures but also rooted in international political and economic forces as well as inequalities in the South (Lund-Thomsen 2004). There is clearly a need to incorporate theories from outside the management literature to more critically assess what CSER initiatives can or cannot achieve in relation to improving conditions of workers/households in the South (Lund-Thomsen 2005).

The Critical Framework on CSER

The critical framework on CSER uses a multi-level approach that investigates the potentials and limitations of CSER initiatives by

---

[40] The integration of economic, social and environmental concerns into policy-making.

outlining optimistic and pessimistic views of how individual firm behaviour, industrial clusters, national governments, and global value chains affect CSER initiatives. The framework first considers the relationship between environmental regulation and firm competitiveness. The incentive for companies to engage in CSER practices is seen as related to strict environmental regulation. An optimistic view sees environmental regulation as a means to promote innovation in companies, reducing costs by using cheaper materials or adopting different processes. A pessimistic view foresees that environmental regulation will force companies to face additional expenditures to curb pollution that will tend to reduce profits (Jenkins et al. 2002). Whereas this literature may be helpful in terms of understanding incentives for CSER engagement at the firm level, it does not address the question of how cooperation and competition between firms may affect what CSER initiatives can and cannot achieve. Here, the literature on industrial clusters offers a useful supplement. Industrial clusters are "geographical concentrations of firms working within the same industry". In an optimistic view, cooperation within clusters will allow firms to upgrade, improving their export potential as well as their social and environmental performance (Nadvi & Barrientos 2004; quotation, p. 1). In a more pessimistic outlook, attempts at cooperating in industrial clusters may be fraught with free-rider problems with some firms opting out of joint action in order to reduce their own costs, putting downwards pressure on their social and environmental performance (Khan et al. 2003). The Achilles heel of the industrial clusters literature is that it does not conceptualise how local industrial clusters in the South are inserted into the global economy. Humphrey & Smitz (2000) thus suggest that the industrial clusters literature can be fruitfully combined with an analysis of how the design, production, and marketing of products involve a chain of activities (the so-called value chain) divided between enterprises often located in distinct localities around the world. In the optimistic view, the diffusion of standards related to quality assurance, health and safety, as well as environmental and labour conditions through global value chains improves efficiency and working conditions, increases market access and upgrades environmental performance. In the pessimistic view, the diffusion of these standards reduces the potential for labour cost advantages and acts as a non-tariff barrier for Southern exports (Nadvi 2003), eventually resulting in a relocation of production to other parts of the world (Hesselberg & Knutsen 2002). This may happen when communities and NGOs in the South use a variety of approaches to apply pressure on firms to improve their CSER performance (see Garvey & Newell 2004). Companies may thus be induced to upgrade the social and environmental aspects of their operations. However, companies may also choose to outsource the most polluting aspects of their operations to other regions where marginalised population groups are unlikely to cause resistance and wind up being disproportionately affected by environmental and occupational risks (Bailey & Bryant 1997). States in the South may promote or hinder this development by adopting a role as a destroyer (through their support for unfettered economic development) or a steward of the natural environment (by making CSER concerns a part of the industrialisation process). The role of donor funding in supporting CSER initiatives which affect the conditions of workers and households will also need to be considered. The question is whether potential benefits generated through donor-funded projects will be sustained once donor support is phased out. In sum, a critical framework on CSER in the South analyses how micro-level struggles over the distribution of social and environmental hazards are linked to local and global political and economic forces. It considers how the relationship between environmental regulation and firm competitiveness, industrial clusters, their insertion into global value chains, community-based accountability strategies, and donor funding provide (dis)incentives for SMEs to engage in CSER practices, and how this affects the conditions of workers and households residing near production sites.

Justification of Industry Selection

Different industries such as the manufacturing of textiles, footwear, and sporting goods could have been used as examples of how micro-levels over the distribution of environmental and social hazards affect the conditions of workers and households. However, the article will investigate the leather tanning industry for the following reasons.

a) The tanning industry has gradually shifted from the industrialised North to countries in the South since the 1970s. The share of developing countries in global production of light leather increased from 35% in 1970-71 to 56% in 1994-96, while their share of heavy leather production went up from 26% to 56% in the same period. Similar trends were evident in relation to exports and employment within the industry, while sourcing is increasingly used as a result of specialisation (Hesselberg & Knutsen 2002).

b) As far as CSER is concerned, the leather tanning industry constitutes an important source of employment and foreign exchange earnings in many developing countries (Varadarajan & Krishnamoorthy 1993). The leather tanning industry has also been ranked as one of the most polluting industries as compared to other manufacturing industries. Its toxic intensity is one of the highest per unit of output (Khan et al. 2003). At the same time, it has traditionally involved a large number of child workers in production (Hesselberg & Knutsen 2002).

The Pakistani Context

The international tanning industry is found in a number of countries across the South, including Bangladesh, Brazil, India, Mexico, Pakistan and South Africa. This article focuses on Pakistan, since it constitutes a challenging case in relation to investigating the potentials and limitations of CSER initiatives. According to Albertyn & Watkins (2002), the effectiveness of voluntary CSER initiatives will – in part – depend upon high degrees of social/environmental awareness, the presence of an active civil society, and government commitment and capacity to enforce existing regulations. Whereas countries such as Bangladesh, Brazil, India, Mexico and South Africa[41] have witnessed the emergence of national or regional social movements, communities in Pakistan are generally not well-organised, which prevents them from exerting continued pressure on companies (NEC 2004). Trade unions have been subjected to severe government repression. Recent data indicate that only 3% of the Pakistani workforce is unionised (Ahmad Khan 2002, p. 163). The lack of a unionised movement has severely undermined the effectiveness of labour rights in Pakistan (NEC 2004, p. 5). Meanwhile, the non-profit sector tends to be seen as promoting the Western agenda of its foreign donors. The government prioritises export promotion ahead of environmental protection and lacks capacity to enforce existing regulations (ibid.). The

---

[41] Bangladesh has the Bangladeshi Rural Advancement Committee; Brazil is home to the Landless Labourers' Movement; India has several movements, including the Chipko Movement; Mexico has become famous for the work of the Zapatistas in Chiapas; and South Africa has witnessed the development of a nation-wide movement for environmental justice.

implementation of national environmental quality standards relies heavily upon industry self-monitoring and reporting (Saeed Alrai 2002). In these circumstances, most CSER initiatives would appear to be severely constrained. However, the experiences of the soccer ball industry, oil and gas, and the surgical instruments industry indicate that CSER initiatives may still have significant impacts. In the soccer ball industry, a public-private partnership between UNICEF, the ILO[42], NGOs, multinational companies and Pakistani manufacturers largely succeeded in eliminating child labour from the industry. However, the project also generated unintended consequences, including a reduction of income for some women, increased sexual harassment, and Pakistani soccer ball producers becoming less competitive as soccer ball production shifted elsewhere (Husselbee 2000, Schrage 2004 and Nadvi 2004). Public-private partnerships are also important in the oil and gas sector. In spite of the frequent non-implementation of environmental and social laws in Pakistan, CSER has been a focused agenda for oil and gas companies, who by law are required to invest in communities and stakeholders in the area of their operations. These include companies such as HUBCO[43], Premier Kufpec[44] and BHP, who are involved in community welfare programmes focusing on local capacity building, health and education initiatives. Shell has moved ahead to prevent deforestation and species conservation in collaboration with World Wildlife Fund (WWF) and The World Conservation Union (IUCN). Another central motivation for international companies such as OMV[45] and British Petroleum seems to be that they are trying to bring their country policies in line with the

---

[42] UNICEF - The United Nations organization responsible for children's issues; ILO - the International Labour Organization

[43] The Hub Power Company, which is listed on Karachi, Lahore, Islamabad and Luxembourg Stock Exchanges has the largest market capitalization of any private company in Pakistan and has over seventeen thousand Pakistani and international shareholders. The Hub power station in Karachi is the first and largest power station to be financed by the private sector in Southern Asia and one of the largest private power projects in the newly industrialised world.

[44] A 50:50 joint venture between Premier, an oil company based in the UK, with Kuwait Foreign Petroleum Exploration Company (K.S.C.) ("KUFPEC"), a wholly owned subsidiary of Kuwait Petroleum Corporation. The joint venture was set up in September 2001 and operates through a joint company Premier-KUFPEC Pakistan B.V.

[45] OMV is a leading oil and natural gas group in Central and Eastern Europe, which is active in exploration and production worldwide and has integrated chemical operations (http://www.omv.com/smgr/portal/jsp/index.jsp?p_site=AT; accessed 15 March 2005).

international policies, although some use customised policies as per local environment and needs. For example, Shell has developed its Shell Tameer Programme in Pakistan as a customised programme for the global Shell Liver Wire Programme.[46] In addition, Premier Kufpec has been under pressure from a range of NGOs including WWF-Pakistan, the Sustainable Development Policy Institute, Shehri, Shirkatgah, and Friends of the Earth International for its plans to initiate gas exploration in the Kithar National Park in the province of Sindh. Finally, many corporations are involved in charitable giving and philanthropy linked to a particular cause. The devastating Tsunami disaster and Shakat Khanum Memorial Cancer Hospital in Lahore are two such instances that gained interest by corporations such as Unilever, Pepsi and Shell. The Pakistani experience with CSER also points to the role of trade sanctions in upgrading export industries. In the mid-1990s, firms from the Sialkot surgical instruments cluster were excluded from the US market for failing to comply with the USA's good manufacturing practices. This forced Sialkot producers to upgrade their quality standards (Halder & Nadvi 2002). Moreover, Pakistani newspapers have frequently reported CSER problems, Pakistanis have filed complaints against polluting companies at local courts, and the military government is increasing cooperation with NGOs. These factors make Pakistan a challenging case for determining the effectiveness of CSER initiatives in an authoritarian context dominated by rapid industrialisation.

Case Study: The Kasur Tanneries

The article employs a case study design to analyse why companies in the Pakistani leather tanning industry engage in CSER initiatives, and how the adoption and implementation of donor-funded projects in the industry affect the conditions of workers and households residing adjacent to production sites. The article concentrates on 237 tanneries located in a large cluster on the outskirts of the city of Kasur. Kasur is an interesting research location for several reasons. First, it has the

---

[46] LiveWIRE is a Shell-supported programme that aims to raise awareness of business startup as a viable career choice for young people. Tameer identifies young entrepreneurs and provides them with the tools to start a business: from preparing for the risks involved, to giving them the confidence to contact avenues for information and funding (http://www.tameer.org.pk/page.php?page_id=81: accessed 15 March 2005).

largest concentration of tanneries in Pakistan. Second, since the industry's expansion during the 1980s, workers and local residents have been exposed to life-threatening substances as a result of tannery pollution. Third, local residents and NGOs have actively been protesting against the impact of the industry since the early 1980s. Fourth, the industry has been the subject of a large-scale donor intervention that consisted of occupational health and safety training of workers, in-house pollution mitigation measures, and end-of-pipe treatment of polluted wastewater. The partnership was initiated with support from the United Nations Development Programme (UNDP). This support will phase out by mid-2005, while a cost-sharing mechanism for the continuation of the project has been developed between various tiers of the government (50%) and Kasur Tanneries Association (50%), prompting questions about the potential for collective action/free-rider problems amongst the tanneries. Finally, environmental and social upgrading within the industry could facilitate increased access to export markers.

Historical Background

In 1947, when Pakistan came into being, very few tanneries existed in Pakistan and were mostly involved in small-scale production of leather for use as soles in shoes. In the 1950s and 1960s, some larger, better-equipped tanneries were established throughout the country. These only produced semi-finished (wet-blue) leather, which was mainly exported to Europe for finishing. In the 1970s, however, the processing of finished leather began on a larger scale. With increasing wage costs and stricter pollution control measures in developed countries, there was a significant translocation of leather production facilities to the developing world, where pollution-control measures were less stringent. Hence, by the late 1980s, the leather industry in Kasur was producing high-quality finished leather. This industry had become the second most important export industry for Pakistan by the end of the decade, growing by 800% in a matter of ten years.[47] However, the bright outlook of the leather industry, especially in the export market, was blighted by the environmental pollution produced by the industry, especially in the tanning subsector. Haphazard industrial growth and the ineffective implementation of environmental legislation had

---

[47] "Five Year Development Plan for the Leather Industry in Pakistan (1992-1996), Volume 1". Prepared by National Management Consultants (PVT), for Government of Pakistan, Export Promotion Bureau. December 1991.

converted Kasur, one of the major tanning clusters in Pakistan, into a town of diseases related with air and groundwater pollution.[48]

Drivers for CSER Engagement and their Effects on Workers/Communities

We will now use the critical framework on CSER to answer our three basic research questions stated in the beginning:

(i) Why do companies in the Pakistani leather tanning industry engage in CSER initiatives?

(ii) How does the adoption and implementation of donor-funded CSER initiatives in the Pakistani leather tanning industry affect the conditions of workers and households residing near production sites?

(iii) Do the benefits associated with CSER initiatives continue once donor funding has expired?

First, we consider the relationship between **environmental regulation and firm competitiveness**. An optimistic view sees environmental regulation as playing a key role in promoting innovation in companies and helping reduce their operating costs, while a pessimistic view would envisage that environmental regulation forces additional costs on firms and hence reduces their profits. Pakistan does have a number of laws that provide a framework for regulating the impact of polluting companies. These include Environmental Acts, Ordinances and Codes, such as the Penal Code of 1860[49], the anti-pollution legislation embodied in the Factories Act of 1937[50], the Environmental Protection Ordinance (1983)[51], and the more recent Pakistan Environmental Protection Act (1997).[52]

---

[48] "An Overview of Common Diseases Resulting from Environmental Pollution in Kasur". Participatory Development Resource Cell (PDRC), Sakano-Lab, Tokyo Institute of Technology, Japan.

[49] The penal code outlawed the release of any noxious or poisonous substances into the atmosphere, with a maximum penalty of three months' imprisonment and/or fine up to Rs. 500 (in 1989, 1 US$ = Rs. 21.4). It was established during British colonial rule.

[50] The Factories Act outlawed the disposal of industrial wastes into bodies of water

[51] It called for the establishment of a high-level Environmental Protection Council at the federal level to form national environmental policy and ensure enforcement of National Environmental Quality Standards (NEQS).

[52] It was enacted as an improvement over the Pakistan Environmental Protection Ordinance and aimed to effectively implement the NEQS, which had not been effective previously due to reasons such as the lack of implementation capacity and resistance in industry.

However, these laws have not been enforced effectively. In the case of Kasur, the UNDP described in 1993 how the four tannery clusters in Kasur were discharging a total of 9,000 cubic metres of heavily polluted tannery waste water per day, out of this 2,500 cubic metres was discharged into the Rohi Nallah (a nearby waterstream). The remaining wastewater formed stagnant pools covering an area of 327 acres and another 311 acres during the monsoon period. The amount of tannery pollution load discharged into the environment (per annum) was: 4,000 tons of BOD_5, 11,000 tons of COD, 10,000 tons of suspended solids, 160 tons of chromium and 400 tons of sulphide. Hence, the environmental and social consequences of the leather tanning production in Kasur were extremely serious before the pollution project intervened. There is little doubt, however, that the pollution control project significantly improved the situation. A win-win situation appeared to exist when in-plant measures and a combined treatment plant were put in place. The capital costs and investments required for reclamation/appreciation of agricultural land was of a one-off character. At the same time, chrome recovery, waste recycling and water consumption reduced production costs. This could be seen "in the relatively short payback periods for in-plant measures, the dispersion of recurring costs associated with end-of-pipe treatment across the cluster and the land reclamation gains. Clean-ups on this scale also yielded impressive environmental and health benefits".[53]

In spite of these gains, it was also obvious that *some* leather tanneries were still ignoring existing environmental regulations in the new millennium. On 25 October 2003, the national daily, *The Dawn*, reported that notices had been served on a cluster of newly built tanneries along the Lahore-Ferozepur Road. Five factories had been constructed without obtaining due permission. While two tanneries had installed treatment plants, the others had been throwing their waste into a nearby drain. The Kasur district environment officer stated that strict action would be taken against these tanners. At the same time, four people – including a tannery owner – died on 26 July 2003 while removing waste from a poisonous chemical well in one of the clusters after a suction machine had broken down.[54] This situation was not an isolated incident but reflected the broader trend towards non-implementation of existing laws related to environmental pollution in

---

[53] Khan, SR, Developing Country Initiatives in Complying with International Environmental Standards – Pakistan's Small and Medium-sized Enterprises, SDPI Research and News Bulletin, vol. 10, no. 3, May-June 2003.
[54] The Dawn, Notices Served on Tanneries in Kasur, 25 October 2005.

Pakistan. For instance, in the city of Multan, the Municipal Corporation verified that it had for the past two years refused to renew the licences of the hide factories on Nawabpur Road due to environmental hazards created by these factories. However, the tanneries were still functioning in the area at the time of the newspaper report.[55] As these examples illustrate, environmental regulation does not appear to have been a central factor that prompted tanneries to innovate and thus upgrade their CSER performance. In other words, although Pakistan has enacted a number of environmental laws and regulations, their presence does not seem to a significant driver for tanneries to engage in CSER initiatives.

If would appear as if the literature on *industrial clusters* offers a more useful alternative to explaining why companies engage in CSER initiatives. In an optimistic view, cooperation within clusters will allow firms to upgrade, improving their export potential, as well as social and environmental performance. In the pessimistic view, industrial clusters will foster free-rider problems, putting downwards pressure on the social and environmental performance of the cluster. The vast majority of the Kasur tanneries are members of either the Tanneries Association Dingarh (for medium to large tanneries) or the Small Tanneries Association (comprising 4-5 workers per tannery).[56] It is worth noting that these associations were even present before the environmental crisis in Kasur started to receive significant media attention. For example, the Tanneries Association Dingarh was formed in 1964 in response to a flood that hit Kasur. The 13 tanneries in operation at the time grouped together in order to seek government help for reconstructing their tanneries. Their request turned out to be partially successful.[57] Collection action within the Tanneries Association has also been central in relation to environmental upgrading within the industry. First, the Tanneries Association tried to

---

[55] The Dawn, MMC Unable to Remove Polluting Tanneries, 27 January 2002

[56] We recognise that clustering can help enterprises compete by both generating intended and unintended benefits. Unintended benefits may be generated through similar or related activities that lower costs for producers. This could include a pool of specialised workers, easy access to suppliers/specialised inputs, and the quick spread of knowledge within the cluster (Nadvi and Schmitz 1999) However, in this case study, we focus on the generation of intended benefits through conscious cooperation between enterprises within the Kasur cluster. Our focus on the role of the Kasur Tanneries Association has to be seen in the light of the important role that trade associations generally play in facilitating cooperation in Pakistani industrial clusters (see also Nadvi 1999).

[57] Interview with the Tanners Association in Kasur, Kasur, 24 February 2005

bring the issue to the attention of the relevant government authorities in Kasur already in the 1990s. Second, the tanneries contributed financially to the Kasur Tanneries Pollution Control project in its initial phase, as indicated in the above figures. Third, since 2002 the Kasur Tanneries Association has contributed 50% of the costs associated with the pollution control project. The common effluent treatment plant constructed with UNDP support during the first couple of years of the project is now being run on the basis of a cost-sharing mechanism between the voluntary contributions of the tanneries (50%) the Government of Punjab (20%), District Government Kasur (15%), and the Tehsil Government Kasur (15%). It is envisaged that the tanneries will pay the full cost of running the common effluent treatment plant by 2007. In relation to the pessimistic view, which suggests that attempts at cooperating in industrial clusters may be fraught with free-rider problems, it would appear as if there are some cases in Kasur where tanneries have not contributed towards the overall running costs of the plant. In these instances, it appears that (i) the tanners might not be aware of the importance of contributing towards the plant; (ii) they might not be interested in paying the additional costs associated with keeping the plant operational; and (iii) the business cycle of the tanners might make it difficult for them to contribute towards its maintenance during particular periods.[58] However, given the fact that the treatment plant has been functional since 2002, it does not appear as if free-riding constitutes a problem that could threaten its long-term survival. In other words, it seems as if the benefits associated with cooperation within the cluster played an important role in terms of explaining why the tanneries engaged in the pollution control project.

Another factor that might explain why tanneries engage in CSER initiatives is their integration into *global value chains*. The optimistic view suggests that global value chains lead to improved efficiency and working conditions, increased market access, and upgrading of environmental performance in SMEs through the diffusion of international standards through the chain. The pessimistic view argues that the diffusion of these standards acts as a non-tariff barrier, leading to the eventual reallocation of production to more competitive regions. On the one hand, it has been argued that the tanneries will have to demonstrate compliance with international trade regulations in order to sustain their access to international markets. Non-tariff regulations

---

[58] Interview with Kasur Government Official. Kasur, 24 February 2005

relating to health, safety and environment can prove to be major barriers in the export of leather if proper measures are not taken to upgrade the existing environmental infrastructure and conform to international standards.[59] On the other hand, it is surprising to note that only two out of 237 tanneries in Kasur have received 9001 or 14001 certification.[60] One of the reasons for this could be the difficulty in accessing information on standards and technology, and difficulty in securing loans for lumpy capital investments, such as water treatment plants.[61] The total investment required for ISO14001 is about Rs. 500,000, while the annual investment required for maintaining the certification is about Rs. 200,000. However, this does not appear to be an unmanageable investment for the Kasur tanneries, since the combined effluent treatment plant is already in operation.[62] Given the very limited number of certified tanneries, it appears that value chains have *not* have prompted the diffusion of standards in the Kasur tanneries. In other words, contrary to the common assumption that global value chains are a significant source of firm upgrading, value chains do not seem to constitute a significant driver that provides incentives for the Kasur tanneries to engage in CSER initiatives. At the same time, we lack data to ascertain whether environmental and social upgrading in the Kasur tanning industry has led to a significant translocation of production to other clusters in Pakistan (or other countries in the developing world). It is worthwhile noting that the two other large tannery clusters in Pakistan (Sialkot and Korangi) are currently engaged in the process of setting up their own treatment plants.[63] This could indicate that the Pakistani tanning industry might eventually pursue a race to the top instead of a race to the bottom as far as CSER upgrading is concerned.

Community pressure may also provide incentives for the Kasur tanneries to engage in CSER initiatives. In the optimistic view, such pressure could lead to the upgrading of environmental and social standards, while the pessimistic view foresees that it would lead to

---

[59] "Upgradation of Common Effluent Pretreatment Plant (CEPTP), Kasur to meet National Environmental Quality Standards (NEQS)" KTWMA

[60] Personal communication from environmental consultant

[61] "Developing Country Initiatives in Complying with International Environmental Standards-Pakistan's Small and Medium Enterprises". Shaheen Rafi Khan

[62] Interview with Environmental Consultant, Lahore, 24 February 2005

[63] Business Recorder, 26 May 2003. "ADB to set up water treatment plant at Sialkot Tanneries Zone"

Business Recorder, 1 June 2002. "Treatment plant for Korangi tanneries to start by year-end"

outsourcing of the most polluting components of tannery operations to other regions where there are less stringent environmental laws and community pressure is absent. In the Kasur case, community pressure played a vital role in the setting up of the project. An example of such community pressure was witnessed in 1993, when the people of Bangla and adjoining villages near Kasur constructed a mile-long bund to keep poisonous tannery wastewaters away from their home. Even in the face of severe opposition from the district administration and police, the villagers refused to budge and soon the administration was forced to concede defeat.[64] Similarly, the communities in Kasur exerted considerable pressure on the tannery owners and workers, through ostracising them and forcing them to live as outsiders in their communities.[65] Furthermore, in 1999-2000, the Committee of Civil Society Organizations in Kasur played a role in organising affected communities and making their pleas heard.[66] More recently, community pressure has been important in terms of convincing the KTWMA to plan a phase 2 of the Kasur Tanneries Pollution Control Project, which strives to fully meet the NEQS. As indicated above, we lack data to ascertain whether significant shifts in tannery production have taken place since the CSER upgrading process began. At present, we do not know whether public pressure in Kasur has led to a translocation of tannery pollution to areas where communities are less capable of fending for themselves. However, it does appear as if the general improvement in environmental conditions has led to a demobilisation of public pressure on the tanneries in Kasur.[67] Since community pressure has been one of the most significant reasons why the tanneries have engaged in CSER initiatives, the lack of continuity in community pressure may raise questions about the future potential for further upgrading within the industry.

Donor Funding

Lastly, it is imperative to consider the role of donor funding in initiating CSER activities within the tanning industry. The optimistic view states that donor funding enables investments in cleaner technology and end-of-pipe treatment, and contributes towards state-

---

[64] SDPI, Citizens Report on Sustainable Development, 1995
[65] Interview with Kasur Government Official, Kasur, 24 February 2005
[66] The Committee of Civil Society Organizations was established in March 2000, and works under the patronage of Mr. Malik Meraj Khalid, educationalist and former caretaker Prime Minister of Pakistan.
[67] Interview with Kasur Government Official, Kasur, 24 February 2005

of-the art know-how. The pessimistic view states that donor funding eventually phases out and the benefits cannot be sustained. The optimistic view holds true for the Kasur tanneries, due to the project environmental and working conditions having improved.

In terms of generating benefits for the tanneries and local communities in Kasur, an outcome of the project has been that working conditions have substantially improved in the tanneries due to several occupational health and training workshops devised for the workers, stressing upon the importance of wearing gloves and face masks.[68] The KTWMA plant has been successful in decreasing water consumption, salt use and chrome use within the tanneries. In 2001, this was reflected in 10-20% decrease in water consumption, 50% decrease in the use of salt, and 25% decrease in the use of chrome[69] The 2005 figures for the overall efficiency of the plant are given below:

Parameter	Incoming Effluent (mg/1)	After Treatment (mg/1)	% Reduction	NEQS (mg/1)
Suspended Solids	2800	100	96.5	200
BOD5	1500	400	73	80
COD	2800	1100	61	150
Cr+3	30	1	97	1
S-2	150	20	87	1
TDS	10,000	10,000	0	3500
SO4	2000	900	55	600
C1	5000	5000	0	1000

Kasur Tannery Waste Management Agency: Upgradation of Common Effluent Pretreatment Plant (CEPTP), Kasur to meet National Environmental Quality Standards (NEQS) 2005

Table 4:1 Overall Efficiency of Common Effluent Pretreatment Plant, Kasur

Other donor-funded programmes in Pakistan, such as Introduction to Cleaner Technologies Program (ICTP) and Environmental Technology Program for Industry (ETPI) are presently successfully operating within the tanneries.[70] It would seem that in the Kasur case the pessimistic view does not hold, as even after the cut-off period of 2002

---

[68] Workshops and seminars organised by Participatory Development Resource Cell (PDRC) during 2000, 2001, 2002

[69] Export Promotion Bureau: 2001

[70] "Operationalizing Corporate Social Responsibility in Leather Sector". Muhammad Musaddiq, Chairman Pakistan Tanners Association. June 21, 2004

the KTWMA plant has still been operational. The project is being sustained by Pakistani (as opposed to donor) contributions towards the running costs of the project.[71] However, although the project succeeded in achieving the environmental standards envisaged in the project document, the plant has only reached 75% of the targets set out in the NEQS.[72] Yet the implementation of the Kasur Tannery Pollution Control Project and its successful operation for the last two years is an indication of the commitment of the tanning community of Kasur, Government of Punjab and the District Government Kasur.

Conclusion

At the beginning of this article, we set out to answer three questions. First, what are the main drivers behind the engagement of CSER in the Pakistani leather tanning industry? Second, how does the adoption and implementation of donor-funded CSER initiatives in the Pakistani leather tanning industry affect the conditions of workers and households residing near production sites? Three, are CSER initiatives sustainable once donor funding expires? In trying to answer these three questions, we argued that the business-oriented CSER literature is trying to turn questions of social, economic and environmental justice into technical problem-solving exercises. We found this unhelpful in understanding the motives and effects of SME engagement in donor-funded CSER practices. We therefore tried to establish an alternative critical framework on CSER that made use of the literature on environmental regulation and competitiveness, industrial clusters, global value chains, community accountability mechanisms, and the role of donor funding in influencing CSER initiatives. On the basis of our case study of the Kasur leather tanning industry, it did not seem that environmental regulation had been playing a large role in providing incentives for SMEs in the industry to adopt CSER measures and/or improve their social and environmental performance. Although Pakistan has a number of relevant environmental protection laws in place, these are largely not implemented. The joint efforts of the Tanneries Association played a key role in upgrading the environmental and social performance of the industry. However, free-rider problems still exist, with some tanners not paying their share of

---

[71] As mentioned above, in the following ratio: Government of Punjab 20%, District Government Kasur 15%, Tehsil Government Kasur 15%, and the Kasur Tanneries Association 50%.

[72] Interview with Senior Politician, Kasur, 24 February 2005

the costs associated with running the joint effluent treatment plant. Whereas global value chains could – in theory – provide incentives for the tanning industry to upgrade its performance, very few enterprises have so far been ISO14000 certified, with hardly any producers adhering to SA8000 standard. Perhaps the most salient pressure on the tanneries to engage in CSER initiatives has been the existence of community accountability mechanisms, such as direct action strategies and court petitions, which pressurised the tanneries to combat the pollution associated with their production. However, the question is whether the pressure on the tanners to upgrade will eventually lead to a relocation of the most polluting aspects of the tannery process. Finally, donor funding has enabled the industry to make the necessary investments to upgrade the CSER performance of the industry. In terms of sustainability, it appears as if the establishment of the KTWMA has provided an organisational structure that is viable in the long term, whereas the tanners are – in spite of some free-rider problems – willing and able to pay their share of the costs related to the running of the joint effluent treatment plant.

However, whereas the project was successful in terms of reducing water and air pollution problems to a considerable extent as well as tensions between the tanners and the communities, the original project design appears to have left a number of issues unaddressed. The project design did not:

1. involve any significant public participation component. In other words, the communities that were bearing the costs of the industry's expansion – women in particular – appeared to have little or no say in how the health risks affecting them should be removed. As a result, important community concerns may have been overlooked in the project design and implementation.

2. seem to provide the citizens or NGOs of Kasur with the tools that could enable them to monitor or hold the industry to account for its economic, social or environmental impacts. As a result, it may be difficult for citizens in Kasur to articulate their concerns, since hard data on the economic, social and environmental performance of the tanneries cannot be independently verified by the communities themselves. This knowledge gap leads to the communities being in an unequal bargaining position vis-à-vis the tanners.

3. upgrade the industry in terms of improved certification within the industry. To date, only two out of 237 tanneries have received ISO9001 or ISO14001 certification, while another ten are about to be certified. Within the context of the WTO and increased economic competition, compliance with international standards may be a necessary condition for improved export performance, since Northern buyers require that Southern exporters adhere to such standards. In other words, non-compliance with standards (e.g. ISO14001) could potentially threaten the survival of the tanneries in an increasingly competitive world economy. This could also result into reduced employment and increased poverty, potentially presenting a significant challenge for the recently introduced local government system.

Future Perspectives

If the Kasur tanneries are to improve their competitiveness and CSER performance, it might be useful to generate more in-depth knowledge about the problems faced by the industry before a possible phase 2 of the project is initiated. This could involve the following themes:

a. the problems faced by the enterprises (e.g. the tanneries) in relation to improving their export performance, working conditions, and external environmental impact. This would also include stakeholder mapping and identification of existing networks/interventions supporting the upgrading of the industry.

b. the problems faced by citizens and communities in increasing their participation in the governance of the industry, creating or gaining access to information, and making use of that information to induce the tanners to upgrade their performance. In particular, the opportunities and constraints faced by women in organising themselves to have their voice heard should be explored.

c. the problems faced by various tiers of the local government in Kasur in terms providing an adequate governance framework that supports the economic, social and environmental upgrading of the industry.

d. the problems faced in creation and functioning of non-formal and formal community empowerment mechanisms, such as monitoring committees, citizens community boards as envisaged under Local Government Ordinance 2001, especially around the theme of corporate responsibility.

Based on the research into the above points, one could envisage that the following components might be worthwhile addressing in a phase 2 of the project. In other words, a phase 2 of the project should not only focus on hardware upgrading but also on software upgrading within the industry and surrounding communities:

e. *exposure visits/toxic tours* for sensitising the policy and decision makers at various levels, as a means to create a demand for implementation of existing social and environmental regulations. These tours could also familiarise the participants with the economic, social and environmental challenges faced by the industry as well as trade-offs required to be understood while formulating development policies, plans and programmes.

f. *facilitating SA8000 and ISO14001 certification of tanneries* – with the aim of helping this sector to remain competitive in the world markets and meet stringent requirements from international buyers, while improving their social and environmental performance for improved community relations and employment.

g. *community empowerment* – with the aim of strengthening the existing civil society networks and, where required, creating new civil society networks. Special attention should be given to women's networks. These networks might then be able to undertake independent, community-based air and water pollution monitoring, as being done in other developing countries.

h. *training and skills development* - with the aim of enhancing the ability of key stakeholders to document, articulate and incorporate public concerns in the policy process.

Bibliography

Ahmad Khan, S. (2002). Socially Acceptable Solutions of the Tanning Industry, in Javed, N. & Z. Abbas, Kasur Tanneries Pollution Control Project, Proceedings of the International Conference on Pollution Control in Tanning Industry of Pakistan, Lahore, KTWMA & UNDP. Lahore, Design Zone, 11-13 June.

Albertyn, C. & Watkins, G. (2002). Partners in Pollution: Voluntary Agreements and Corporate Greenwash, South African People and Environment in the Global Market Series. Pietermaritzburg. Groundwork.

Blowfield, M.E. (2005). CSR – Reinventing the Meaning of Development, International Affairs, 81[3], forthcoming 2005.

Blowfield, M.E. & Frynas, J.F. (2005). Setting New Agendas: Critical Perspectives on Corporate Social Responsibility in the Developing World, International Affairs, 81[3].

Bryant R.L. & Bailey, S. (1997). Third World Political. Ecology Routledge New York.

Christian Aid (2004). Behind the Mask: The Real Face of CSR, Christian Aid, The United Kingdom, [28 February 2004]. httn://www.christianaid.org.uk/indet)th/0401csr/index.htm

Economist, The (2005, 22-28 January). A Survey of Corporate Social Responsibility, The Economist, 374[8410].

Garvey, N. & Newell, P. (2004). Corporate Accountability to the Poor – Assessing the Effectiveness of Community-based Strategies, IDS Working Paper 227. Brighton, IDS, [October2004].

Halder, G. & Nadvi, K. (2002). Local Clusters in Global Value Chains: Exploring Dynamic Linkages between Germany & Pakistan, IDS Working Paper 152. Sussex, IDS.

Harvard Business Review et al. (2003). Harvard Business Review on Corporate Social Responsibility (Harvard Business Review Paperback Series). Cambridge, Harvard Business School Press.

134

Hemingway, C.A. & MacLagan, P.W. (2004). Managers' Personal Values as Drivers of Corporate Social Responsibility, Journal of Business Ethics, 50.

Hesselberg, J. & Knutsen, H.G. (2000). Leather Tanning, Environmental Regulations, Competitiveness and Locational Shifts, in Jenkins et al. (eds), Environmental Regulation in the New Global Economy. Cheltenham, Edward Elgar.

Hopkins, M. (2003). The Planetary Bargain: Corporate Social Responsibility Matters. London, Earthscan Publications.

Humphrey, J. & Schmitz, H. (2000). Governance and Upgrading: Linking Industrial Cluster and Global Value Chain Research, IDS Working Paper 120. Sussex, IDS.

Husselbee, D. (2000). NGOs as Development Partners to the Corporates: Child Football Stitchers in Pakistan, Development in Practice, 10[3-4].

International Confederation of Free Trade Unions (ICFTU) (2003). Export Processing Zones: Symbols of Exploitation and Development at a Dead End, Brussels. Accessed 28 February 2004. http://www.icftu.orz(disvlaydocument.asp?lndex--991218374&Languase=EN

Jenkins, R. et al. (2002). Environmental Regulation in the New Global Economy – The Impact on Industry and Competitiveness, Cheltenham, Edward Elgar.

Khan, S.R. et al. (2003). The Costs and Benefits of Compliance with International Environmental Standards: Pakistan Case Study, in Sustainable Development Policy Institute, Sustainable Development and Southern Realities - Past and Future in South Asia. Karachi, City Press.

Klein, N. (2000). No Logo: Taking Aim at the Brand Bullies, Knopf. Toronto, Canada.

Lund-Thomsen, P. (2004). Towards A Critical Framework on Corporate Social and Environmental Responsibility in the South: the Case of Pakistan, September 2004, Development, 47[3].

Lund-Thomsen, P. (2005). Corporate Accountability in South Africa: the Role of Community Mobilizing in Environmental Governance, International Affairs, 81[3], forthcoming 2005.

Middlemiss, N. (2003). Authentic Not Cosmetic: CSR as Brand Enhancement, Journal of Brand Management, 10[4-5].

Nadvi, K. & Schmitz, H. (1999). Clustering and Industrialization: Introduction, World Development, 27[9].

Nadvi, K. (1999). Collective Efficiency and Collective Failure: The Response of the Sialkot Surgical Instrument Cluster to Global Quality Pressures, World Development, 27[9].

Nadvi, K. (2003). The Cost of Compliance – Global Standards for Small-scale Firms and Workers, IDS Policy Briefing, Issue 18. Sussex, IDS, [May 2003].

Nadvi, K. (2004). The Effect of Global Standards on Local Producers: A Pakistani Case Study, in H. Schmitz (ed). Local Enterprises in the Global Economy: Issues of Governance and Upgrading. Cheltenham, Elgar.

Nadvi, K. & Barrientos, S. (2004). Small Firm Clusters: Working to Reduce Poverty, IDS Policy Briefing, Issue 21. Sussex, IDS, [May 2004].

NEC (2004). Operationalizing Corporate Social Responsibility in Leather Sector. Lahore, NEC.

O'Brady, A.K. (2003). How to Generate Sustainable Brand Value from Responsibility, Journal of Brand Management, 10[4-5].

Oxfam (2004). Trading Away Our Rights: Women Working in Global Supply Chains, United Kingdom, Oxfam. Accessed 28 February 2004. http://www.oxfam.org/ene/prO40209 labour report.htm

Porter, M. & Linde, C.V. (1996). Green & Competitive: Ending the Stalemate, in Welford, R. & R. Starkev, The Earthscan Reader in Business and the Environment. London, Earthscan.

Prakash, A. (2000). Greening of the Firm - the Politics of Corporate Environmentalism. Cambridge, Cambridge University Press.

Prakash, A. (2001). Why Do Firms Adopt 'Beyond-Compliance' Environmental Policies, Business, Strategy and the Environment, 10.

Saeed Alrai, M.I. (2002). Environmental Policy and Practice in Pakistan and Possibility of Modifications, in Javed, N. & Z. Abbas, Kasur Tanneries Pollution Control Project, Proceedings of the International Conference on Pollution Control in Tanning Industry of Pakistan, Lahore, KTWMA & UNDP. Lahore, Design Zone, 11-13 June.

Schrage, E.J. (2004). Promoting International Worker Rights Through Private Voluntary Initiatives: Public Relations or Public Policy?, UI Center for Human Rights. Iowa, University of Iowa.

Utting, P. (2000). Business Responsibility for Sustainable Development, Occasional Paper no. 2, United Nations Research Institute for Sustainable Development.

Varadarajan, D.H. & Krishnamoorthy, S. (1993). Environmental Implications of Leather Tanneries. New Delhi, Ashish Publishing House.

CHAPTER 5

CORPORATE CITIZENSHIP AND HUMAN RIGHTS

REALITY AND PROSPECTS OF THE PROPOSED CONSTITUTIONAL CHANGES IN KENYA

Kiarie Mwaura

Lecturer in Law, School of Law, Queen's University, Belfast, Northern Ireland

Abstract

Globalisation has enabled businesses to assume a central role in both the domestic and international economies. This has offered both unprecedented opportunities for corporations and grave threats to human rights. Companies that are not socially responsible are facing considerable pressure from consumers and NGOs and the reputation of those that are not socially responsible is being damaged easily by the widespread consumer activism in the global market. Apart from assessing the extent to which companies have been responsible for violations of human rights in Kenya, this paper examines the effect that the proposed constitutional changes are likely to have in terms of changing the managerial practice of directors. It also assesses whether these laws are sufficient to deal with the rising global corporate social responsibility (CSR) standards. Apart from raising awareness and helping company directors to understand their legal obligations towards CSR, this paper will also formulate other reforms which can be implemented by policy-makers in order to promote CSR and the respect for human rights by corporations.

Introduction

Globalisation has enabled businesses to assume a central role in both the domestic and international economies. This has offered both unprecedented opportunities for corporations and grave threats to human rights. Companies that are not socially responsible are facing considerable pressure from consumers and NGOs and the reputation of those that are not socially responsible is being damaged easily by the widespread consumer activism in the global market. For example, Del Monte Kenya suffered heavy losses in 2001 when the workers' unions, local NGOs, and the representatives of the Catholic Church organised a boycott of its products in Italy, a key destination of the company's products, as a result of the failure on the part of the company to heed the concerns of employees and the local communities (Kent, 2001). Although Del Monte paid its employees relatively well and offered some social facilities, the wider community felt that the company was not doing enough. As a result of the publicity of the boycott, the company suffered great losses, which could have been avoided by reducing the conflict between the management of the company, its employees, and the community. The boycott was only called off when the company bound itself to invest in social facilities, like schools, health and education to benefit the workers, their families and the neighbouring communities.

Although the recent developments ought to encourage company directors to shift their focus from the traditional role of profit maximisation, a number of factors, such as insufficient stakeholder activism, lack of legal awareness amongst the victims of human rights violations, and lack of effective remedies to redress the wrongs committed by companies, continue to encourage directors to pursue socially irresponsible activities. In addition to these factors, the complex, burdensome and uncertain regulatory framework makes it difficult for company directors to understand what is expected from them. For instance, whilst the Kenyan Companies Act (the "Act") provides that the duties of directors are owed to the company, directors are often at a loss to understand the extent to which they ought to take stakeholder interests, such as human rights protection, into account.

As it will be seen, although the current regulatory framework does not protect adequately the interests of stakeholders, there is a new Draft Constitution in Kenya which seeks to make companies liable for all constitutionally protected fundamental human rights, including environmental, consumer and labour rights. Given that this type of mandatory regulation has not been implemented in many countries, Kenya will be a step ahead of others in moving corporate social responsibility (CSR) into the realm of corporate social accountability.

Apart from assessing the extent to which the Draft Constitution, if implemented, will change managerial practice in Kenya, this paper explores measures that company directors can adopt in order to prevent breaches of their fiduciary duties and to meet the standards set by labour, environmental and company laws in Kenya. It also assesses whether these laws are sufficient to deal with the rising global CSR standards. Apart from raising awareness and helping company directors to understand their legal obligations towards CSR, this paper will also formulate other reforms which can be implemented by policy-makers in order to promote CSR and the respect for human rights by corporations. The paper will first consider the theoretical framework that underlies the need for companies to assume social responsibilities. It then proceeds to consider the extent to which companies have been responsible for violation of human rights in Kenya. In doing so, the article will focus largely on the effects that the Export Processing Zones (EPZs) have had on human rights standards. It will then assess whether Kenyan corporate law is effective in protecting the interests of corporate stakeholders. To illustrate its effectiveness, the paper will consider whether the interests of employees are adequately protected and the extent to which donations have been abused by company directors to further their personal and corporate interests to the detriment of other wider societal interests, such as the need to eradicate corruption. In addition, the paper looks at the efficacy of the legislative framework on corruption in order to determine how effective it is in deterring company directors from engaging in corruption. The paper concludes by considering the suitability of the current Constitution in entrenching corporate citizenship and the extent to which the proposed Constitutional changes are likely to impact on corporate citizenship.

Theoretical Framework

As investors, shareholders expect companies that they invest in to give them a return on their investment. To achieve this objective, directors of a company seek to maximise the profits of a company because the failure to do so may lead to their dismissal. Contractarian theorists justify wealth maximisation on the basis that the firm is a unit for all bargaining arrangements which the participants in a company seek to use so as to maximise wealth through beneficial bargains (Jensen and

Meckling, 1976). So, shareholders, as participants in a company, are considered by contractarians to have no other objectives apart from profit maximisation. Besides, the firm is considered incapable of having other objectives, such as social responsibility, because it is a nexus of contracts, and not an individual with motivations and intentions.

Although stakeholders may suffer when the sole objective of directors is to maximise the wealth of shareholders, contractarian theories do not regard that as a sufficient basis for affording legal protection because corporate stakeholders, such as creditors and employees, are considered capable of protecting themselves through contracts (Millon, 1995). This view does not recognise the inequality of bargaining power between rational economic actors within a company. It is for this reason that communitarian theorists regard the company as an entity having both a public role and a private one (Stokes, 1986). The communitarian theory recognises the need to protect non-shareholders on the basis that disparities in bargaining power and lack of information make it impossible for some non-shareholders to protect themselves through contracts.

Whilst profit maximisation may well benefit shareholders, it may also harm them when the profitability of a company suffers because of its bad reputation. As such, it is important to have a legal system which allows directors to take into account the interests of stakeholders because this not only enables them to safeguard the reputation of the company and, in turn, its long-term productivity, but it also plays a key role in promoting human rights and other societal interests which are critical stakeholder interests.

Effect of Corporations on Labour Rights

In the recent past, companies in Kenya have incurred heavy losses as a result of closures which have been necessitated by workers' strikes. Workers, especially those in the EPZs, have taken actions against their companies as a result of their socially irresponsible conduct. In 2003, for instance, workers in the EPZ sector went on strike demanding "higher wages, entitlement to leave, including maternity, annual, sick and compassionate leave, and protesting against overwork and compulsory overtime, lack of protective clothing, inaccessibility to emergency exits, sexual harassment, unfair suspension and summary dismissal, unexplained deductions and suppression of their right to organise into trade unions" (Kenya Human Rights Commission, 2004).

Companies operating in the EPZs sometimes adopt inhumane policies because they are under considerable pressure to meet unrealistic targets set on them by sourcing companies in the USA and Europe. The failure to meet such targets results in the supplying company meeting the cost of shipping the goods abroad.

The effect of EPZs on labour rights standards in Kenya has been a major concern due to the number of people affected by their policies. The EPZ is the fastest-growing sector of the manufacturing industry in Kenya and it employed 26,447 people by 2004 (Kenya Human Rights Commission, 2004). The EPZs were first established in 1990 by the Export Processing Zone Act with a view to creating jobs, enhancing the transfer of technology, diversifying export products and markets, and promoting industrial investment for export. By virtue of the Foreign Investment Protection Act 1964, investors who establish businesses in the EPZs are guaranteed the right to transfer profits, dividends and capital out of Kenya. Although the government earns around ten billion Kenyan shillings from the sector, it loses much more through the social cost borne by the persons working in the sector.

Companies in the EPZs have been able to get away with violations of human rights because the government has been reluctant to impose stringent regulations on such companies, on the premise that they would relocate to other countries and others which are not already present would be reluctant to enter the Kenyan market. Indeed, the Export Processing Zone Act, which is supposed to regulate the employment in the sector, is skewed in favour of foreign investors and does not therefore address adequately the rights of workers. Other labour law statutes have also not been protective of workers. For instance, it was not until 2003 that the application of the Factories Act to the EPZs ceased to be exempted. Before then, inspectors under the Factories Act had no authority to inspect factories in the EPZs. The government has also contributed to the violations of workers rights through the Finance Act No. 4 of 1994, which amended certain provisions of the Employment Act and the Regulations of Wages and Conditions of Employment Act to deny trade unions the right to be involved in redundancy procedures. The statute introduced the concept of retrenchment, which made it possible for workers to be laid off without involving trade unions; a procedure that was not available before 1994.

It is as a result of such lax laws that companies in the EPZ sector have adopted inhumane policies, such as having long and unpredictable working hours for employees and carrying out pregnancy tests for new female employees with a view to denying jobs to those found to be pregnant. Such policies have compelled women who become pregnant in the course of their employment to procure abortions in order to keep their jobs (Kenya Human Rights Commission, 2004). These practices have drastic effects on the rights of women, who comprise 75% of employees in the EPZ sector. Women are often preferred because they are considered to be "easier to work with, patient, keen and careful ... hence less mistakes and rejects, unlike men who are aggressive, easily bored and always looking for trouble" (Kenya Human Rights Commission, 2004).

Apart from the pressure from workers, the growth of democracy in Kenya has made it possible for consumers and NGOs to demand accountability and respect for human rights from companies operating in the EPZs. Although local companies are also under pressure to conduct business responsibly, much of the pressure has been exerted on foreign companies in the EPZs because they have often been exempted from labour laws in the past, when local companies have had to comply with such laws. In addition, most foreign companies abandon responsibilities that they have to assume elsewhere when they set up business in Kenya.

Given that labour laws have been ineffective in protecting the rights of workers in Kenya, it is important to assess whether Kenyan corporate laws do offer adequate protection to workers and other stakeholders.

Effectiveness of Corporate Law

Its outdated nature
The main regulatory framework governing companies and the responsibilities of company directors is contained in the State Corporations Act 1987 and the Companies Act 1962. Whilst the State Corporations Act 1987 governs the operations of parastatals, the Act regulates public and private companies. It is notable that as a former British colony, Kenya's regulatory framework for directors, and company law as a whole, was inherited. The Act is based almost entirely on the 1948 English Companies Act. The English Act was introduced in Kenya in 1959 and adopted in 1962 virtually verbatim. Despite significant changes in the English Companies Act since 1948 and the substantial economic development in Kenya since 1962, the regulatory framework for directors has remained as it was in 1962. In

contrast, several former British colonies in Africa, such as Ghana and Nigeria, have changed their companies legislation. Given that Kenya's circumstances have greatly changed since 1962, it is doubtful whether the law created in England during the nineteenth century to meet the objectives of capitalists operating in a laissez-faire environment would adequately govern modern-day commercial organisations in Kenya.

Kenya's Judicature Act (section 3) permits the application of the common law and doctrines of equity in force in England as at 12 August, 1897. As such, the Kenyan courts apply English common law principles and have hardly adopted a Kenyan approach to the interpretation of the Companies Act (*Flagship Carriers Ltd v Imperial Bank Ltd*). Whilst decisions of English courts given after the reception date are not of binding authority in the courts of the territory, they are entitled to the highest respect if the English law has not been subsequently modified. The current English judicial pronouncements on company law are, therefore, highly persuasive in interpreting the Kenyan provisions. It is notable that the duties of directors are not codified in the Act. As such, most principles underlying them are found in the English common law. Due to lack of codification, the common law principles applicable to Kenya are largely inaccessible and, as such, directors and practitioners have to search through a maze of case-law to understand their responsibilities.

Its failure to effectively recognise CSR

The Act is silent on the legal obligations that directors have. One would therefore have to look at the common law to establish whether company directors have obligations to take into account stakeholder interests. To ensure that companies are administered fairly, the common law requires directors to act *bona fide* in the best interests of the company and not for any collateral purpose (*Re Smith v Fawcett Ltd*). They are also not allowed to make secret profits or allow their personal interests to conflict with their duties to the company (Trevor *Price and Another v Raymond Kelsall*). They have a duty to act *bona fide* in what they consider, not what a court may consider, is in the interests of the company.

The duty to act *bona fide* in the interests of the company requires directors to exercise their powers for the purpose for which they are given and not for collateral purposes. As such, they must keep within the proper limits and avoid using powers given to them for a totally different purpose from the one originally intended. Any exercise of the powers of directors for an improper purpose can be set aside even though the directors may honestly have believed that they were acting in the interests of the company (*Australian Growth Resources Corp Pty Ltd v Van Reesema*). A shareholder, for instance, may challenge in court a company's resolution allowing directors to pursue activities that are not reasonably incidental to the carrying on of the company's business. For an act to be incidental to the business of the company, the benefit to the company must be direct and not "too speculative or too remote" (*Evans v Brunner Mond & Co*). In addition, a matter can be challenged for not being expressly or impliedly authorised by a company's objects clause as contained in its Constitution, on the basis that it goes beyond the capacity of the company (*ultra vires*).

Since the duty to act in the best interests of the company requires directors to use powers conferred on them by the articles of association, construction of the articles determine the criteria used by the courts to determine whether a particular purpose is proper (*Re Smith v Fawcett Ltd*). In the event that the articles are not explicit, proper purpose, according to the decision in *Re The Highlands Commercial Union Limited,* may be implied from the "general obligations and duties which directors incur by the very nature of their appointment." The proper purpose test fosters the accountability of directors by allowing courts to monitor the directors' decision-making more closely.

The Act does not specify whether the duty to act *bona fide* in the interests of the whole company requires directors to consider the interests of the corporate entity with present members or the company as a whole, including employees, creditors and other stakeholders.

According to the English common law, any act considered to be *bona fide* by the director must be geared towards promoting the business. Gratuitous payments or gifts out of the assets of the company (*Re Smith v Fawcett Ltd*) and provision of a pension to a widow of a former employee have been rendered not to be in the best interests of the company (*Parke v Daily News Ltd*). Similarly, crediting sums to directors as a "bonus" at a time when there were no profits available for such purposes was held in *Re The Highlands Commercial Union Limite* to amount to breach of trust or duty because it was not in the best interests of the company. However, gratuitous gifts out of a company's assets for the purposes of education and charity were allowed in *Evans v Brunner Mond & Co* because they were directly beneficial to the company. The passing of a resolution to give grants to scientific institutions was held to be *intra vires* the objects of the company because the company intended to make use of the reservoir of experts trained from those grants and therefore the expenditure was necessary for the continued progress of the chemical manufacturing business of the company.

Although directors who assume some social responsibilities might be considered to be acting within their powers when they undertake activities that are reasonably incidental to the business of the company (*Evans v Brunner Mond & Co*), it is worth noting that lack of codification of the common law rules regulating the responsibilities of directors makes it cumbersome for directors to ascertain their actual role in social responsibility. For instance, it is unclear whether a director who sacrifices the profits of a company in the short term by assuming some social responsibilities would be liable for the breach of his duties if his objectives were to enhance the profits of the company in the long term. According to *Evans v Brunner Mond & Co*, such a director would be liable for breach of his duties if he undertakes activities whose intended benefits to the company are too speculative or too remote. As such, there is a need for the Act to specify expressly in whose interests directors are supposed to act and to whom they owe their duties, so as to enable directors to ascertain their obligations easily. The drafting may follow the developments in the USA, where courts have held that a board of directors owes duties not only to shareholders, but also to the corporate enterprise, including creditors, when the company is in the vicinity of insolvency (Keay, 2001). Some states in the USA have also passed legislation requiring directors to consider non-shareholder interests. The British Company Law Review Steering Group also proposed that the statutory codification of directors' duties should require directors to "promote the success of the company for the benefit of its members as a whole" (Keay, 2001). The Final Report of the Company Law Review Group recommended that a director should act in what he decides is the way most likely to promote the success of the company. In making such a decision, he is required to consider relevant factors, such as relationships with employees, suppliers and customers, impact on the community or environment or the good reputation of the company (DTI, 2001). By defining expressly the term "company as a whole" to mean the interests of all shareholders or other requisite interest groups, such as employees, creditors and the society within which the company operates, the Act would effectively deal with the problem associated with the interpretation of the said term.

Obligations to employees

To a certain extent, some companies already consider interests of employees by encouraging them to purchase shares, offering gratuities, and medical attention (Thomas, 1969). Although the Act has no provisions requiring directors to consider the interests of employees, directors can still take such interests into consideration if the interests are reasonably incidental to the carrying on of the business of the company. However, taking the interests of employees into account is unlawful if doing so conflicts with the interests of a company or if it is not reasonably incidental to the carrying on of the business of the company. The common law gives directors the discretion to decide the matters that they ought to consider in such circumstances. In *Hutton v West Cork Rly*, Bowen L.J. observed:

> "A railway company, or the directors of the company might send down all the porters at a railway station to have tea in the country at the expense of the company. Why should they not? It is for the directors to judge, provided it is a matter which is reasonably incidental to the carrying on of the business of the company; and a company which always treated its employees with Draconian severity, and never allowed them a single inch more than the strict letter of the bond, would soon find itself deserted - at all events, unless labour was very much easy to obtain in the market."

Directors are therefore likely to ignore wider stakeholder interests that are not directly beneficial to the company, especially in a market place, such as the Kenyan one, where stakeholder activism is not well entrenched. This is congruent with the contractarian view which argues against the consideration of the interests of employees on the basis that it undermines shareholder supremacy.

Although employees have a right to join trade unions, their capacity to make demands from companies is undermined by discretionary powers that the Minister for Labour has to declare strikes illegal under the Trade Disputes Act. As such, the efficacy of trade unions as representatives of employees is questionable. Employees are also vulnerable because there is no statutory protection which permits directors to offer compensation by making *ex gratia* provision for employees. Moreover, directors are not under any obligation to establish pension schemes for employees or to safeguard the long-term interests of employees by running a company efficiently. However, this position might change if the Draft Constitution proposed by the

Constitution of Kenya Review Commission is implemented. Clause 59 of the Draft Constitution guarantees everyone's right to fair labour practices, including the right to: strike, a fair remuneration, reasonable working conditions, and participation in the activities of a trade union.

Although requiring directors to consider employees' interests might be beneficial to workers, the British Company Law Review Steering Group deems such a requirement unnecessary because consideration of the interests of employees undermines the principle of shareholder supremacy (DTI, 2001). Although such a requirement might undermine the supremacy of shareholders to some extent, there is a need to recognise and protect such class interests within the public because of the inequality of the bargaining power between the employees and the company. Although contractarians argue against such protection, it is submitted that they assume wrongly that workers are in a position to protect themselves through the contracts entered into with the company (Millon, 1995).

The Nigerian Law Reform Commission also declined to recommend the adoption of a provision obliging directors to have regard to the interests of employees on the basis that it would affect adversely the developing economy of the country and, in turn, lead to loss of jobs, as the requirements would deter foreign investors (Nigeria Law Reform Commission, 1987). Although it might be the case that requiring directors to have regard to the interests of employees would not be suitable for a developing economy which is keen to attract investments, it should also be borne in mind that foreign companies are not always factors in the promotion of developing economies, as their success is usually at the expense of local companies and the economy. In fact, direct and indirect employment gains made by foreign companies may be offset by induced job losses in the local companies, human rights abuses and environmental degradation (Griffiths & Wall, 1995). Empirical study has shown that entry of transnational corporations in a market contributes to short-term economic growth, but also reduces long-term growth performance (Bornschier & Stamm, 1994). Since transnational corporations are foreign-owned, they often seek to maximise profits for their Western owners and not to improve the welfare of the host countries (Dine, 2001).

Given that companies and the society as a whole stand to benefit from consideration of the interests of employees by directors, it is important to require directors to have regard for such social responsibilities. It is thus submitted that the duties of directors ought to focus on the long-term interests of the enterprise rather than the narrow interests of members. Directors ought to weigh the interests of stakeholders while making decisions because companies can enhance their long-term productivity by sacrificing profits in the short term (Viller, 1998). This view was supported by 57% of respondents to a survey conducted by the author in Nairobi in 2001-2002 (the "Survey") (Mwaura, 2002). The respondents felt that directors ought to consider social responsibilities so as to facilitate participation of employees in economic activities, as the failure to take the interests of employees into consideration adversely affects their productivity and, in turn, the performance of the company.

The interests of employees that might need to be respected by a company include: consideration and consultation expectations; fair labour practices; financial matters, such as salary and pensions; and the opportunity to enjoy continued employment with the business (Milman, 1996). Requiring directors to have regard to the interests of employees would not be difficult to implement because there already exists some legislative measures to the same effect. Such legislative measures regulate "minimum wages, maximum hours, employment of women, children and young persons, industrial accidents, hospitalisation, and payment in cash as opposed to kind" (Thomas, 1969).

Given that it would be impossible to enforce a provision requiring directors to have regard to the interests of employees, as directorial duties are owed to a company rather than employees, it would be preferable to give employees full voting rights within a company by allowing employees to nominate representative directors (Vagts, 1966). Such representative directors would be able to protect the interests of employees by voicing their concerns on the board. In the event that representative directors are outvoted and directors continue with misconduct, the representatives would be able to challenge managerial conduct as minority shareholders, where the employees own shares. Further protection might be given to employees by enabling employees to call for the investigation of the company by the Registrar of Companies where misconduct of directors affects the interests of employees. It is notable that the Act is prohibitive, as section 165 (1) only allows a member to call for the investigation of a company. It is submitted that employees ought to be given this right without being required to provide the security for costs.

Effectiveness of Anti-Corruption Legislation

Although the onerous duties of directors as fiduciaries obliges them to act in good faith, for the benefit of the company, and to avoid conflict of interest situations, rampant corruption in the country has contributed to the abuse of duties by directors (Kibwana, 1996). When directors abuse the resources of a company through corruption, they not only threaten the liquidity of the company, but also contribute to the stagnation of the economy, inadequate physical and social infrastructure, poorly functioning political systems, loss of investment and general economic instability (Kimberly, 1998).

To reverse this trend, the Kenyan Government has enacted the Anti-Corruption and Economic Crimes Act 2003, which repeals the Prevention of Corruption Act. The Kenya Anti-Corruption and Economics Crimes Act 2003 widens the scope of the definition of corruption to include not only the public sector but also the private sector. Under the 2003 Act, directors are not only required not to compromise the interests of companies by accepting gifts or donations, but they are under a duty not to corrupt others with donations irrespective of their intended benefits to the company. Breach of these duties has the effect of making a person liable to anyone who suffers loss (section 44) and can also lead to suspension of a public officer (section 55) and disqualification from holding public office for ten years (section 57). Although these measures will curb corruption to an extent, there is a need to disqualify corrupt persons from serving as directors in private companies as well. Such disqualification would not only protect creditors and employees, but would also serve as a deterrent to those who might be tempted to engage in fraudulent activities.

Given that some donations made by a company may be reasonably incidental to the business of a company (*Evans v Brunner Mond & Co*), such donations are *intra vires* the company and lawful since "the law does not say that there are to be no cakes and ale, but there are to be no cakes and ale except such as are required for the benefit of the company" (*Hutton v West Cork Rly*).

However, despite their direct benefits to companies, some donations can also have some detrimental effect on companies, especially when they are used to further corruption. It is notable that 39% of respondents to the survey carried out by the author in 2002 felt that donations given by companies encourage corruption; 15% of respondents felt that donations enhance the image of companies; and 46% took the view that donations promote certain purposes, such as charity and education. Those who felt that donations encourage corruption attributed their views to the fact that directors of parastatals in Kenya have given donations in the past for political reasons in return for political favours, such as appointment to lucrative government positions. In fact, Kenya Cooperative Creameries, which gave large donations to a former government, was a good springboard into political positions, as many of its former directors benefited in this respect.

As a safeguard against abuse of political donations, there is a need to limit the amount of money that can be donated by directors, oblige directors to disclose donations in the accounts of the company, or require the consent of shareholders to be given before substantial donations are made.

While it may be partly true to say that any benefit that accrues to a company is "reasonably incidental to the carrying on of the company's business.... and is done for the benefit of and to promote the prosperity of the company" (*Re Lee, Behrens and Co Ltd*), there can be no doubt that benefits procured through corrupt means by directors amount to breach of their fiduciary duties.

Although the pursuit of corrupt practices by directors might be justified on the basis that the objectives of the firm are to maximise profits (Jensen & Meckling, 1976), rather than acting in a socially responsible manner, corrupt practices cannot be pursued for the proper purpose because they undermine the economic well-being of the country. Thus, acting on the basis of what is for the economic advantage of the company in such circumstances may not only be detrimental to the country but also to the company. This is because the profitability of companies is also affected by the well-being of the national economy.

Besides, it can be argued that corrupt practices by directors are not in the interest of the company on the basis of their illegality. The articles of association cannot confer powers on directors to pursue illegal practices. Given that directors are required to exercise their powers for the purpose for which they are given and not for collateral purposes, corrupt practices by directors cannot fall within lawful objectives of the articles of association.

Due to the rampant nature of corruption in Kenya, it is submitted that the Act should enhance the responsibility of directors by enabling the use of the proper purpose doctrine to ensure that any exercise of power for corrupt purposes by directors is set aside for not being in the best interests of the company.

Whilst changes in the Kenyan law may help alleviate corrupt practices associated with fiduciaries, it is also important for the international community to implement regulations that will discourage foreign investors from engaging in corrupt practices. Due to the increase of corruption in the post-Cold War period as a result of the scramble for new markets, industrialised countries have increasingly allowed their transnational corporations to engage in corrupt practices. In some countries, such as Germany and Belgium, bribes have been tax deductible. Sometimes, companies that are under strict regulations have lost out on competitive businesses abroad. A vast majority of foreign governments have been reluctant to legislate against bribery of foreign public officials.

Since the international regulatory framework is not effective in proscribing acts of corruption and breach of fiduciary duties in general, changes in the Kenyan law may well not eliminate corrupt practices associated with fiduciaries; the reason being that the inequality of bargaining power between the State and transnational corporations makes it possible for the corporations to flout rules and discourages the government from imposing stringent measures. In the past, British American Tobacco (BAT) has had strong influence on the policies of the Kenyan government that the government allowed it to draft anti-tobacco legislation which was later endorsed by Parliament.

The failure of some industrialised countries to oblige transnational corporations, which have a seat in their jurisdictions, to implement the OECD Convention on Combating the Bribery of Foreign Public Officials in International Business Transactions also enables the corporations to engage in corrupt practices. Rigorous enforcement of the Convention is also lacking in some countries which have incorporated the Convention into their national laws. Uniform global regulations for transnationals which recognise transnational corporations as international law subjects with obligations towards good governance, environment and society, would foster transparency and encourage companies to comply with the regulations, especially if the enforcement mechanism is effective.

The implementation of the OECD Convention can make it less tempting for foreign officers to corrupt public officials. Although the Convention can reduce corrupt practices, its effectiveness can be hampered by the fact that it remains unenforceable in countries that have not incorporated it into their domestic legislation and that it fails to restrict the value of gifts given to foreign officials. This displays a great variation from the standards set for transnationals in their home countries. In the USA, for instance, some regulations prohibit private individuals or companies from giving gifts of more than $50. Failure of the Convention to have similar requirements reflects negatively on its effectiveness in the fight against corruption.

Effectiveness of the Current Constitution

Although there are some good laws and provisions in the current Constitution that seek to protect stakeholder interests, they have not been of much use because they have not been strictly enforced by the government. For example, while section 82 of the present Constitution prohibits discrimination, discrimination, especially against women, is still prevalent in the EPZs. While section 80 of the Constitution also guarantees freedom of association and the right to collective bargaining, companies in the EPZs do not recognise the right and often intimidate those who join trade unions. In addition, while section 73 (1) and (2) proscribes forced labour, slavery or servitude, workers in the EPZs continue to be subjected to this. Lastly, while section 74 also protects persons against inhuman and degrading treatment, harassment is still prevalent in the EPZs.

One of the main reasons for the lack of effective enforcement of the above provisions is the fact that section 84 of the Constitution requires leave of the High Court to be granted before any action under the Bill of Rights is entertained in court. This requirement has impeded greatly the application of the Bill of Rights in Kenya.

Another factor that has impeded the realisation of rights protected under the Bill of Rights is the fact that the current Constitution only imposes the responsibility to respect these rights on the State but not on companies. Failing to oblige companies to honour societal interests is both biased and discriminatory because it exonerates many of them from standards that they have to meet in other countries. Such discrimination is an attack on the fundamental principle underlying the State's obligations under the International Covenant on Economic, Social and Cultural Rights (ICESCR) and the Universal Declaration of Human Rights 1948, which is given treaty effect by the International Covenant on Civil and Political Rights (ICCPR).

The ICCPR provides that human rights are everyone's birthright and apply to all without distinction. Since the protected rights under ICCPR include the social rights of employees, the present laws and practices are not in conformity with the Covenant. Conformity with human rights international standards can only be achieved by obliging companies to consider the economic interests and fundamental rights of corporate stakeholders, as has been proposed by the Constitution of Kenya Review Commission in the Draft Constitution.

Prospects of the Proposed Constitutional Changes

The new Draft Constitution is different from the current Constitution in that it will oblige not only State institutions but also companies to respect these rights. Human rights, as such, will have direct horizontal effect on private bodies and more cases are, therefore, likely to come before the courts. The Draft Constitution makes the provisions in the Bill of Rights binding on both natural and juristic persons. Clause 29 (1) of the Draft Constitution provides that "the Bill of Rights applies to all laws and binds all State organs and all persons."

If the Draft Constitution is adopted, all constitutionally protected fundamental human rights, whose main purpose is to protect the individual from the State, will also be available against any person (company). For instance, liability would attach for the failure to respect employees' privacy, right to assemble, and right to fair labour practices, including striking, clean environment and consumer rights.

This is a welcome initiative because it departs from the stance adopted by the present Constitution and the international human rights law, which protect any legal person from abuse of its rights by a state but do not require the legal person to observe similar standards in the course of its business.

Entrenching human rights obligations on companies in the Constitution is a step in the right direction because, unlike an ordinary statute, it would not only be difficult for any government in power to change the Constitution, but it would be onerous to exempt companies in the EPZs from constitutional labour standards the same way that they have been exempted from ordinary statutes in the past.

However, having constitutional provisions to protect human rights is not an end in itself because they can fail to have effect if the people are ignorant of such rights. As such, there is a need to raise awareness so that the people can participate effectively in the realisation of these rights. Indeed, the lack of awareness of socio-economic rights in South Africa has been cited as one factor that has affected the realisation of those rights (Liebenberg & Pillay, 2000).

In addition, the failure to enforce the Bill of Rights can render the rights worthless. The failure to enforce such provisions in Ghana and South Africa has allowed violations to continue. Generally, the lack of enforcement of such rights in countries where they exist can be attributed to lack of awareness, lack of political will on the part of the government to exert pressure on strong transnational corporations, and lack of resources. It is because of these reasons that it is contended that having in place binding international regulations and a body to enforce such rights against corporations would provide redress to victims who fail to get any recompense when national states fail to enforce human rights.

Conclusions

Given that Kenyan labour laws, corporate laws and the current Constitution have not protected the interests of stakeholders, the government has a role to play in providing a regulatory framework that holds corporations to account for violations of human rights. It is insufficient to rely solely on extra-judicial means, such as consumer activism and CSR, to safeguard stakeholder interests, because stakeholder activism is not widespread in Kenya. In addition, given that companies have shown the tendency of assuming socially irresponsible conduct, even when they assume higher standards in other countries, there is a need for companies to be bound by legally binding norms.

Although shareholders may sometimes benefit when directors ignore the interests of corporate stakeholders, they also stand to incur long-term losses when the reputation of a company suffers. Thus, honouring community interests might be in the best interests of a company because such responsibilities nurture good customer relations, motivate employees, and contribute to the well-being of the national economy.

Although the honouring of some social responsibilities by directors may benefit the company in the long term, some actions, such as the giving of political donations, ought to be closely regulated because they are prone to abuse by corrupt directors. Abuse of donations can, for instance, be controlled by limiting the amount that can be given by directors or by requiring prior consent of shareholders before the donations are given.

Codification of the common law principles is necessary because it would not only be useful to the courts and make it easier for directors and stakeholders to understand their responsibilities but also provide an opportunity to correct defects in the present law. For instance, the duty of directors to act in the best interests of the company and for a proper purpose should be expanded to include matters that are not only related to the company, but also other incidental matters, such as corruption and violations of human rights, that are a danger to the society. The same approach also needs to be adopted at the international level so as to regulate transnational corporations effectively. This would complement the standards that will be imposed by the new constitutional provisions and, in turn, promote corporate citizenship.

Bibliography

Bornschier, V. & Stam, H. (1994). Transnational Corporations in S. Wheeler (ed.), The Law of the Business Enterprise Oxford: Oxford University Press.

Daily Nation (2001, 18 March). Lobbies call off Products Boycott.

Department for Trade and Industry (2000). Modern Company Law for a Competitive Economy: Developing the Framework. London, [URN00/656].

Department for Trade and Industry (2001). The Company Law Review Steering Group: Final Report, London.

Dine, J. (2001). Company Law, London: Sweet & Maxwell.

Dodd, E.M. (1932). For Whom are Corporate Managers Trustees?" Harvard Law Review, 7, p. 1145–1163.

Griffiths, A. & Wall, S. (1995). Applied Economics: An Introductory Course, London and New York: Longman.

Jensen, M. & Meckling, W. (1976). Theory of the Firm: Managerial Behavior, Agency Costs, and Ownership Structure, 3 Journal of Financial Economics, 3, p. 305-360.

Keay, A. (2001). The Director's Duty to Take into Account the Interests of Company Creditors: When is it Triggered? Melbourne University Law Review, 25, p. 315-339.

Kent, T. (2001, December) CSR Investment is not a Choice, Ethical Corporation Magazine, 1.

Kenya Human Rights Commission (2004). Manufacture of Poverty: The Untold Story of EPZs in Kenya, Nairobi, Kenya Human Rights Commission.

Kibwana K et al. (ed.) (1996). The Anatomy of Corruption in Kenya: Legal, Political, and Social Economic Perspectives, Nairobi: Claripress.

Kimberly, A. E. (1998). The Problem of Corruption: A Tale of Two Countries (Kenya, Uganda), Northwestern Journal of International Law & Business, 12, p. 524-534.

Liebenberg, S. & Pillay, L. (Eds.) (2000). Socio-Economic Rights in South Africa, University of West Cape, South Africa: The Socio-Economic Rights Project, Community Law Centre.

Millon D. (1995). Communitarianism in Corporate Law: Foundations and Law Reform Strategies in Lawrence Mitchell (ed), Progressive Corporate Law Colorado: Boulder.

Milman, D. (1996). From Servant to Stakeholder: Protecting the Employee Interest in Company Law in D., Feldman and F., Meisel (eds.), Corporate and Commercial Law: Modern Developments, London: Lloyds of London Press.

Mwaura, K. (2002). Regulation of Directors in Kenya: An Empirical Study" International Company and Commercial Law Review, 13, p. 465-479.

Nigeria Law Reform Commission (1987). Working Papers on the Reform of Nigerian Company Law: Volume 1 - Review and Recommendations, Lagos: Government of Nigeria.

Stokes, M. (1986). Company Law and Legal Theory in W., Twinning (ed.), Legal Theory and Common Law Oxford: Blackwell.

The Draft Constitution of Kenya.
http://www.kenyaConstitution.org/

Thomas P.A. (1969). Private Enterprise and the East African Company, Dar es Salaam: Tanzania Publishing House Ltd.

Vagts, D.F. (1966). Reforming the 'modern' Corporation: Perspectives from the German", Harvard Law Review, 80, p. 23-89.

Villiers C. (1998). European Company Law: Towards Democracy Aldershot: Ashgate Publishers.

Cases

Australian Growth Resources Corp Pty Ltd v Van Reesema (1988); 6 ACLC 529.

Bennet's Case (1854); 5 De GM and G 284 at 298.

Evans v Brunner Mond & Co. [1921] 1 Ch 359.

Flagship Carriers Ltd v Imperial Bank Ltd, High Court Civil Case No 1643 of 1999 (Unreported).

Greenhalgh v Arderne Cinemas Ltd [1951] Ch 286.

Hutton v West Cork Rly (1883) 23 Ch D.

Parke v Daily News Ltd [1962] Ch 927.

Re City Equitable Fire Insurance Co (1925) Ch 407.

Re Lee, Behrens and Co Ltd [1932] 2 Ch 46 at 51.

Re Smith v Fawcett Ltd [1942] Ch 304.

Re The Highlands Commercial Union Limited [1957] EA 851.

Trevor Price and Another v Raymond Kelsall [1957] EA 752.

Statutes

Trade Disputes Act, Chapter 234, Laws of Kenya.

The Employment Act, Chapter 226.

The Employment of Women, Young Persons and Children Act, Chapter 227.

The Regulation of Wages and Conditions of Employment Act Chapter 229.

The Shop Hours Act, Chapter 231.

The Workmen's Compensation Act, Chapter 236.

The Factories Act, Chapter 514.

PART TWO

NEW PARTNERSHIP
PERSPECTIVES

CHAPTER 6

FROM LONDON TO STOCKHOLM AND BEYOND

THE ROLE OF DEVELOPMENT COOPERATION AGENCIES IN CSR

Tom Fox[73]
International Institute for Environment and Development

Abstract

Development cooperation agencies (donors) are interested in the CSR agenda as an entry point into discussions about the contribution of the private sector to their development objectives. This paper draws on discussions at two key events in which donor agencies came together to exchange experiences and to discuss the unique roles that they could themselves perform in relation to CSR. The first meeting, hosted by the UK Department for International Development in January 2002, was held behind closed doors to allow donors to compare notes on their respective strategies, whereas the second, hosted by the Swedish Ministry for Foreign Affairs in March 2004, was a large, multi-stakeholder conference. The paper describes the key outcomes of both events and discusses how donor approaches to CSR have developed, and what this means for the future of development assistance in this area.

[73] The author is grateful to the co-author of one of the background papers on which this chapter draws, Dave Prescott, and also to Halina Ward, Jonas Moberg, Elenore Kanter and the Swedish Partnership for Global Development, Eddie Rich and Holly Wise for their advice and inputs. However, the opinions expressed are those of the author alone.

Introduction

Development cooperation agencies[74] have worked on many of the issues encapsulated within the concept of corporate social responsibility (CSR) for many years. They have significant experience in the fields of enterprise development, labour standards, human rights, environmental protection and so on. But as CSR has emerged as a policy area in its own right – at least in the eyes of some businesses, non-governmental organisations (NGOs) and policy-makers – development agencies have started to explore what it means for them. In particular, they are interested in whether CSR offers a useful entry point into discussions about the contribution of the private sector to their development objectives.

This chapter discusses how development agencies' approaches to CSR have developed. It draws in particular on the proceedings of two key events in which donor agencies came together to exchange their experiences and to discuss the unique roles that they could themselves perform in relation to CSR. The first event was organised by the Canadian International Development Agency (CIDA) and the UK Department for International Development (DFID) and hosted by DFID in London in January 2002.[75] The Swedish Ministry for Foreign Affairs hosted the second event in March 2004 in Stockholm.[76] This was organised in collaboration with the Swedish International Development Cooperation Agency (Sida), the World Bank, the International Business Leaders Forum (IBLF) and the International Institute for Environment and Development (IIED). This chapter describes the objectives and key outcomes of both events, notes some further developments since the Stockholm meeting, and discusses some implications for the future of development assistance in this area.

From London...

The objective of the 2002 London meeting was "to assess the role of bilateral development agencies in promoting pro-poor CSR and

---

[74] This chapter uses the terms 'development cooperation agency', 'development agency' and 'donor' interchangeably. We refer primarily to bilateral agencies such as the UK's DFID and Sweden's Sida, but also in certain cases to multilateral agencies such as UNDP and the World Bank.

[75] See Fox (2002) for a summary of the proceedings of the London meeting, available at http://www.iied.org/docs/cred/cred_roundtable.pdf.

[76] See Fox and Prescott (2004) for a report based on discussions at the Stockholm conference, and its appendices for a more detailed record of the proceedings, available at http://www.iied.org/cred/pubs.html#devcoop.

explore how development agencies could interact with the international business and development communities and developing countries". It was held at a time when the Johannesburg World Summit on Sustainable Development (WSSD) was looming large on the horizon. Discussions were therefore shaped in part by a sense that CSR would be on the WSSD agenda, and that donors might use the WSSD process as an opportunity to develop or highlight their CSR-related activities.

The instigators of the meeting were Eddie Rich and Ellen Hagerman, at that time the officials with responsibility for CSR within DFID and CIDA respectively. Their invitation to a two-day round-table meeting was welcomed by many of their counterparts within other agencies. Officials with CSR-related remits from nine bilateral development agencies took part in the meeting, alongside observers from six multilateral agencies. Seven other bilaterals and four other multilaterals expressed interest but were unable to attend.

Apart from formal speeches by the then UK Secretary of State for International Development, Clare Short MP, and by Sir Mark Moody-Stuart, then Chair of Business Action for Sustainable Development (BASD), the meeting was run in workshop style. The dynamic was informal, exploratory and interactive. Most of the first day of the meeting was given over to information sharing, with the bilateral agencies describing their work on CSR, and the multilateral agencies offering lessons from their own experience.

This was the first time that the group of officials had come together. There was a strong sense of individuals connecting with others in similar positions in other agencies. Although the proceedings of the meeting were subsequently published, there was a feeling that the meeting was 'behind closed doors', which encouraged participants to talk candidly. Some of the participants described how their agencies had really only just started to think about CSR, while others with more experience talked openly about their successes, dilemmas and difficulties. One participant noted that the meeting established "a newly created environment of trust between bilateral agency representatives on CSR", no doubt helped by the absence of other participants. Other than the facilitators and a few observers, the only people in the room were the agency representatives themselves.

... to Stockholm

In contrast, the Stockholm meeting was a full-blown international conference. It was presented as the continuation of a series of international meetings on responsible business practice and public policy, which included the London meeting and a conference organised by the World Bank in October 2003 on the role of governments in encouraging CSR. The policy arena on the horizon this time was the June 2004 UN Global Compact Leaders Meeting; it was their support for the Compact that formed the subtext for some of the discussion between donors in the corridors in Stockholm.

The stated objectives of the Stockholm conference were "to explore the role that development cooperation agencies can play in the promotion and implementation of responsible business practices" and to "discuss how to improve the development impact of CSR". The organisers hoped that the meeting would "provide an opportunity for donor agencies to informally share experiences and discuss ideas on how their activities can promote, facilitate and enable responsible business practices in the South."

The conference was instigated by the Swedish Partnership for Global Responsibility, a unit within the Swedish Ministry for Foreign Affairs.[77] It was formally hosted by the Swedish Minister for International Development Cooperation, Carin Jämtin. Sida, the Swedish development agency, was among the co-organisers. Sida has subsequently developed its own guidelines for its CSR work, which draw in part on the outcomes of the conference (see the following chapter).

In contrast with the London meeting, the Stockholm conference was a large, multi-stakeholder affair, with over 200 participants from the private sector, NGOs, trade unions, academia and from development agencies themselves. By necessity, the agenda was much more formal, with keynote speeches and panels. There were some breakout workshop sessions, and some time for discussions with the floor within plenary sessions, but it was much more of a set-piece event, with some speakers – including development agencies – using it as an opportunity to showcase their work.

The stated objective of the Stockholm conference was remarkably similar to that of the London meeting. But it was the difference in style and form that marks the two meetings apart, and this reflects to some extent the evolution of donors' approaches to CSR. In 2002, many of the development agencies were cautiously starting to explore the concept and what it meant to their work. Of course, we should be careful not to generalise – even in Stockholm, some donors were there

---

[77] See www.ud.se/ga

primarily to learn from others. But by 2004, it was clear that many donors were much more confidently taking the platform to talk publicly about what they had already done. In the words of one development agency official: "By then, they had something to say".

Which way this evolution will go next is less clear. Some development agency insiders fear that the Stockholm conference signified an uncritical acceptance by donors of the current CSR agenda. Many agencies appear to have been won over by the argument that CSR will help them to support their development objectives, and are looking for ways to bring it into their work. But CSR is an ambiguous concept, and it is far from assured that everything that is called CSR will necessarily be positive for development.

These insiders argue that what is needed is a space for 'behind closed doors' discussion among donors, to establish how they should engage with CSR, away from the pressure to showcase their work that international conferences create. It may be appropriate to create a standing institutional framework for this purpose. We return to a discussion of the future of donor activity on CSR below. To inform this, first we outline some of the key outcomes of the London and Stockholm meetings.

Why development agencies are interested in CSR

The London meeting explored the various starting points for donors' engagement with the agenda. It should be noted that the positions put forward at the meeting were in part defined by the interests and responsibilities of the individuals attending, and these did not necessarily reflect the overall institutional approaches. But broadly, there were two key starting points.

The first reflected an interest among donors in working in partnership with businesses. Most of the agencies noted that they had more experience of working with governments and civil society organisations than with the private sector, and the CSR agenda offered new opportunities to explore what value collaboration with businesses could bring. For example, the German agency GTZ described how its 'Centre for Cooperation with the Private Sector' had touched a nerve within the German business sector, attracting a significant number of applications for assistance in creating partnerships with companies in developing countries. USAID described the work of its 'Global Development Alliance', which sought to create public-private alliances on economic growth, health, governance, conflict and humanitarian assistance.

The second starting point related to the scope for the CSR agenda to influence how business operates, particularly in developing countries where governance structures may be weak. For example, DFID helped to establish the Ethical Trading Initiative, which addresses labour standards within global supply chains. Various agencies expressed their support for the OECD Guidelines as a basis for ensuring that companies operating in developing countries adhere to minimum standards. In some cases, the Guidelines were linked explicitly to government grants or subsidies offered to companies.

These two broad starting points remained valid by the time of the Stockholm conference. But they were complemented by a stronger sense that businesses needed to be brought into the development agenda more comprehensively. Various high-profile policy documents produced since the London meeting had emphasised that international objectives such as those represented by the Millennium Development Goals (MDGs)[78] would not be met by government action alone. The 'Monterey Consensus', a document produced after the International Monetary Fund (IMF) meeting in early 2002, had explicitly recognised the role of business in development. By the time of the Stockholm conference, a UN Commission had produced an influential report entitled *Unleashing Entrepreneurship: Making business work for the poor.*[79]

Thus, while the precise nature of the role of business in development remained a subject of debate, the Stockholm conference seemed to offer an emerging consensus on two key issues: firstly, that a responsible, values-driven private sector can be an important actor in development; and secondly, that new forms of cooperation between the public sector, the private sector and civil society – with all the complexities and tensions that these entail – offer enormous potential for achieving development objectives. At the Stockholm conference, it was recognised that to maximise this potential, it would be necessary

---

[78] The eight Millennium Development Goals were formulated with specific targets in order to guide the development community's efforts to implement the Millennium Declaration, which was signed by over 190 countries in September 2000, committing them to fight poverty, hunger and other development challenges.

[79] Launched in 2003, this High-Level Commission aimed to engage the private sector in efforts to achieve the Millennium Development Goals. See Commission on Private Sector and Development (2004), available at www.undp.org/cpsd.

to bring together the development and business communities on a far more systematic basis.

Taking CSR to the South

A number of substantive issues were raised at the two events. One of the most prominent was the need to relate the CSR agenda more closely to the needs and circumstances of developing countries. This was described at the London meeting as 'taking CSR to the South'. It consisted of two aspects, the first being to reduce or avoid any negative impacts of CSR initiatives in developing countries. This was founded on the concern among donors that the drivers of CSR, particularly reputational issues in Northern consumer markets, are not necessarily in line with priorities and corporate impacts in developing countries, and that CSR-related standards could represent barriers to export markets, especially for small and medium-sized enterprises (SMEs).

The second aspect was more proactive. Donors identified the need to ensure the strategic involvement in the CSR agenda of businesses and other stakeholders in developing countries, and to encourage a 'bottom-up' approach to CSR initiatives. In part, this meant building the capacity and awareness of governments, the private sector and civil society in developing countries to engage with the agenda more actively. Participants at the London meeting suggested that many civil society organisations in developing countries had not yet made the link between CSR and poverty reduction, the private sector had little knowledge of CSR codes and standards, and Southern governments' thinking had not developed far beyond concerns about the potential protectionist impacts of CSR. These all represented gaps that donors could help to tackle. But making progress on CSR also meant tackling the divisive relationships in many developing countries between civil society and the private sector, and sometimes between governments and businesses.

At the London meeting, donors identified a number of activities that they could pursue in order to support CSR in the South. These included support for local ownership of CSR and helping others to understand what CSR means in local contexts; awareness raising and mentoring; specific capacity building for government, private sector and civil society; and facilitating Southern stakeholders' informed participation in meetings and forums for standard-setting, negotiation and information sharing.

Taking CSR to the South was still a major issue at the time of the Stockholm conference. The conference report noted that "discussions about corporate responsibility largely take place in the US and Western Europe, and relate mostly to the activities of big companies operating in international markets. SMEs and the domestic private sector in developing countries have rarely figured in the debate, except as actors within the supply chains of multinational enterprises. There are of course exceptions, and distinctive local agendas have emerged, for example in Brazil, South Africa and the Philippines. But from the point of view of a development cooperation agency, there is an urgent need to focus the corporate responsibility debate on SMEs, the informal sector, and the domestic private sector in developing countries" (Fox & Prescott, 2004). The following donor activities in relation to this issue were identified at the conference:

- *Supporting the development of responsible SMEs*. For example, Sida is supporting a project in Bangladesh, which is working with SME chambers of commerce and NGOs to promote the enforcement of national environmental and social regulations, including core labour standards. And UNIDO is working in Vietnam to integrate social and environmental standards into SME operations, in order to show the link between responsible business conduct and enhanced productivity and competitiveness.
- *Encouraging business links between multinational companies and the domestic private sector in developing countries*. For example, DFID has created a series of 'challenge funds', which provide grants to enterprises that help to develop sustainable business links with companies in developing countries; and USAID is involved in an 'enterprise development alliance' with UNDP and ChevronTexaco, which is providing technical assistance and financial support to small enterprises in Angola, with an emphasis on the agricultural and water sectors.
- *Supporting specialist local intermediary organisations* that can provide advice and support on corporate responsibility, not only to companies but also to governments and other actors. Such organisations can catalyse action and bring together companies and local stakeholders. They can also help to ensure that corporate responsibility is relevant to the local context.

Building an enabling environment for CSR in the South

The second major substantive issue raised at the two meetings was the role of donors in helping to create conducive conditions for responsible business in developing countries. Donors can do this in various ways. The first is building government capacity and public governance frameworks, for example by:

- *Strengthening the implementation of existing laws and guidelines* by helping governments to translate international principles, for example on labour and the environment, into national legislation; building the capacity of policy-makers and regulatory authorities; and encouraging partnerships between public inspectors and private auditing, monitoring and certification schemes.
- *Strengthening compliance and monitoring capacity, and supporting grievance mechanisms,* to help manage the impacts of foreign direct investment (FDI) through multi-stakeholder processes at a national or local level, and to resolve issues when things go wrong.
- *Strengthening revenue management mechanisms and increasing transparency*, so that FDI can be attracted, and the revenues invested in legitimate social and economic development, supported by public expenditure reviews and initiatives such as the Extractive Industries Transparency Initiative.
- *Strengthening financial markets and corporate governance*: As well as supporting the capacity of financial sector regulators, donors can support and share lessons from innovative mechanisms that seek to link access to finance with good corporate governance. They can also lead work on improving corporate governance standards in a developing country context. For example, the IFC is undertaking work on the responsibilities of board members of small private companies.

As well as building government capacity, development agencies can support other institutions that contribute to an enabling environment for responsible business activity in developing countries. These institutions can variously act as intermediaries, advocates, technical advisers, whistle-blowers and pressure groups. They can also play a valuable role in managing or disbursing aid funding to the private sector, particularly where direct transfer of funding from a donor to a company would be inappropriate. Donor activities in this area include:

- *Supporting labour unions.* CIDA, for example, is funding the Canadian Labour Congress to strengthen the capacity of developing country trade unions to defend workers' rights and promote core labour standards and codes of conduct.
- *Supporting business associations* that can share good practice and provide peer pressure. These include chambers of commerce, progressive business leadership groups, or trade associations.
- *Supporting civil society organisations* that can encourage corporate responsibility locally. These include universities, media bodies and other civil society groups that can gather and disseminate information on business activity and represent the interests of companies' stakeholders. Donors can also help to raise awareness of rights and norms such as those of the ILO core conventions and the OECD Guidelines for Multinational Enterprises.
- *Supporting multi-stakeholder dialogues* at local, national and international levels, which bring together businesses, intermediary organisations and civil society organisations to find solutions for sectoral or cross-cutting issues, such as codes and standards, corruption, conflict, health and education. Donors can help to ensure that each stakeholder group is adequately represented in such dialogues, and also act as facilitators.
- *Recognising and sharing good practice.* While it is difficult for public sector bodies to endorse private sector entities, donors can catalogue and share good practices in corporate responsibility without going beyond their public sector remit. For example, the Dutch government has created the 'CSR stimulation award' for companies in the Dutch agribusiness and food industry, and Sida has worked with the Swiss-Swedish company ABB to identify good practice in rural electrification projects in developing countries.

As well as building the capacity of enterprises and various institutions, there is a need to invest in individuals who can take forward a development-oriented CSR agenda. Effective development activity and successful business activity are both highly dependent on the leadership and risk-taking of individuals, which in turn requires a clear information flow on these issues between sectors and countries.

Development agencies can therefore usefully invest in leadership development programmes and other forms of human capacity. These include developing the capacity for brokerage services. For example, through its 'Growing Sustainable Business' initiative, UNDP is creating a cadre of brokers who can bring together actors from business, government and civil society to create alliances and mediate solutions. CIDA works with UNDP to develop a brokerage mechanism to support two-way information exchanges, linkages and partnerships between private sector actors in developing and developed countries.

Other areas where donors can support human capacity include training in CSR and cross-sector partnership, particularly for their own country officers and commercial attachés. For example, the UK's Foreign and Commonwealth Office has a two-day training programme for its commercial officers on aspects of corporate responsibility, including combating bribery and corruption. UNDP, ILO, the Swedish government and the British government have all sent representatives on a training course on cross-sector partnerships. Finally, development agencies can use their convening power to encourage leadership and as a platform for developing new partnerships, such as the Swedish Partnership for Global Responsibility, an initiative developed by the Sweden Ministry of Foreign Affairs to promote CSR based on internationally agreed principles.

Practical challenges faced by donors working on CSR

The CSR agenda has undoubtedly attracted considerably more attention within development agencies in recent years, partly due to the fact that many issues and approaches that existed in individual projects before the CSR agenda emerged are now being recognised as part of a wider programme of work. There is some evidence of 'mainstreaming' CSR within some development agencies. But discussions at the two events highlighted a number of practical challenges that must be dealt with when discussing CSR from a donor perspective.

Some of these challenges are internal, relating in particular to the task of integrating CSR into existing development agency agendas and operations. Participants at the London meeting stressed that there was still a great deal to be done if the CSR agenda was to become fully integrated in agencies' work. Part of the job of individuals working on CSR was described as helping other agency staff understand and relate to the agenda. But full integration remained hampered by institutional resistance, patchy support and high workloads for individuals working on CSR as they tried to get to grips with the diverse issues involved. Participants described a need to ground CSR policy in operational practice, and to work more closely with key individuals in country offices.

A breakout group at the London workshop described this process of integration as a question of change management, which requires leadership and facilitation. In some agencies, as elsewhere in the development community, there remained a reluctance to work with and a suspicion of the private sector. Participants suggested various responses to such resistance, including:

- Taking a gradual and staged approach
- Having coherent communications and robust arguments to explain to colleagues why the agency should engage with the private sector
- Using relevant case studies and offering practical guidance to colleagues rather than using abstract terminology
- Avoiding getting hung-up on definitions, including that of CSR, instead thinking in terms of objectives and common principles and then finding ways to work to them.

In addition to these internal difficulties, participants at the London meeting identified three sets of external challenges in their work on CSR.

Firstly, a number of participants felt that they needed to find better ways to ensure coherence and coordination between initiatives, and to share information between agencies. Some had difficulty defining the boundaries of responsibility for dealing with CSR issues, both within and between institutions. Some participants were not sure how particular initiatives related to each other, and how best to build on current initiatives.

Secondly, the agencies' role as funding bodies was raised. Some participants were interested in finding how they could move beyond being simply a provider of subsidies that encourage responsible business, to a situation in which companies themselves make a direct contribution. Others noted challenges in ensuring that their funds are spent in a socially responsible way.

Thirdly, some participants felt the need for guidance on selecting and managing partnerships. In particular, they sometimes found it difficult to decide which companies and industry associations they should work with, and on what terms. And engaging with other stakeholders on CSR issues – including governments and civil society in developing countries – also raised challenges, especially if these organisations are sceptical about the value of engaging with business.

The potential for donor coordination and collaboration on CSR

Given that both the London and Stockholm meetings were designed to bring development agencies together to discuss their work on CSR, it is unsurprising that the issue of donor coordination and collaboration was discussed at both events. In London, suggestions for mechanisms to facilitate such coordination included regular exchanges of information on programmes, lessons learned and ideas for common approaches, at both head office and country office levels. There was also a suggestion that a regular consultation group, including bilateral and multilateral agencies, would be useful.

A formal mechanism such as this still did not exist by the time of the Stockholm conference. Some speakers mentioned the possibility of creating one, for example within the OECD's Development Assistance Committee framework, though no firm decisions were reached on this issue. More generally, discussions suggested that the potential for development agencies to share good practice in supporting corporate responsibility, and for coordination, becomes more manageable if their activities are grouped around particular industry sectors, themes or countries.

Since the Stockholm conference, the prospects and opportunities for leadership and coordination among development agencies and governments more generally on CSR have been explored further.[80] But the need for coordination remains, as underlined by a position paper recently produced by Sida, which states:

"The coordination of governments and development agencies in their efforts to promote responsible business practices has been given little attention, although the private sector and NGOs are engaged in many initiatives aimed at understanding and furthering corporate social responsibility. There is a need for a more coordinated international approach by development agencies and their respective governments. The development agencies need to share their experiences. The OECD's Development Assistance

---

[80] See, for example, Bigg & Ward (2004) and Calder & Culverwell (2005).

175

Committee (DAC) has so far not convened the donors in an effort to coordinate policies relating to responsible business practices specifically, although it has held joint meetings with other functions of the OECD to explore how it can address corporate behaviour in developing countries." (Sida, 2005: Appendix 2)

Conclusion: The future of development agency engagement with CSR

The London and Stockholm meetings provided snapshots of donor activity on responsible business issues. They allowed individuals within different agencies to learn more about others' approaches, and they helped to create a sense of a shared agenda. But we should not overstate their significance. For one, they do not tell the whole story. There is much donor activity on various aspects of private sector development, human rights, environmental protection, and so on, which has not been viewed through the lens of CSR as such, although it could be. And the meetings do not appear to have led to any significant consolidation or coordination of CSR work across different agencies as yet.

However, the proceedings of the meetings do provide useful, if partial, insights into how donors' approaches to CSR have developed. Indeed, it is possible to track the emergence of some current donor initiatives since the London meeting. For example, one of the suggestions made at that meeting was the notion that multinational companies should be encouraged to stimulate economic activity in one or more of the 49 least developed countries. Mark Moody-Stuart of BASD proposed this to donors on the basis that one of the main challenges for the World Summit on Sustainable Development was to work out how to achieve sustainable development in the poorest countries of the world. This idea subsequently formed the basis of the UNDP/UN Global Compact 'Growing Sustainable Business for Poverty Reduction' (GSB) initiative.[81]

---

[81] The GSB initiative grew out of the 2002 Global Compact policy dialogue on "business and sustainable development". It is founded on the understanding that economic development of the poorest countries is of fundamental long-term interest to the global community. The aim is to encourage and facilitate investments in poor countries in ways that contribute to poverty reduction and the MDGs. This includes in particular promoting employment creation, business linkages, local economic development, and growth of small and medium-sized enterprises.

Such initiatives might be seen as the new generation of donor activities on CSR, which integrate traditional development agency approaches (in this case enterprise development and business linkages[82]) with new themes within the CSR agenda and business theory (here the notion of business at the 'bottom of the pyramid'[83] in particular). Similarly, future donor activities might integrate aspects of CSR into investment promotion; an approach that has been explored by the World Bank Group's CSR Practice in its work with developing country governments.

More generally, development agencies' CSR work will continue to be conditioned by wider policy frameworks. The current focus of the development community on the MDGs is likely to form the basis for many donors' CSR approaches. Possible interventions here might include those that explicitly seek to align business incentives with the achievement of the MDGs, or that translate the individual targets into what they mean for the private sector.

Although the London and Stockholm meetings, and developments since them, have raised the profile of CSR among development agencies, we must sound a note of caution here. CSR is by no means a widely accepted or understood concept within the development community. Development agency officials who have worked on CSR over the last few years stress its challenges and its limitations.

It is currently fashionable for donors to proclaim their support for CSR, and to use platforms like the Stockholm conference to draw attention to their commitment to working with the private sector. But if CSR is to be anything other than a fad within the development community, it is necessary to continuously examine how donors are engaging with the agenda. Donors have accepted that they must deal with CSR somehow, but that should not mean wholeheartedly accepting everything that it can stand for. In the words of one development agency official, "CSR could be a force for good if it shifts thinking. We should be shaping that debate". And even if CSR does turn out to be a fad, it will no doubt be reinvented in another form. The need for development agencies to consider the private sector's contribution to development will not go away.

---

[82] 'Business linkages' refers to the use of local suppliers and outsourcing where possible; in doing so, maximising the transfer of assets and skills to local communities, and creating a multiplier effect that increases local business activity, employment and income.

[83] This generally refers to the consumer market represented by the four billion people with a per capita income of less than US$1,500 (Prahalad, 2004).

Bibliography

Bigg, T. & Ward, H. (2004). Linking Corporate Social Responsibility, Good Governance and Corporate Accountability through Dialogue, London: IIED.

Calder, F. & Culverwell, M. (2005). Following up the World Summit on Sustainable Development Commitments on Corporate Social Responsibility: Options for action by governments, London: Chatham House.

Commission on Private Sector and Development (2004). Unleashing Entrepreneurship: Making business work for the poor, New York: UNDP.

Fox, T. (2002). Development Agency Round Table on Corporate Social Responsibility: Round Table Report, London: IIED.

Fox, T. & Prescott, D. (2004). Exploring the Role of Development Cooperation Agencies in Corporate Responsibility, London: IIED/IBLF.

Prahalad, C.K. (2004). The Fortune at the Bottom of the Pyramid: Eradicating Poverty Through Profit, Philadelphia, Penn.: Wharton School Publishing.

Sida (2005). Guidelines for Sida's support to corporate social responsibility, draft position paper, Stockholm: Sida.

CHAPTER 7

CORPORATE SOCIAL RESPONSIBILITY - A NEW TOOL IN DEVELOPMENT AID

CAN BILATERAL DONORS MAKE BUSINESS WORK FOR THE POOR?

Marie Thrane
Head of Section, Danida, Ministry of Foreign Affairs of Denmark

Helle Johansen
Head of Section, Danida, Ministry of Foreign Affairs of Denmark

Linda Jakobsen
Business Consultant, Denmark

Abstract

Several bilateral donors have taken on corporate social responsibility (CSR) support as a new tool in development aid. This involves cooperation with new partners and with old partners in new ways. On the one hand, this new instrument creates possibilities of supplementing traditional development aid with new resources, partners and interventions – making the total contribution to poverty reduction larger. On the other hand, closer cooperation with the private sector involves new challenges for the donor. The development effects of CSR do not come automatically; it is the responsibility of the donor to support CSR in a way that is not just business support but real development aid. Donors must make CSR work for the poor. This poses challenges on the internal organising of the donor agency and on ways of cooperating with external partners.

This chapter deals with the possibilities and potential problems for the bilateral donor when working with CSR support as a new instrument in development aid. It is made clear that donors are working with it in an experimental manner. No clear answers exist yet as to how to overcome the challenges and make the most of the opportunities. But it is clear that high commitment to CSR at the leadership level of the donor agency has the potential of making CSR support an integrated and effective part of development aid.

Introduction

Background: Why business is important to development

Donors and business need each other. That is the fundamental premise of this chapter. Just ten years ago, the private sector was looked upon with a degree of suspicion by the development aid community. Today, donor agencies are strengthening their cooperation with the private sector. How did the role of business in development aid change and why is it interesting to explore the challenges and possibilities in the cooperation between donors and business?

First of all, Western business plays a real role in development – with or without the presence of donors. The commercial activities of Western businesses in the developing world have effects on local businesses, competition, the level of technology, wage levels etc.

Secondly, the importance of the local private sector and economic growth in developing countries is widely recognised and donors have supported the economic development of local business for years.

Thirdly, companies are under pressure to do business in the developing world in a socially responsible way. To assist the CSR of the business sector, the UN has formulated ten Global Compact principles for responsible business. The principles cover human rights, labour rights, the environment and anti-corruption – areas where business can make a real difference. To implement these principles in the developing world under difficult social, economic and political circumstances, the companies need partners with local knowledge. *Business cannot do it alone.*

Lastly, the Johannesburg Summit in 2002 stated that public-private partnerships (PPPs) are effective supplements to traditional development aid. In 2003, UN Secretary General Kofi Annan went a step further by saying that the eight Millennium Development Goals (MDGs) cannot be reached by 2015 without the support of the private sector. GNPs of developing countries amount to just pennies in comparison with the annual revenues of multinational companies such as General Motors, Coca Cola and Shell. The Foreign Direct Investments (FDI) of these companies also far exceed aid from national donor agencies. In times of cuts in the budgets of donor agencies, the resources, competencies and active involvement of the private sector are necessary for solving the problems of the developing world. *Donors cannot do it alone.*

The advance of corporate social responsibility (CSR) amongst Western companies brings new opportunities for donors to engage them in development aid. Several bilateral donors take up the issue of CSR in a development context, such as Danida (in Denmark), GTZ (in Germany) and Sida (in Sweden). Donors can help Western companies make CSR activities in developing countries more focused and effective. Companies can help donors by bringing additional resources to the developing countries.

CSR is carried out at business level. The term refers to the actions of the company to improve social and environmental standards in the company, subsidiaries or in the surrounding community. When we talk about CSR efforts of donors, it does not mean that donors themselves practise CSR themselves as an organisation, but rather that donors help create enabling environments for CSR and support concrete CSR activities of companies operating in the developing world. As such, CSR is not in itself a goal for the donor – it is a new instrument of development aid to reach the existing goal of poverty reduction. The question for donors is how to align the CSR activities of Western business with development goals to the benefit of the poor.

Most donors are beginners in the field of CSR and there is a need to collect best donor practices and share experiences, as well as evaluate and develop systematic and methodological approaches to CSR in the donor community. No clear answers exist as to what the best donor approach to CSR comprises. This chapter presents opportunities and possible problem areas as well as some reflections on how the donor can deal with CRS in a way that unleashes its full potential contribution to development.

The focus of the chapter: Bilateral donors and their CSR partners

Bilateral donors can cooperate with a range of partners to support CSR in developing countries. In the following model, the institutions listed in the left column are from Western countries, whereas the institutions listed in the right column are from developing countries.

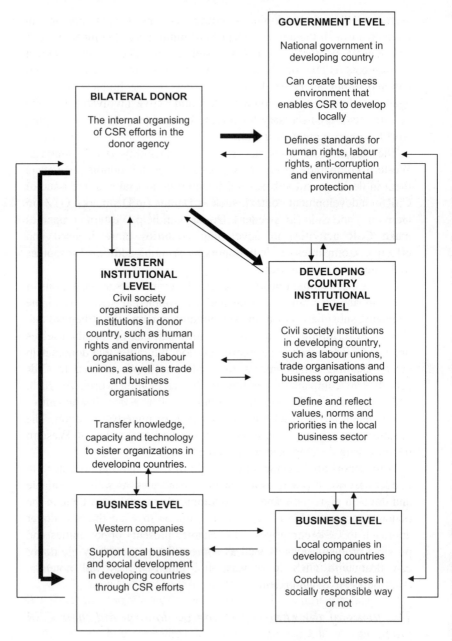

Figure 7:1 The bilateral donors' cooperation with partners to support CSR as a development tool in developing countries

Figure 7:1 illustrates the donor cooperation with main CSR partners. The arrows illustrate the support, dialogue and advice that flows amongst the different partners. With the bilateral donor as the point of departure, this chapter focuses on the relationships illustrated by the thick arrows. Each actor has its own role to play in strengthening CSR in a given developing country. Typically, a CSR partnership involves multiple partners. If the donor has a coherent approach to CSR that includes all levels in this figure, synergies can be obtained and the effects of the donor support to CSR will be maximised.

The donor's aim behind CSR support is to encourage as many enterprises as possible to engage in effective CSR activities. Therefore the core of CSR support is the public-private partnerships (PPPs) that the donor enters into with enterprises. The close cooperation with companies regarding CSR creates new possibilities in development aid and new challenges. To ensure a maximum positive effect on poverty reduction, the donor has a responsibility to carefully design PPP programmes and to supplement PPPs with activities at government and institutional level. The challenge for the donor is to work with CSR as a new development aid tool in a way that maintains core principles for effective development aid.

The first section in this chapter deals with the possibilities and challenges of PPPs when the donor supports the CSR activities of enterprises in developing countries. These possibilities and challenges are based on the differences in objectives, means and comparative strengths of the donor and the enterprise. It is discussed how the donor can construct PPP programmes that take these differences into consideration to the benefit of the donor, the enterprises and the development in the recipient country.

The second section deals with the possible donor efforts at government and institutional level in the developing country aimed at strengthening an enabling environment for CSR.

1. The institutional level: The donor can support civil business organisations in developing countries that can promote norms, standards and priorities of CSR in the local business.
2. The government level: The donor can support the efforts of national authorities in developing countries to formulate a CSR agenda and set up regulations, incentives and institutions to promote human rights, labour rights, anti-corruption and environmental standards in the local business.

The third section deals with the challenges of the internal organising of the donor agency when incorporating CSR support as a new instrument of development aid. Before placing demands of CSR on external partners, the donor itself must live up to a range of demands to be a professional and credible partner in CSR activities, and an effective organising of CSR efforts must be in place.

Challenges and possibilities of cooperation with companies

The core of a "public-private partnership" or "cross-sector partnership" is the principle of additionality. This means that the partnership leads to a larger and better contribution to poverty reduction and sustainable development than what the individual actor could achieve alone. In a partnership, each partner's comparative advantages should be fully utilised to create "win-win situations".

When entering into a new market in the developing world, the enterprise lacks local experience, network and expertise. It faces a business environment that is very different and more problematic than what is the case in the Western world: corruption, economic uncertainty, political transition, poor working conditions, poor human rights records etc.

The comparative advantage of the donor is the experience in how to work in the developing world and how to assist local stakeholders in improving existing structures to the benefit of everybody – including the private company. The donor has access to the national, local and regional policy level in the host country.

The comparative advantage of the company is capital, know-how, technology, technical skills, business knowledge, and the power of employing people. Private investments in developing countries are necessary for economic and social development. Higher investments lead to increased production and job creation to the benefit of the local population. The Western enterprises also possess technical skills and know-how that are highly needed in many companies in the developing countries.

The donor agency should design PPP programmes that utilise the comparative advantages of both the donor and the enterprise. This is easier said than done. When PPPs are established, the difference in objectives and means imply potential conflicts.

The challenges faced by donors in the cooperation with companies must be understood in the light of the changes in principles laid down

184

in the means of development aid during the last decades. The issues raised in this section are summed up in Figure 7:2.

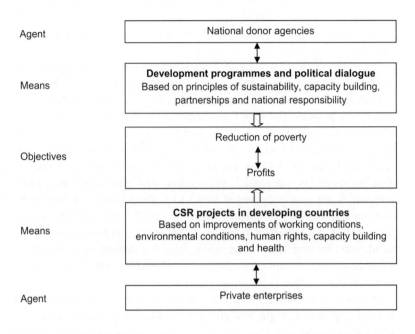

Figure 7:2 The different objectives and means of private companies and national donor agencies

Possibilities of merging the objectives of donors and enterprises

The main objective for donors is poverty reduction, while the overall objective of the private company is maximising profit. However, factors that contribute to profits must be understood broadly. Even though CSR is not considered a part of core business, CSR efforts can be part of a strategy to ensure profits in the long term. This can be illustrated by a recent survey from World Economic Forum (2005) that points to the most common reasons for enterprises to engage in partnerships for development:

- Commitment to the values and principles of the company
- Protection of corporate reputation and brand
- Meeting funding requirements
- Investing in a sound and secure business environment
- Entering into underdeveloped markets

The challenge for the donor agency is to construct PPPs that merge the objectives of profits and poverty reduction and create win-win situations. The mentioned reasons for companies to enter into partnerships should be taken into consideration when designing the PPPs.

There are many examples of PPPs where the donor agency and the enterprise have mutual interests of improving the local business conditions. This helps the local community on the one hand and minimises business risks for the enterprise on the other hand. Creating better labour conditions leads to higher productivity, which at the same time contributes to social and economic growth. Improving the local business climate means that it is easier for companies to operate, which should result in increased production and job creation. More companies are also encouraged to start up if the costs of establishing new businesses are reduced. Offering healthcare services to the workers and perhaps their families will also contribute to better living conditions for the local community, whilst offering new and more advanced products and technology at affordable prices can lead to better living conditions for the population.

On the other hand, there are situations where the objective of maximising profit might not go hand in hand with the objective of poverty reduction.

One area could be differences in the choice of the geographical focus of interventions. Western companies will only engage in commercial activities and practise CSR in countries with market and business potential. The important emerging markets for companies are China, India, Brazil, Mexico, Indonesia, Turkey, South Africa and Thailand (Prahalad, 2005). These countries are home to about three billion people representing 70% of the developing world population. The economic development of these markets offers huge possibilities for Western companies and many of them have an interest in entering the market at an early stage before it is fully developed. The donor, on the other hand, will direct the development aid to the poorest countries, and these countries might not be identical to the countries with the biggest business potential.

To facilitate the establishment of PPPs in development aid, the donor will in some cases have to broaden the normal range of partner countries to include countries with a business potential. On the other hand, the donor can also raise the businesses' awareness of new markets and, by its local presence, contribute to minimising the businesses' risks of entering unknown markets. The donor agency might set maximum GNP levels of these countries to justify the allocation of development aid. Furthermore, donor agencies will normally need to have local knowledge and networks in the specific country in order to be an attractive partner to companies.

The means of donors and enterprises in developing countries

Traditionally, development aid consisted of a large number of individual projects within various fields. A project usually lasted 1-2 years and was directed towards a single institution or organisation in need of assistance.

To optimise the effects of development aid, donor agencies have shifted from development cooperation via project activities to sector programme support.[84] Some of the fundamental means in today's development cooperation are challenged when donors enter into partnerships with enterprises because the companies' CSR activities are characterised by individual projects. When entering into partnerships with private enterprises, the donor agency should ensure that core aid principles are considered to optimise the development effects.

The sector programme approach means that development aid is directed towards governmental level and often deals with the framework within which a business/organisation is acting. The main approach for today's development aid is to seek improvements in relation to policy regulation, barriers and opportunities within selected sectors and to bring about an overall structural change in the partner country. Consequently, a programmatic approach is much more comprehensive than individual projects and has a much longer timeframe.

The main agreed principles behind sector programme support are: sustainability, capacity building, partner cooperation in the recipient country in order to create local and national ownership, alignment of development programmes with national policies, and donor coordination. The following figure summarises how these principles are challenged by differences in the approaches by the donor and the enterprise to activities in developing countries. The last column shows examples of specific aspects that the donor can cover in PPP programmes to maintain aid principles.

---

[84] Sector programme support is defined as a long-term framework for a broader development assistance to a national endeavour, including various and flexible modalities of support at different levels within agreed objectives and management procedures (Danida, 2005).

It should be noted that these challenges are seen from the perspective of the donor. The enterprises would probably see a number of other challenges when entering into partnership with donors. These challenges could be bureaucracy, the donor's lack of understanding of how businesses work, and reluctance to create new and innovative solutions to development problems. This chapter will, however, focus on the challenges from the donor's perspective.

Aid Principles	National donor approach	Enterprise approach	Requirements to elements in the PPP in order to maintain the aid principles
Sustainability	The continuation of benefits from a development intervention after major development assistance has been completed (Danida, 2005).	Lack of need and capacity to consider the sustainability of the benefits of CSR efforts longer than what is needed by the enterprise.	An exit strategy must be formulated Capacity building must take place to ensure that local partners can take over when the PPP is terminated. An agreed long-term timeframe for the intervention must be reached.
Capacity building	Capacity building amongst central actors in the developing country is based on analysis of local and national needs in order to support long-term sustainability.	Capacity building supports the commercial activities of the enterprise.	The donor demands that capacity building is part of the PPP activities. The donor can offer economic support to the transfer of knowledge and technology between enterprises.
Local and national ownership in recipient country	Strategic national partners are involved in the formulation and implementation of the programme.	CSR projects involve partners related to the enterprise.	The donor demands that local partners are involved. PPP programmes must include guidelines that ensure alignment with national policies and sector programmes. PPP interventions must focus on sectors and problem areas that are agreed upon with national partners.
Programme alignment with national policies	Donor support aligns with national policies.	Lacks the incentive and capacity to align with national policies.	
Donor coordination	Donors seek to coordinate activities with other donors.	Lacks the incentive and capacity to coordinate with other donors or CSR activities.	Both donor programmes and CSR initiatives must be coordinated.

Figure 7:3 Challenges in aid principles and elements in PPP programmes to overcome them

189

The donor can try to overcome the above-mentioned challenges in a public-private partnership by designing guidelines for PPPs that include requirements to the activities that are supported. These requirements can be formulated as part of the criteria for enterprises to obtain donor support and in the cooperation agreements between donor and enterprise. Examples of requirements are: minimum time period of the project, sector focus, priority of training and technical assistance, and an exit strategy.

In the following, it is discussed how the core aid principles can be supported by the design of the PPP programmes. The issue of donor coordination is not discussed separately.

Sustainability and capacity building

Sustainability is the overarching aid principle. It is ensured by capacity building, a long-term strategy, the strengthening of institutions, and an exit strategy.

An important means to ensure sustainability is to support capacity building. Central local actors in development cooperation who receive training and education within specific fields can continue and further improve the structural changes initiated by the donor. Capacity is also a precondition for a successful exit strategy. This has to be mutually agreed upon by the donor and the recipients and also describe how the recipients gradually take over the programme responsibilities before the day the donor withdraws.

One of the donor's tasks in a PPP is to ensure sustainability of the joint efforts, including capacity building of local partners. In most cases, the company would not attach the same importance to an activity's long-term development effects as a donor. Hence, this important factor can be overlooked simply because it is outside the scope of the company's core business. It is, however, also in the interest of the company that their CSR activities create the greatest possible development effects.

The donor can assist the companies and provide economic support to training and technical assistance carried out in local companies, so the knowledge and newly acquired skills stay in the local companies. Especially for small and medium-sized enterprises (SMEs), the economic support from the donor can mean a difference to how many resources are used on training and education in the local company.

The PPP project needs to be carried out over a longer time period to increase the chances of creating sustainability. Requirements to the length of the project from the donor's side are important because the time span of enterprises' CSR initiatives is usually shorter than that of donors. CSR decisions made in enterprises depend mainly on market trends and not on local needs and considerations about sustainability alone. Unless CSR is integrated within the core business strategy of the enterprise, it is likely that in times of shortage of resources companies will focus on core competencies within the company and not on CSR (UNIDO, 2004).

The donor can also use its knowledge about exit strategies for developing activities in partnership with the company. In project preparation this question can be raised and the training and education activities can be designed accordingly. At this time the exit strategy can also be discussed with the local partner and the partners' expectations can be integrated in the PPP project.

An example of a PPP project where sustainability is sought incorporated is a joint project between Inmobia, a Danish producer of mobile contents (e.g. news and commercials); Celtel Kenya, the local mobile operator, National Aids Control Council in Kenya; and Danida. The project aims at raising the awareness of HIV/AIDS among young Kenyans via quizzes and FAQ on the mobile phone. The companies do not charge for the HIV/AIDS information. In an early phase of the project, it was discussed how the local partners would be able to create similar information campaigns without assistance from Inmobia after the end of this project. When the issue was raised, Inmobia had in fact already thought of the importance of transferring know-how to the local partner so that the intervention would not be dependent on Inmobia's presence in Kenya in the long run. Danida could assist the company on how to integrate the wish for sustainability and capacity building in the project. This cooperation is also a good example of a partnership where all partners use their comparative advantages. The specific project would not have been possible without the competencies and technical capabilities of the individual partners.

Local and national ownership in recipient country

Ownership is the appropriation or taking of responsibility for a certain endeavour. Ownership implies formal or real authority as well as effective self-authorisation to assume management responsibility (Danida, 2005). In practice, this means that national partners in the developing country should be involved in the formulation and implementation of development aid programmes.

In PPPs, the donor should therefore ensure that the local companies and organisations are actively involved in preparation as well as implementation of the activities. With the creation of local ownership, the chances of creating sustainable effects are increased.

The partnership agreement could be used to divide the responsibilities of local as well as Western partners.

Align programmes with national policies
Traditional donor programmes are formulated in cooperation with and in support of the priorities of the local and national stakeholders in the recipient country in alignment with national policies.

As CSR is a rather new type of activity for most enterprises, especially SMEs, they can be expected to have an incremental approach to CSR. Experience shows that enterprises either cooperate directly with other institutions or enterprises in the developing world or concentrate their CSR activities within their own company. Many enterprises have no incentives or experiences in cooperation with policy level in a developing country and only in rare cases will they enter into partnerships at the institutional level. Hence, it is the donor's responsibility to lay down guidelines for PPP activities to ensure they are in alignment with national policies.

The donor has to make decisions about in which sectors and areas the PPPs should be established. Some donors choose to focus their partnership activities towards a specific sector which has been identified in cooperation with the local government. Concentrating on one sector could imply the establishment of multi-stakeholder partnerships to create economic and social development in that specific sector. Other donors, such as Danida, choose to use the UN Global Compact as a framework for their PPP activities. The UN Global Compact is a set of universal principles covering labour and human rights, environmental improvements, and anti-corruption.

It is important that the donor agency makes these strategic decisions due to the criteria of alignment with national policies and due to marketing aspects. It will be easier to market the PPP programmes to the businesses if they are focused as well as related to the problems experienced directly by companies doing business in developing countries.

To sum up, this section has stressed the importance of designing PPP programmes where the basic principles for traditional development cooperation are taken into account. It is possible to include some of these principles in the PPP. However, to optimise the development effects of the CSR activities at business level, the institutional and governmental levels need to be involved.

CSR work at institutional and government level

Even the most optimal construction of a PPP programme cannot ensure full compliance with the core principles of development aid. It is in the nature of things that cooperation with enterprises does usually not lead to structural or political changes in the developing country.

The ability to affect the policy and structural level is exactly the comparative advantage of the donor. It is the responsibility of the donor to have an overall approach to CSR where efforts are set in at all levels to lift the CSR work to a programmatic level. As a supplement to the PPPs, the donor should use its network, experience and access to the institutional and governmental level in the developing countries to support the PPP interventions and ensure their scaling-up effect. Efforts at these levels in the developing country affect the business environment, norms, policies, institutions, structures and competencies with regard to CSR that last longer than the individual PPP projects. For example, the individual project of a company to adhere to human rights could support general standards and norms affecting all companies.

By working at these levels, the donor can support all the principles of development aid: sustainability, capacity building, local ownership and alignment with national policies.

The institutional level needs to be included in order to optimise the CSR efforts

To optimise the CSR efforts, it is essential to include local business organisations as well as other private organisations, like human rights and environmental organisations, in the work in order to create an enabling environment for responsible business. The local business organisations are important because they can assist in ensuring broader effects and scaling-up effects of the CSR efforts. The organisations can put CSR on their agenda and encourage and support member companies to work with CSR and enter into PPPs. Furthermore, the organisations should be engaged in policy dialogue and planning of development activities, and thereby ensure local ownership in the organisations.

The human rights and environmental organisations are important players as they possess specific knowledge and expertise that is important to the development task. These organisations often have a strong local presence and with that good contact to the local communities. Hence, the environmental and human rights organisations can be strategic partners in partnerships for development.

The CSR capacity of trade and business organisations in developing countries needs to be strengthened so they can advise their members about how to work with CSR. Especially SMEs need to be encouraged and supported in their CSR work. SMEs are the mainstay of most economies in terms of employment creation, and their cumulative social and environmental impacts are highly significant (Fox, 2004). Hence, this group plays an important role in strengthening CSR. Even though SME involvement is important, the local bigger companies should not be left out. There might be a need for assisting the companies in focusing their CSR efforts towards more long-term activities and investments and in adopting CSR as a core business strategy. A recent study on CSR in Kenya showed that the majority of the executives interviewed seem to equate CSR to philanthropy, charitable giving and community involvement (Trust, 2004). CSR was seen as an add-on activity rather than a core business strategy.

In practice, building CSR competencies in the local organisations should be linked to other capacity building areas. In continuation of capacity building within other functions of the business organisation, the development agency could assist the organisation in strengthening its capabilities in relation to ethical guidelines, codes of conduct and certification processes.

Working to improve environmental and social standards through the UN Global Compact principles is another way companies can work with these issues. Hence, these principles could also be raised in discussions with the business organisations. The business organisation could be assisted in forming partnerships with local NGOs within fields that require specific knowledge. How to create awareness of the importance of CSR among the members is another issue that could be included in the capacity building of the business organisation. Finally, the organisation could be helped to assist companies in forming CSR networks where information and experiences can be exchanged.

It is not expected to be an easy task to engage local business organisations in CSR work, as there are many other areas of concern, and often basic working conditions in the organisations need to be strengthened. However, with an increasing global focus on CSR, the companies in the developing countries have to respond to the requirements from the Western business partners. Therefore, the local business organisations need to be able to support their members sooner or later. If the capacity building takes place via a twinning arrangement (organisation-to-organisation), there might not be a long tradition in the Western organisations to work with these issues either. Establishment of partnerships with environmental and human rights organisations is a way to bring in more expertise and capacity within CSR fields.

The government level ensures sustainability

The possibility of CSR to become a sustainable development engine depends on the national political commitment. If the government takes ownership for the CSR agenda, chances are that CSR is supported by rules, institutions and incentive structures.

Donors can play a facilitating role for raising CSR awareness and institutional capacity at government level in developing countries, and also help governments create an enabling environment for CSR in local business. This is important because CSR only has a real and sustainable effect on development if rooted in the local business sector. If CSR is not supported, guided and rewarded by the government, it has fewer chances of finding a place on the agenda of local business, where more pressing needs may be dominant.

Clearly, donors cannot direct the national policy level in a CSR direction overnight. Weak and corrupt national institutions, no sense of urgency for CSR, and a lack of resources in developing countries are real challenges. Building a CSR agenda at government level and facilitating government dialogue with civil society on CSR will take time, capacity building and the power of good examples.

Therefore, CSR should not be introduced to the development agenda as a new independent area of work, but as a cross-cutting issue relating to the development of the business sector, to the role of the private sector in the development of other sectors, and to issues of human rights, anti-corruption etc. The question of the role of the private sector in development and its ability to act in a socially responsible way is a natural consequence of an ongoing focus on human rights etc.

CSR is a means to reach development goals and reduce poverty by strengthening the role of the private sector as a development partner for local government. CSR at business community level can make real changes and helps attract FDI. If government does not see the CSR agenda in such a positive light, the danger is that CSR becomes a Western concept that is forced upon the South.

It will be important for the donor to distinguish between different developing countries and to link the CSR agenda to the concrete level of development, national development goals and political willingness to work with CSR. Furthermore, it will be important to consider whether to use the CSR terminology at all. When CSR is mentioned in the following, one should bear in mind that the practical implementation at government level might not be about the term CSR but about socially responsible business in traditional areas such as human rights and the environment.

CSR as an element in the bilateral development partnership

One tool for the donor is to put CSR issues on the agenda of the annual bilateral negotiations between the donor and the government in the developing country where shared understandings of development challenges and goals of the development cooperation are reached. Another tool is to incorporate goals for CSR into the long-term strategies that are agreed upon by the donor and the partner country.

CSR goals and regulations

In the developing world, CSR can be about securing minimum standards within areas where business operates and create externalities, and about creating an enabling environment for voluntary socially responsible business.

Firstly, donors can assist in translating international standards into national legislation, for example on workers rights, corruption and the environment. National regulation should be based on national levels of development and needs. It is important to be aware that these standards are not a priority for many developing countries. One example is the failed attempt of the EU to put labour rights on the agenda of the current WTO Doha Round. Secondly, donors can support institutional capacity building in public institutions that should enforce these regulations and help the business community to observe them. Often the problem is not lack of regulations but lack of capacity to enforce regulations. Thirdly, donors can advise the state to create positive incentives for CSR, such as CSR investments, tax incentives, visibility for the social entrepreneurs etc. Finally, the donor can share experiences with the state on how to present oneself as a professional partner for the business sector and how to create possibilities for PPPs.

Participation of local business

The donor can encourage government to base its CSR efforts on an understanding of local business conditions and development needs. CSR happens at business level. To ensure local ownership and commitment to CSR, it is important that the state formulates and implements its CSR policy in a participatory manner involving the business community. Many countries, such as India and Russia, have local traditions for socially responsible business that might not have been labelled CSR. The donor should encourage government to explore these traditions and build CSR policies on them. One danger is that government cooperation is primarily orientated towards larger enterprises. As the business community in developing countries is most often dominated by SMEs, the full CSR effect can only be reached if drivers of social entrepreneurship are also found in this segment.

The internal organisation of the bilateral donor agency

When a political decision has been taken that CSR should be part of development aid, it is the responsibility of the donor agency to organise itself internally to be able to work with CSR as a development aid tool that satisfies core principles of development aid. The internal organising and allocation of resources to CSR will depend on one fundamental question. Does the leadership of the donor agency see CSR as just another 'flavour of the month' or is the donor seriously committed to make CSR a central part of development aid – or is the commitment somewhere in between?

The main argument is that the donor must make a decision about how to weigh CSR relative to other development aid instruments and make conscious choices about the allocation of resources and efforts to CSR accordingly. This does not mean that the donor cannot use CSR support as a means for development if the presented maximum requirements are not met.

Strategic decisions to match the level of commitment must be made about a) the working definition of CSR, b) the strategy for CSR support, c) the placement of CSR responsibility, and d) the programmatic level of the CSR approach and internal capacity building.

There are two good reasons for dealing with these areas in a comprehensive and strategic way. Firstly, it will make it easier to fit the CSR efforts into a programmatic approach and make the sustainability of the interventions more likely. Secondly, to be a credible partner to enterprises, the donor must present a level of competencies and professionalism that makes the input from the donor valuable to the enterprise when dealing with CSR. PPP is not just about the economic donor support to the CSR projects of the enterprises; the idea is also that the donor can offer knowledge and experience that can lift the CSR efforts to a higher level.

CSR is not the same in the North and the South

The CSR terminology is much discussed, and the donor must choose a working definition of the term that makes sense in a context of development aid.

From a donor perspective, it is important to differentiate between a 'Do no harm' and a 'Do good' definition of CSR. 'Do no harm' refers to companies just observing regulations and norms in the society in which they operate. As regulations of business, human rights and the environment are often weak and poorly enforced in developing countries, a 'Do no harm' CSR approach on behalf of Western companies will not contribute to development - and might even support existing structures.

A donor cannot legitimise supporting clean-cut business activities for the Western company – as this would be considered business support and not development aid. For the donor to be able to define the support to Western business as development aid, the CSR support must be related to the 'Do good definition'. The CSR of Western companies in developing countries has been defined by the organisation, Business for Social Responsibility, as 'operating a business in a manner that exceeds the ethical, legal, commercial and public expectations that society has of business'. This refers to companies expanding their core business activities to include investments in improving, for example, working conditions for local employees in their subsidiaries or in the companies of suppliers.

This understanding of CSR could be combined with a definition that includes both voluntary and regulated activities and also illustrates that business often conducts CSR in cooperation with others. One option is the World Bank working definition of CSR:

> "CSR is the commitment of business to contribute to sustainable economic development – working with employees, their families, the local community and the society at large to improve the quality of life, in ways that are both good for business and for development."

Considering the weak rules and institutions for regulating business and the harsh conditions for doing business in developing countries, it will not always make sense to apply a 'Do good' CSR definition to the local companies. At this stage of business development in developing countries, it is more realistic to direct the CSR efforts of donors towards helping the government create not only an enabling environment but also rules and institutions that motivate and force local companies to adhere to minimum standards of human rights, labour rights, anti-corruption and environmental protection. Just formulating standards and getting the companies to abide by them will make a real difference. As such, 'Do no harm' definitions of CSR might be more appropriate and realistic when talking about socially responsible behaviour of local companies.

A CSR strategy reflects donor commitment

The CSR support of the donor will always involve business as a central actor. Most donors have a range of programmes for involving business in development work. Synergy and complementarity of CSR interventions could be strengthened by incorporating them into an overall strategy for all activities involving business and by relating them to sector programmes and existing development goals, such as poverty reduction. An action plan for CSR support will not suffice in this respect. A strategy implies clearly defined goals for CSR that are made operational and measurable on a yearly basis. Measurable goals make CSR efforts transparent and it becomes possible to hold the donor agency accountable for CSR activities. The Canadian donor agency CIDA has gone a step further and made a policy framework for activities related to the private sector and sustainable development together with other Canadian government departments (IIED, 2002).

Placement of CSR responsibility and allocation of resources must be clear

CSR activities involve the business community, but the effects of CSR are not limited to the business sector. For example, a partnership between a donor and a company can aim at supporting HIV/AIDS information campaigns, cooperation with business organisations can aim at formulating standards for human rights, and negotiations at the political level can focus on how CSR can contribute to the overall goal of poverty reduction. Therefore, it should be possible to involve different expertises of the agency in CSR interventions according to the sector and development problem in question.

If the donor chooses to deal substantially with the enterprises when entering into PPPs, a CSR coordinator could be placed in each unit – be it organised country, sector or otherwise. Another option is to draw in sector experts from relevant units into each CSR programme/project depending on sector focus. The agency can also consider setting up a team of CSR specialists, who rotate amongst units according to the particular intervention. Whatever organisation model is chosen, it is important that clear responsibilities for this area of work are allocated, but that CSR work is rooted in the whole organisation.

A programmatic approach ensures sustainability

As CSR activities are always linked to specific sectors and development goals, they could be integrated in sector programmes which also include a private sector component. For example, if the goal is to build local CSR capacity with the assistance from Western companies, it is a good idea to fit this specific activity into the overall donor efforts to strengthen the local business sector. This could ensure a synergy effect and scale up the effects of the CSR activity to fit in with the development of a whole sector, as opposed to the development of one or a handful of local companies.

If the donor wants a strong position for CSR, it can be considered to mainstream CSR as a cross-cutting issue in all sector programmes. Mainstreaming can also involve incorporating CSR into different programmes as conditions for lending, procurement and project support to business, as done by the Swedish donor agency, Sida (IIED, 2002).

The incorporation of CSR into sector programmes should happen progressively over the coming years. Experiences with PPPs and other CSR-related activities should be shared between donors and within the donor agency across borders of developing countries, with a view to developing a more methodological approach and to identifying interventions that are known to work. This can contribute to moving from a project approach where concrete activities are tried and tested to a more programmatic approach. As sector programmes are reformulated and new programmes are initiated, CSR support can be built in as a component or a cross-cutting issue. Still, it will be important to ensure flexibility of CSR support to allow for innovative ideas and initiatives from the private sector.

Internal capacity building ensures incorporation of CSR in development aid practices

CSR is a new area of work for most donor agencies. Therefore, capacity building amongst donor staff should be carried out both for home-based and stationed personnel. CSR knowledge and awareness across the organisation is a prerequisite for CSR to be taken seriously and for the staff to be able to incorporate CSR measures into relevant interventions.

Real CSR understanding and capacity is also important for the business community plus institutions and governments in developing countries to see the donor as a competent partner in CSR matters. A way to build donor capacity is to set up structures for CSR dialogue between the donor agency and business representatives in order to come closer to an understanding of each other's CSR definitions, motives and goals. The Danish agency, Danida, has established an informal dialogue forum with representatives from companies and business organisations. Lessons learned from the discussions are that misunderstandings are cleared and knowledge is shared in a constructive way.

Conclusion

CSR is a new tool in development cooperation that has to be taken seriously by donors and companies in order to create real development and win-win situations. PPPs are a useful way of creating cooperation between companies and donors, and can result in positive changes for companies and communities in the developing world. However, PPPs on their own might result in "islands of development" within the developing country, and not a general national development.

One way of optimising the outcome of the CSR efforts is to include the fundamental principles of development aid, such as sustainability, local ownership and capacity building, in the CSR work. The donor has to utilise its comparative advantage and ensure that the PPP activities are supported by a programmatic approach where local organisations and the government in the developing country are included in the CSR efforts. In this way, CSR will not jeopardise the traditional principles of development aid and outcome will be optimised.

Another important aspect is that the donor organisation would have to be seen as a serious and credible cooperation partner in the eyes of the companies. This means that the donor, besides being a "door opener" for the company and a financial partner, should also be able to offer expertise, networks and local knowledge to the partnership. The businesses should perceive the partnership with the donor as value added to their project activities.

The use of CSR as a development tool is itself a concept under development. At the present time, no comprehensive methodological approach widely has been agreed upon amongst donors on how to engage businesses via their CSR activities in the development cooperation. There is only a limited knowledge and understanding of the development effects of PPPs. It is necessary to increase the understanding of CSR and PPP by sharing knowledge on best practices and lessons learned. This work would have to be carried out by companies and donors in cooperation.

Bibliography

Danida (2005). Aid Management Guidelines.

Fox, T. (2004). Corporate Social Responsibility and Development: In quest of an agenda, Development, 47[3].

IIED (2002). Development Agency Round Table on CSR.

Prahalad, C. K. (2005). The Fortune at the Bottom of the Pyramid. Wharton School Publishing, Upper Saddle River, NJ, 2005 , 401 s.

Trust, U. (2004). Report on the status of corporate social responsibility – on behalf of UNDP Growing Sustainable Business Initiative in Kenya.

UNIDO (2004). Corporate Social Responsibility and Developing Country SMEs.

World Economic Forum (2005). Global Corporate Citizenship Initiative: Partnering for Success: Business Perspectives on Multi-stakeholder Partnerships. Geneva: World Economic Forum

CHAPTER 8

COMBINING INTERNATIONAL CONSISTENCY WITH LOCAL PRESENCE

NOVOZYMES, CORPORATE RESPONSIBILITY AND THE UNITED NATIONS GLOBAL COMPACT

Michael Hougård Pedersen

Adviser, Novozymes' Sustainability Development Center,
Copenhagen, Denmark

Abstract

This article outlines Novozymes' utilisation of the United Nations Global Compact as a reference framework for upholding international consistency and appreciating local cultural traditions, when further integrating corporate responsibility into the company's way of doing business. Since this reference framework is particularly useful when doing business in developing countries, the article includes a number of examples on the way that Novozymes applies it in China.

Introduction

As the vast majority of companies, Novozymes is a part of many global value chains with customers, employees, suppliers and other partners in many different countries, each having their own particular cultural traditions, laws and regulations. This fact makes it particularly challenging to uphold international consistency and to appreciate local cultural traditions, when further integrating corporate responsibility into Novozymes' way of doing business.

In balancing these often contrasting objectives, Novozymes has found United Nations Global Compact a most useful reference framework for the company's mission and values statement, policies, and management standards. Not only does the universality of the international conventions, which the Global Compact principles are derived from, enable Novozymes to operate with international consistency without rightly being accused of engaging in a crusade. The framework character of the principles, which provides room for local clarification and interpretation, also enables Novozymes to adapt to and appreciate local cultural traditions across the world without being unprincipled.

Key facts about Novozymes

Novozymes is the biotech-based world leader in enzymes and micro-organisms. The company is headquartered and listed in Copenhagen, Denmark. With an estimated share of 44% and 50% of the global markets respectively, Novozymes has 4,000 employees, an annual turnover of USD 1 billion and a net operating profit of 18%. The company's eco-productivity index[85] is 116 for water and 113 for energy, while its frequency of occupational accidents[86] is 7.1 and the one of occupational diseases[2] 1.1. (2004 figures).

Ever since Novozymes was formed as a result of the demerger from Novo Nordisk in 2000, the company has remained very committed to further integrating corporate responsibility into its way of doing

---

[85] Eco-productivity index (EPI):

$$\frac{\text{Production (2004)}}{\text{Production (2003)}} \quad \text{x} \quad \frac{\text{Consumption (2003)}}{\text{Consumption (2004)}} \quad \text{x} \quad 100$$

[86] Frequency of occupational accidents and occupational diseases:

$$\frac{\text{No. of occupational accidents x 1,000,000}}{\text{No. of employées x 1,600}}$$

or

$$\frac{\text{No. of cases of occupational disease x 1,000,000}}{\text{No. of employées x 1,600}}$$

business. As a result of these efforts, Novozymes, among other things, continues to be a sector leader in Dow Jones Sustainability Indexes for the fifth consecutive year.

Novozymes' quality management system reflects the company's commitment to corporate responsibility. Along with corporate responsibility policies and management standards, the company has set up a cross-functional, high-level strategy group called 'Sustainability Development Strategy Group'. This strategy group, which reports to Novozymes' corporate executive management team, is responsible for devising the company's overall corporate responsibility strategy, including target setting and monitoring progress. Comprisng vice presidents from across Novozymes' organisation, who are appointed by the company's functional and geographical management groups, the strategy group is supported by a corporate responsibility unit called 'Sustainability Development Center'. This center comprises specialists in the disciplines of social responsibility, environmental matters, bioethics and business integrity.

Along these lines, corporate responsibility is a fixed item on the agenda at Novozymes' board meetings twice a year. Furthermore, corporate responsibility performance and development targets have been integrated into a corporate responsibility bonus scheme for the corporate executive management team, vice presidents and directors. Novozymes also publishes an integrated annual report, and key corporate responsibility indicators are reported quarterly, both internally and externally, along with financial data.

In terms of assurance, Novozymes' business units across the world are regularly assessed by a group of facilitators. These facilitators assess compliance with the company's values, policies and standards by the means of interviews with employees at all levels. Their findings are reported to Novozymes' corporate executive management team. Novozymes also has a special ombudsman, who provides an opportunity for all employees to have cases heard which they believe to be in conflict with the company's values, policies and management standards.

China is one of Novozymes' fastest growing markets and already takes up the position as the company's second largest national market. Novozymes has had operations in China for ten years with headquarters and research & development in Beijing and production sites in Tianjin, Hongda and Shenyang. The country, which now hosts 600 of the company's employees, remains of utmost importance to

Novozymes; both in terms of future market potential, production potential as well as research & development potential.

Not least in China, where Novozymes has won several corporate responsibility prizes, the company attaches great importance to further integrating corporate responsibility into its way of doing business. Among other things, Novozymes has a local sustainability development unit in China, and the company has been engaged in setting up the China Business Council for Sustainable Development. Novozymes' Site President in China is a member of the company's Sustainability Development Strategy Group and also holds the position as a Vice President of China Business Council for Sustainable Development.

Further information about Novozymes is available at www.novozymes.com. This website also includes additional information about the company's approach to corporate responsibility (see 'About us > Sustainability') and more information about Novozymes' operations in China (see 'About us > Publications > Site reports').

A brief introduction to United Nations Global Compact

The Global Compact is a unique United Nations initiative. Among other things, it originates in the perception that governments alone cannot effectively achieve the United Nations goals of poverty eradication, peace and security in a new and globalised social order, the premises of which are based upon a broad circle of civil society actors that have grown bigger and more influential than many governments.

Following inauguration in 2000, which was initiated by Kofi Annan, United Nations Secretary-General, approximately 2,000 companies from across the world have now become signatories to the Global Compact. Along with a range of non-governmental organisations, United Nations agencies, research institutes, cities, unions and employers' associations, these companies have committed themselves to, within their sphere of influence, working towards fulfilling ten principles on human rights, labour, the environment and anti-corruption:

The ten principles of the United Nations Global Compact

Human rights

Principle 1: Businesses should support and respect the protection of internationally proclaimed human rights.

Principle 2: Businesses should make sure that they are not complicit in human rights abuses.

Principle 3: Businesses should uphold the freedom of association and the effective recognition of the right to collective bargaining.

Labour standards

Principle 4: Businesses should support the elimination of all forms of forced and compulsory labour.

Principle 5: Businesses should support the effective abolition of child labour.

Principle 6: Businesses should support the elimination of discrimination in respect of employment and occupation.

The environment

Principle 7: Businesses should support a precautionary approach to environmental challenges.

Principle 8: Businesses should undertake initiatives to promote greater environmental responsibility.

Principle 9: Businesses should encourage the development and diffusion of environmentally friendly technologies.

Anti-corruption

Principle 10: Businesses should work against all forms of corruption, including extortion and bribery.

Further information about the Global Compact is available at www.unglobalcompact.org.

Novozymes' global and local approach to corporate responsibility

In Novozymes' mission and values statement, the company states that: "we imagine a future where our biological solutions create the necessary balance between better business, cleaner environment and better lives." Novozymes' commitment to the Global Compact is part of this mission and values statement, which is called 'The Novozymes Touch'. It also includes a commitment to United Nations Universal Declaration of Human Rights, the United Nations Convention on Biological Diversity and International Chamber of Commerce's Charter for Sustainable Development. Accordingly, the Global Compact guides Novozymes' efforts to further integrate corporate responsibility into the company's way of doing business.

In practice, Novozymes' continuous corporate responsibility integration constitutes a mix between a global and a local approach. On the one hand, our business units across the world have to comply with Novozymes' corporate policies, standards and strategies to ensure international consistency. On the other hand, the business units clarify and interpret Novozymes' corporate requirements by devising their own local rules, initiatives, and strategies to adapt to and appreciate local cultural traditions and to encourage targeted initiatives around particular local corporate responsibility issues and stakeholders. Since this combined approach is particularly useful when doing business in developing countries, practical examples of its application are listed below with China as reference case. These examples are by no means exhaustive.

Internal compliance measures

As part of Novozymes' quality management system, the company has introduced a social minimum standard to ensure compliance with basic human rights and core labour standards. Among other things, this minimum standard includes the right to freedom of association and collective bargaining. It also prohibits forced labour, discrimination in any aspect of employment, and the employment of children below 15 years of age. All business units' compliance with Novozymes' social minimum standard is monitored continuously, e.g. by requiring business units across the world to carry out annual self-assessments and to account for management systems in place to ensure compliance. Furthermore, compliance with Novozymes' social minimum standard will be integrated into the company's internal audit scheme as of 2006.

One of the particular challenges that Novozymes is facing in China in regard to the minimum standard is the *de-facto* prohibition against unions. Due to this particular Chinese circumstance, Novozymes China complies with the company's minimum standard by ensuring employee representation in relevant internal management bodies in China.

Local strategies

Novozymes' largest business units across the world are not only required to comply with the company's social minimum standard. They are also required to devise their own social responsibility strategies, e.g. to identify local stakeholders and prioritise focus areas within human rights and labour standards that are particularly relevant locally. Besides ensuring local relevance and ownership, such local strategies for social responsibility are also used to identify examples of best practice for internal knowledge sharing. To facilitate the development of local strategies for social responsibility, Novozymes has launched an Intranet, which constains comprehensive guidance on social responsibility and access to various tools.

Novozymes' Chinese strategy for social responsibility allows the company to identify and address particular local issues and stakeholders in China. Accordingly, Novozymes' recent Chinese social responsibility strategy particularly addresses the issue of employee health and safety, e.g. through comprehensive annual company-paid health checks and through information on HIV/AIDS protection. Charitable donations are also addressed in this strategy. They include donations to senior citizens' universities and scholarships for the universities in Tianjin, Nankai and Jiangnan.

Responsible purchasing

Novozymes launched a scheme called 'Purchasing with Decency' in 2003. This scheme was primarily introduced to increase suppliers' awareness about compliance with basic human rights and core labour standards. It takes the form of a standardised self-evaluation questionnaire, the contents of which have been derived from relevant international conventions. Suppliers across the world are required to fill in the questionnaire with an account for management systems in place to ensure compliance. Acknowledging the fact that solving issues of non-compliance simply by terminating business would be everything but responsible, Novozymes does its utmost to resolve any issues of non-compliance through dialogue and collaboration with the suppliers. However, if eventually a supplier refuses to cooperate in solving issues of non-compliance, Novozymes reserves the right to terminate business on these grounds.

While the scheme covered 35% of Novozymes' raw material suppliers for the enzymes production in 2003 (measured in raw material purchasing value), Novozymes met the target of covering 80% of raw material suppliers in 2004. In the long term, the scheme will be integrated into Novozymes' purchasing supply chain management system in line with the evaluation of suppliers' environmental performance that is already anchored in this system. Suppliers' environmental performance was also integrated into Novozymes' supplier audit scheme in 2005.

Along the lines of Novozymes' scheme for responsible purchasing, the company's purchasing department in China is responsible for asking suppliers to Novozymes' Chinese production sites to fill in the self-evaluation questionnaire. In order to facilitate this process, the questionnaire has been translated into Chinese, and Novozymes' Chinese purchasers have undergone training in its use. So far, a few of Novozymes' Chinese suppliers initially refused to fill in the questionnaire, and there have been a few initial cases of non-compliance related to disciplinary measures and working hours. On these grounds, Novozymes' Chinese purchasing department has initiated a dialogue with the suppliers in question with a view to solving the issues of non-compliance.

Business integrity

As an integrated part of Novozymes' quality management system, the company has devised a management standard on business integrity. The standard, which clarifies Novozymes' values of responsibility, accountability, openness and honesty, lists six business integrity principles. These principles cover bribes, facilitation payments, money laundering, protection money, gifts, and political and charitable contributions. Acknowledging the fact that cultural traditions vary across the world, not least in terms of giving and receiving gifts, Novozymes' business integrity principles take the form of framework principles with room for local clarification and interpretation.

In order to make the principles effective, a business integrity management system has also been put in place. Accordingly, all employees have access to guidance and to anonymously raise concerns about possible breaches of the principles. Employees are also required to report facilitation payments given and big gifts given and received. A corporate Committee on Business Integrity oversees implementation, provides principal guidance, and assesses and reviews the effectiveness of Novozymes' management standard on business integrity.

Last but not least, several awareness activities have been carried out. These activities include a booklet on business integrity to all employees and training of relevant employee groups.

In China, gifts are particularly important as a common and widely accepted token of appreciating a relationship; or 'guanxi' as the Chinese tend to call it. Consequently, Novozymes' Chinese rules for giving and receiving gifts reflect this fact without compromising the company's business integrity principles. Furthermore, a Chinese version of the booklet on business integrity ensures that also Chinese employees know what is expected of them.

Conclusion and implications

The case of Novozymes indicates that the United Nations Global Compact constitutes a most useful reference framework for corporate values, policies and management standards. Not only does the universality of the international conventions, from which the Global Compact principles are derived, enable companies to operate with international consistency without engaging in a crusade. The framework character of the principles, which provides room for local clarification and interpretation, also enables companies to adapt to and appreciate local cultural traditions across the world without being unprincipled.

Balancing such often contrasting objectives, when further integrating corporate responsibility into the way of doing business, increasingly seems a prerequisite to companies that want continuous growth in the global marketplace. Not least, this seems to be the case in major future growth markets of developing countries such as China and India, which are characterised by cultural traditions, laws, and regulations that tend to be very different from the ones of conventional markets in developed countries.

Chapter 9

MAINSTREAMING OF STANDARDS AND STANDARDS FOR THE MAINSTREAM:

EXPERIENCES OF STANDARD INITIATIVES IN PUBLIC-PRIVATE PARTNERSHIPS AND MULTI-STAKEHOLDER APPROACHES

Carsten Schmitz-Hoffmann

Senior Project Manager, Deutsche Gesellschaft für Technische Zusammenarbeit (GTZ)

Introduction

In a globalised world, business and public actors both neet guidelines and rules for their international activities. Legal frameworks are mainly limited to nations, but transnational companies act globally. This gap of legal frameworks meets the realities of global markets. Products – such as textiles or agricultural commodities – are often produced in developing countries of the South, but consumed in industrialised countries of the North. However, consumers demand a transparency how and under which conditions the products they buy have been produced. Companies understand it as a management of risks to know more about the conditions under which their suppliers produce and how actors along the supply chain perform. Which company can afford a scandal or a negative campaign of NGOs? Business actors obviously reflect that scandals may be avoided by supporting producers in providing best production practices and requiring transparency along the chain to know more about production practices and the function of the supply chain. Companies understand the establishment of good conditions in producing regions of the South as "risk-management", minimising the risk to have their business affected by scandals or negative campaigns. At the same time, legal institutions often already require identity preservation or "traceability" of products, especially produced in the agricultural sector. Obviously, companies have to meet these requirements to not lose market opportunities.

The public sector is in a different position. Development insitutions welcome efforts of private companies to invest in developing countries and often support these approaches financially and with know-how. As studies have shown, private investment is the main catalyst for development in developing countries. With the pragmatic approach of public-private cooperation, it seems to be possible to create real "win-win-win" situations: a business plus for the private partner, a realistic and effective public approach, and all for the benefit of the project partners in the South. Standards may play an important role in this type of cooperation, potentially a) establishing the environment for safe investment, b) ensuring high product quality, and c) supporting partners of the South to position themselves on the markets with high efficiency and productivity.

Market surveys show that consumers accept and support standard development processes. More and more, they demand a holistic product quality that includes the quality of a product and the quality of sound social and environmental production practises. Although a small percentage of market resources are already absorbed by niche markets of sustainability products, the huge majority of consumers worldwide is still buying mainstream products. But also this group of consumers wants to be assured that the products they buy have been produced with respect for the environment and society. And certainly without employing worst production methods, such as cutting down rainforest trees or use of bonded labour. It seems to be that their interest does not lie in sustainability as a value or a policy vision, but in their responsibility as consumers.

I will show that standard-setting processes play an important role in modern development cooperation. The instrument of public-private partnerships even provides a better ground for standard-setting. But what are the motivations for differents actors to collaborate in standard-setting approaches and what might these activities comprise in the future? As the experiences of GTZ (Deutsche Gesellschaft für Technische Zusammenarbeit) show, standards and codes of conduct establish the broadest basis for implementation in so-called multi-stakeholder cooperations, where all relevant actors are involved in the development of the guidelines. Facing the growing demand for products manufactured with respect for the environment and society, those standard-setting approaches are already addressing the "mainstream" of products. Only with economic viability on the producing side will standards be accepted as market development. For this reason, a credible, effective and productive development of standards requires collaboration between public actors and private companies. But how can development cooperation provide the basis for this positive environment for standard-setting?

Public-private partnerships in German development cooperation – general background and experiences

Public-private partnerships (PPPs) are financed through funds provided by the German Federal Ministry for Economic Cooperation and Development (BMZ). PPP projects between GTZ and private actors are jointly planned, financed and implemented. GTZ contributes staff, experience, know-how and sometimes funding to these projects. As a government-owned enterprise for international cooperation, GTZ is active in more than 120 countries around the world and provides a global network of offices in more than 60 countries. Approximately 11,000 GTZ experts offer wide-range expertise and extensive experience in several areas. Advisers on the site maintain close contact with governments, authorities, institutions and organisations in their host countries. When used appropriately within the framework of a PPP, these competencies and contacts can significantly accelerate private actors´ success. Especially in activities with a broad scope, such as standard development processes, this network is valuable and introduces broad experience, expertise and know-how to our partners.

Since 1999, GTZ has been supporting private companies´ long-term activities in developing countries through PPPs. Behind these partnerships stands the conviction that if both parties pool their resources, they can achieve their respective objectives better, faster and at lower cost. Above all, small and medium-sized enterprises (SMEs) that are active in developing and newly industrialising countries currently enjoy the benefits of the PPP programme. Whether training experts on location, entering new markets using technology and know-how, or improving the quality of locally produced goods, the programme offers a wide range of opportunities. Private sector investment creates jobs, enhances know-how and generates income for the people in the region. This is precisely the goal of German cooperation with developing countries.

Criteria for cooperation in public-private partnerships

Four criteria must be met before GTZ can contribute to a PPP project: 1) the projects must have solid economic and development policy objectives while making tangible contribution in the partner country; 2) the scope of the project must extend beyond the company's core business, as PPP contributions are not subsidies; 3) the partner companies must bear a significant proportion of the project costs, generally at least 50%; and 4) the projects must be in line with the German government's development policy guidelines.

In the first five years of the PPP programme, in cooperation with German companies and associations, GTZ launched some 300 projects in around 70 countries worldwide. PPPs are possible with virtually all kinds of companies, whether large, medium or small, and work in practically all economic sectors. More than €120 million was allocated to these projects, with a public contribution of approximately 40%.

The success of previous development partnerships with the private sector has prompted GTZ to increasingly involve private sector companies in general technical cooperation (TC) with developing countries. This will enable private sector business activities to be conducted in parallel with TC projects as part of PPP measures. Private sector companies can thus benefit directly from government arrangements with the Federal Republic of Germany and its partner countries. In addition, strategic alliances with companies and business associations are viewed as vehicles for launching long-term, broadly based measures that take into account both the companies' economic interests as well as the development policy objectives of TC.

Standard development processes are often part of such strategic alliances, expanding the PPP concept also to the further involvement of representatives of partner countries, civil society and further donor organisations or development agencies.

Development of standards in public-private cooperation

"Standards: Document that provides for common and repeated use, rules, guidelines and characteristics for products or related processes and production methods, with which compliance is not mandatory. It may also include or deal exclusively with terminology, symbols, packaging, marking or labelling requirements as they apply to a product, process or production method."[87]

Standards ensure that products have been produced under specific conditions with respect to standardised quality, social conditions or environmental requirements. They support the comparability of different products and production methods of all kinds. Thus, they help to position products being produced in underprivileged environments to compete with those that have not. International product standards and production standards have market power and are important factors of international competition. In general, two main characteristics emphasise the impact of standardised process and production methods: a) it can affect the characteristics of a product itself, so that the product may have an impact when it is consumed or used; or b) the process or production method itself has a (social or environmental) impact during the production, harvesting or extraction phase that does not have a discernible impact on the product or service.[88] Worldwide, the International Standard Organization (ISO) accepts and registers standards. Their own activities refer to standardised procedures.

Consumer interest in standardised products

However, buyers of products often require compliance with standards, although of course with different perspectives and different motivations. The compliance with standards often means a better market position for producers and the training in standards implementation means to support producers in their marketing ability.

Consumers demand the acceptance of specific conditions. Basically, they want to use their products in a standardised way. It reduces costs and efforts for business companies if, for example, their international offices can use the same sheets for printing in the USA as they do in Europe. But consumers also want to be assured that the products they buy have been produced under specific conditions with respect for the environment and society. It is a fact that scandals on quality (more)

[87] World Trade Organization, "Technical Barriers to Trade" (TBT) Agreement, Annex 1

[88] OECD GD (97) 137: Process and Production Methods (PPMs): Conceptual Framework and Considerations of Use of PPM-based Trade Measures.

and on unacceptable social and environmental production conditions (less) have negative effects on consumers and therefore on the marketability of products. As examples show, when consumers campaign against one product, they do not distinguish between brands, companies or sources. During the cocoa scandal on worst forms of child labour in West Africa, consumers reduced their consumption of chocolate no matter where the cocoa for the chocolate was coming from. These cases have even more effects on companies' products if there is a more direct link between the raw product and the end-product. The more processing and manufacturing, the less direct the link between the raw product and the end-product. Therefore, from the end-buyer's perspective, the supply chain has to be seen in a different light.

The example of coffee

An interesting example is coffee: Although the beans are roasted, they will still be the same beans in the end-product on the shelves as they were on the coffee tree. In processed products, the last step of processing is the most interesting one to consumers. This fact is obvious in the textile industry, where conditions of cotton production are less interesting to consumers than conditons in Asian textile companies, where the products are manufactured. This has an influence on the consumer's buying decision and influences companies to introduce production standards as a part of their risk management. Especially products from developing countries are in the focus of companies. In industrialised countries, legislations on working conditions, workers' safety and health as well as ecological conditions are mainly well known, monitored by public institutions, and sanctionated by non-compliance. But with globalisation bringing markets closer together, many primary products are sourced in developing countries. Although in these countries the same legislative basis is given, its application is often not monitored – and even if so, non-compliance often has no consequence. To avoid negative press on production practices in developing countries and to optimise the conditions along their supply chains, companies often require, for example, the application of core labour standards laid down by the International Labour Organization (ILO). Environmental aspects as well as the economic dimension of product chains are not covered by the ILO core labour standards, but are of equal importance to companies. Therefore, it is in their interest to refer to comprehensive production standards covering all three dimensions: the social conditions, the environment and economic aspects.

In a nutshell: The Common Code for the Coffee Community (4C)

The 4C initiative is a multi-stakeholder process to develop a sustainability system for the production, post-harvest processing and trading of "mainstream" green coffee. Building on a PPP comprising the Deutsche Kaffee-Verband (DKV) and GTZ on behalf of the BMZ, funding provided the 4C Group of the European Coffee Federation, BMZ and the Swiss SECO is currently supporting the initiative financially.

In a tripartite steering committee, three stakeholder groups are guiding the process: trade & industry, producer organisations and civil society. All activities of the initiative are reflecting this balanced structure. A neutral Management Unit, consisting of representatives of GTZ and the 4C Group of the European Coffee Federation, facilitates the process and ensures a participatory and transparent development of the initiative. The 4C sustainability concept draws on the combination of an inclusive code of conduct, reflecting minimum requirements and enabling continuous improvement, together with sustainability practices. Through excluding unacceptable practices and applying good agricultural and management practices, actors along the chain optimise their performance and make the coffee production sector more efficient and profitable. As a baseline standard, the initiative has a low entry level and supports farmers on their continuous path towards sustainability. Transparency enables the transfer of value along the product chain. A network of supporting companies and organisations focuses on capacity building and training of small producers.

The 4C is a business-to-business model that will not be used for on-pack marketing or labelling of products. It shall establish a new understanding of coffee quality: the intrinsic and sensoric quality of the product plus the quality of sustainable production and processing methods. Therefore, it is an interesting example for the development of a "mainstream" standard in a multi-stakeholder group.

More information: www.sustainable-coffee.net

Motivation to develop and implement standard initiatives

At the beginning of the organic movement, numerous guidelines to produce organic products already existed. Although nowadays there exists only one standard on organic agriculture for the entire EU, there exist further organic agriculture standards in the USA, in Japan and even in Switzerland. Producers of organic products are confused and often have to attain numerous certifications, meeting different requirements. Obviously, in organic agriculture a standardisation of standards seems to be necessary. However, also in conventional agriculture, consumers want to be assured that safe social, environmental and quality standards have been met. This demand resulted in different internal production standards being required by the different sourcing companies. Marketing efforts such as "This product has been produced with respect to our high quality production standards" are still existing, but do not build on credibility. These voluntary standards – often known as codes of conduct – do not provide a common baseline or even address the same issues. However, these internal production standards for the sourcing of companies did not provide the comparability of products as required by consumers. Therefore, critics say these codes of conduct are just marketing tools, required by the companies and used for PR to consumers without any benefit for producers or production systems. On the other hand, codes of conduct often serve as the starting point for developing a broadly accepted international standard – and their requirements are often more comprehensive than national legislations. But to achieve this, credible institutions need to be involved and considerable experience of the application of codes is necessary. Thus, in standard development processes, codes of conduct referring to multi-stakeholder discussions play an important role. At all events, the acceptance of standards often means either to expand in niches with high-value markets or to stay competitive, because a critical mass of the market uses a specific standard. Therefore, from a company's perspective, standards can imply both a negative impact on those not applying a standard or a positive impact on those not doing so.

Why are NGOs interested in the development of standards and codes?

Civil society actors demand compliance with standards at both ends of the chain (and also in between): the supplying side and the buying side. In globalisation theory, national legislations are no longer effective instruments to guide business development. With transnational and multinational companies investing, producing and buying in numerous countries all over the world, national legislations cannot provide the framework for legal business. New tools are needed. From the perspective of human rights organisations or environmental non-governmental organisations (NGOs), standards often are the only way to introduce decent social conditions and protection of the environment to business actors. By using the power of buyers, the demand to comply with specific requirements of standards is followed along the chain. The weak parts of the chain shall be empowered by complying with standards. Decent working conditions, access to health care for workers, written contracts for seasonal workers and minimum wages provide a basis to improve the situation of millions of workers worldwide. Cutting down rainforest trees, using extremely hazardous pesticides, and hunting of endangered species are worst ecological practices that can be eliminated by implementing codes of conducts and standards.

Motivation for producers to be involved in standard initiatives

At production level, better competitive conditions often build on unacceptable social or environmental conditions. Low wages for workers, no access to health care or unsustainable use of natural resources may provide better competition because of low costs of production in the short term. Codes of conduct and standards aim to exclude these practices and allow a common basis for competition based on quality: the quality of the product, but also the quality of socially and environmentally sustainable production and processing methods.

From the perspective of producers in developing countries, the compliance with specific requirements such as company codes of conduct or production standards on the one hand does imply keeping access to import markets. Especially in some buyer-driven markets, it seems to be a must to meet specific standards if one leading standard has been chosen by the majority of market actors (or by some market leaders in an oligopolic market). On the other hand, producers can position themselves on markets by complying with standards, which is often a process of product differentiation. They may be an add-on in some markets. In commodity sectors, organic production results in price premiums. Suppliers selling products by meeting the requirements of the "Fair Trade" standards receive fixed prices (in periods of low world-market prices) or at least fixed premiums (in periods of high world-market prices). Even by using mainstream standards, such as the Utz Kapeh coffee standard, price premiums are recommended. But basically, codes of conduct and standards support producers in standardising their performance. They do not only demand compliance with specific requirements, but also provide best practices and tools to optimise business performance. By using best management and production practices, production systems minimise costs, make their production systems more efficient and work more profitably. As long and medium-term approaches, codes of conducts and standards are tools to improve production conditions. They also allow the measurement and assessment of performance. For high-quality products, they provide a comparable marketing tool to consumer markets by using neutral measurements.

To conclude, codes of conduct and standards are tools in a globalised world to standardise mechanisms on production levels or even in whole product chains. They empower consumers, in the sense of enabling them to refer to comparable products and to keep themselves informed about specific conditions under which products have been produced. By reducing the buyer's risk of buying products that have been produced under unacceptable social or environmental conditions, crisis is avoided in whole sectors. Compliance with codes of conduct provides marketing aspects and makes markets work more efficiently and profitably for producers, not to mention more transparent. Products are traceable along the chain and therefore the performance of all actors along the chain is transparent. Obviously, there is a risk of non-credible standard development. With involvement of all relevant actors in the standard development in multi-stakeholder processes, this lack of credibility can be preserved. From a trade prespective, standards in mainstream markets may also be seen as market barriers. Although most of the codes of conduct and standards have been developed in private or public-private activities, the World Trade Organization (WTO) is working on this issue. Although a decision has not been taken so far, the reference document that is serving as the basis for this discussion is the WTO's Technical Barriers to Trade Agreement, Annex 3 "Code of good practice for the preparation adoption and application of standards".

German development cooperation and standard initiatives

GTZ as a development agency has no direct interest in a particular sector. Its objectives are to meet the development goals of the German government, to reduce poverty, to protect the environment and to cooperate with interested actors to build coalitions for sustainable development. With this neutral role, GTZ can provide the ground for standard-setting processes. In the PPP programme, the development of standards has always been an important topic. As shown above, standards can create "win-win-win-situations". It is not only that GTZ can play the role of a neutral broker without direct stakes in a sector, it also provides the network a) on an international level to all relevant donor organisations, governments and international institutions, and b) to its decentralised structure, where experience is given in numerous projects and standard requirements can be tested under realistic conditions. With the PPP programme of the German government, a valuable tool to bring together interested stakeholders and facilitate their process to develop a standard has supported the scope of GTZ´s activities in standard-setting approaches.

Broad cooperation as basis for broad impact

"Standard-setting organisations shall ensure that participation reflects a balance of interests among interested parties in the subject matter and in the geographic scope to which the standard applies. Participants in the standard-setting process should have expertise relevant to the subject matter of the standard or be materially affected by the standard. (...) Parties that will be directly affected by the implementation of a standard are the most important stakeholders in a standard-setting process. As such, it is important that the standard-setting organisation takes a proactive role in supporting these stakeholders to participate."[89]

Motivations for parties involved in standard-setting processes may be different or even conflictive. However, it is important that all relevant stakeholders are active and have been consulted in standard-developing procedures - i.e "multi-stakeholder approaches" must be adopted. In the future, it may also be required by legal institutions. During the last months, a discussion in the WTO took place to define standards that have been developed without broad stakeholder involvement as trade barriers. But it is not only this legal perspective that makes multi-stakeholder approaches valuable.

---

[89] ISEAL Alliance: "Guidance on ISEAL Code of Good Practice for Setting Social and Environmental Standards".

Dynamics of the sector being subject to the standard and different perspectives need to be reflected by the stakeholders involved. Only with a balanced view will the standard gain credibility. Especially in mainstream approaches, the requirements need to be realistic, applicable and marketable. Otherwise, the standard will be limited to niches and its impact will only refer to a small group of applicants. These niche approaches are undoubtedly important and valuable, but their effects do not stimulate broad development impacts. However, different stakeholders also introduce different perspectives, different experience and different know-how. Retailers, manufacturers, traders, importers, exporters, processors and producers can contribute with different expertise. To formulate realistic and applicable product and production standards, an initiative has to build on this expertise. As a matter of fact, the optimisation of supply chains can only draw on these different perspectives to stimulate a positive benefit for all actors involved. However, if those actors see no prospect of economic benefit for themselves along the chain, they will ignore the approach.

The role of civil society

Not only actors along the chain – business actors – are important as stakeholds in standard-setting initiatives, but also civil society groups, such as social and environmental NGOs or trade unions, play a valuable role. It is not only their remarkable expertise and know-how in specific sectors, but also their function as pressure groups or "watchdogs". Often, they are the ones pointing at worst practices and demanding better conditions in public announcements, campaigns and discussions. With their specific interest, they perfectly fit into the gap between the production chain and consumers. Within the worldwide net of NGOs and unions, they may be the leverage to disseminate a concept or to adjust its content. Especially with decentralised structures, the function of civil society as catalyst to a concept should not be underestimated. Workers and small-scale producers trust their activities. Therefore, skills development and training activities, to roll out a concept, may also be linked to those civil society structures. Additionally, other important actors without direct stakes in the sector of a standard may play an important role as sponsors, implementing agencies or supporters on different levels. Development banks, UN institutions or development agencies may be involved in multi-stakeholder collaborations as well.

Involvement of different stakeholders

In its standard-setting activities, GTZ has extensive experience of multi-stakeholder approaches. The most valuable experience was made with a tripartite involvement of stakeholder representatives in the coffee sector: coffee trade and industry, producer organisations and civil society were active in the development of a code of conduct for social, environmental and economic sustainability along the "mainstream" coffee chain. This "Common Code for the Coffee Community" (4C - see box above) is also supported by a group of extraordinary members, including the World Bank, the International Coffee Organization and the International Institute for Sustainable Development. As this case shows, consensus building is possible even with such different actors involved. Although this process was funded by the international coffee industry together with GTZ in a PPP, also producers and civil society developed an "ownership" of this approach, gaining also high credibility for this balanced initiative. The 4C initiative builds on a comprehensive undersanding of sustainability, addressing all three dimensions in a balanced manner. To still develop an applicable and realistic code of conduct with positive impact for all actors along the chain was mainly possible because of the challenging, yet positive, discussions between the different stakeholders. One could even say the exchange of arguments stimulated the whole process.

Neutral broker to facilitate, organise and support the process

However, GTZ's experience emphasises that for multi-stakeholder cooperation to take place, a neutral platform – to speak with ISEAL, the "standard-setting organisation" – needs to be facilitated, supported and organised. In the coffee case, a project secretariat, consisting of two representatives of both partners each was provided by GTZ and the private partner (Deutscher Kaffee-Verband e.V.). Members of this project secretariat put together the different strings of the very complex, sometimes even fragmented, standard-developing process. Funding is necessary not only to provide a unit to facilitate and administer the process, but also to provide input to the development process, to cover travel costs of producers and civil society representatives, to organise meetings, to contract external experts (e.g. for studies) and to produce information material. In the ideal situation, this builds on public-private funding on an "eye to eye basis." A PPP to create the basis for a standard-setting initiative underlines the credibility of the process and emphasises the responsibility of both the public and the private sector. With GTZ as a neutral body of the project secretariat, it was possible to involve further governments as donors of the initiative and also to link the 4C-related activities with other tools or approaches of other sectors as well as in the coffee sector itself, such as a study on how risk management tools can relate to the implementation of sustainability practices. In further standard-setting activities of GTZ, e.g. in the textile industry together with the Aussenhandelsvereinigung des deutschen Einzelhandels (AVE), it was a success factor to cooperate with a pre-competitive association. With standard-setting processes being a pre-competitive issue, it was positive that also the private partner – with an association – provided a pre-competitive platform.

Companies may also identify further pilot projects – probably together with partners of the multi-stakeholder cooperation – as part of their sustainability policy. These pilots refer also to their competitive interest, because they may support specific suppliers or regions of great interest to the company.

Experiences of GTZ in standard initiatives – comprehensive understanding of sutstainability with highest positive impact

Since the 1970s, GTZ has elaborated numerous different codes of conduct and standards in agricultural sectors, the textile sector and indutrial sectors. The impact is not often easy to measure or assess. But one fact is clear: with all players demanding compliance with a standard, the standard becomes a factor for competition; a must in the market and a benefit for the conditions in the sector. Product chains work more transparently and efficiently. But the more complex a sector becomes, the more limited the effects of standards. GTZ´s experience is that broader effects in a sector can be achieved by introducing comprehensive production and product standards, covering all three dimensions of sustainability. In highly competitive markets, sound social and environmental conditions will only be accepted if they provide a decent economic basis for actors along the chain. With a balance of social, ecological and economic conditions in comprehensive production and product standards, standards may be implemented on a broad basis in a whole sector. With the establishment of the Programme Office for Social and Envoronmental

Standards in 2002, GTZ brought together different perspectives of standard-setting processes. The social perspective of the textile industry, the experience of forest certification, and the knowledge of standard-setting processes with organic agriculture together stimulated synergies and the development of comprehensive standards. But although production and product standards elaborated in development cooperation efforts are gaining significant market share, they still often seem to be limited to niches. High costs of compliance with the requirements, expensive certification schemes, and the exclusive character of many systems hinder the broad implementation of standards. But with the PPP programme and successful cooperation with multinational companies, the interest of major players in sectors has grown to adapt production standards and to request the application of production standards or codes of conducts by their suppliers. With greater economic knowledge than actors of the development cooperation sector, private partners further requested the economic benefits of codes of conduct and standards. This is not a question of competition with niche markets; consumers demand compliance with minimum standards, but are not willing to pay the (often significantly) higher prices of certified products that meet the high standards. At the same time, niche market approaches cannot be transferred to mainstream production. The current quantity of some fruits or vegetables would not be available if organic agriculture were used comprehensively. Basically, two main arguments have been formulated in respect to this fact: a significant positive impact of standard-setting requires either a "mainstreaming" of the process in technical cooperation or the involvement of a critical mass to stimulate broad market effects – standards for the "mainstream".

Mainstreaming of standard initiatives or standards for the mainstream?

In a challenging discussion with companies and policy actors, GTZ has broadened its field of engagement. Building on the involvement of different stakeholders, transparent and participatory standard-setting processes have been developed, facilitated and guided. To stimulate broad effects on production sectors worldwide, the interest to develop standards for the mass market, the so-called "mainstream", has grown and finally successfully ended in collaborations with market leaders such as Nestlé, Kraft Foods or the Otto Group. Obviously, those standards do not imply the same depth of change, but they have the ability to improve the production process on a broad level. To reduce the poverty of 80% of actors in a sector has another quality than improving the living conditions of 5% of actors in a sector by 80%. But it also has other quantity effects: Based on its experience in the textile sector, in the fruit and vegetable sector, and most recently in the coffee sector, three main theses must be emphasised:

1. Without the experience of standard-setting processes for niche markets, a "mainstream" standard cannot be developed successfully. The knowledge, the practical application experience and the intellectual basis of niche standards is the basis for "mainstream" standards to build on. There should be no competition between niche and "mainstream" standards. The standard-setting organisation has to acknowledge this fact and develop certain rules concerning communication and marketing. It is important to emphasise that these "mainstream" standards are rather seen as the basis for competition and therefore the basis also for niche standards to build on.

2. "Mainstream" standards are basically still drawn on a crisis situation. Whereas niche standards meet the demand of a limited group of consumers, specific conditions in "mainstream" sectors stimulate the interest of business actors to set a standard. Often, these conditions refer to critical reporting of the press or NGOs.

3. "Mainstream" processes, whilst not only addressing the critical mass to stimulate broad market effects, also have to involve a critical mass. Only by respecting the viewpoint of different major actors in the sector is a common understanding of changes for the benefit of the sector realistic. Multi-stakeholder processes provide this basis. With a credible mixture of stakeholders and the experience of all actors along the chain, significant market effects may be achieved.

In parallel, GTZ is working on a "mainstreaming" of standard-setting in development cooperation. On behalf of the German Ministry for Economic Cooperation and Development, GTZ conducts numerous projects and programmes of interest for implementation of standards. Since the PPP programme's establishment, many collaborations with companies have been building the basis for developing standards relating to codes of conduct. The next step of this development is to transfer the development and implementation of standards into the reality of bilateral technical cooperation. Initially building on a pioneer character, standards are now broadly accepted and welcomed also by partner countries of the German technical cooperation. Therefore, a "mainstreaming" of standards implementation into the "daily business" of technical cooperation is a major topic. Only with "mainstreamed" standards is linkage to existing activities that have been negotiated between governments feasible. Standard implementation can easily be attached to projects already running. Often being combined with the activity of private business partners, standards implementation may support efforts to integrate PPP into regular technical cooperation. Synergies and dynamics of public-private cooperation – or even the collaboration of a multi-stakeholder initiative – have positive impact on technical cooperation. Especially actors in the German partner countries are often interested in implementing standards to meet the requirements of market demand and position themselves in highly competitive markets.

In the common understanding of a standard, protection of the environment, poverty reduction and optimisation of supply chains can jointly be implemented in existing programmes and projects. With stakeholders' interest, standard-setting initiatives also bring together different actors to invest in a better future for the benefit of a whole sector. Many stakeholders who are involved in the standard-setting do not have any implementation experience. Public development cooperation provides the ground to implement those standards, because they a) have the experience on "grassroot level", b) have access to public systems in the partner countries and c) refer to the network of national and international institutions. With multi-stakeholder initiatives being the most promising approach to developing and setting a standard, public-private cooperation provides a solid ground for implementation of standards. This enables linkage between the situation in the country of production and the global market.

Conclusion

Standards play an important role in the future of development cooperation. Specifically, private partners are interested in introducing product and production standards in business activities. This stimulates public-private cooperation in PPPs. Multi-stakeholder approaches are challenging, yet they represent the most credible and balanced way to develop standards. From a development perspective, the question should not be: standards for the "mainstream" or "mainstreaming" of standards, because both aspects are important for modern development cooperation – especially in PPPs. Although standards for "mainstream" production have the broadest effects, niche approaches are important and provide the basis for broader standards. They may also stimulate and create the interest of the "mainstream" industry in developing standards. With specialised standard-setting initiatives and their associated high requirements, the "big business" will become sensitive to standards in production chains. Consumers are obviously willing to pay significant amounts of money for differentiated products, but they in fact demand compliance with basic standards. On the other hand, "mainstream" standards will have broad effects if they allow for a significant benefit to producers and workers. A "mainstreaming" of standards in technical cooperation shall be the basis for further activities concerning standard-setting approaches. The existing range of options for collaboration in development cooperation – e.g. PPP, programme-based approaches and regular technical or financial cooperation – provides an ideal basis for standard-setting. Therefore, all options may be used to anchor standards as important tools to support the positive development of a whole sector. Especially in international supply chains, standards even provide the environment to meet legal requirements. They are guidelines for international trade. With trade being one major focus of cooperation between industrialised and developing countries, these standards shall further be an important element of development cooperation in the future.

CHAPTER 10

CORPORATE CITIZENSHIP, LABOUR RIGHTS AND THE DEMOCRATIC DEFICIT

Jesper Nielsen

Working Environment and Advocacy Adviser,
The United Federation of Danish Workers (3F)

Abstract

Corporations are not democratically accountable and it may be wrong to encourage them to make their own rules. They should rather comply with common rules, such basic labour rights, developed by democratic processes. The article identifies different positions of the union movement concerning corporate citizenship, especially between North and South. Two cases, in the banana and clothing industry, are explored to compare advanced CSR ambition and reporting with practices in the South (Central America). Severe contradictions between statements and practice are found. Union participation and international cooperation between unions and NGOs has produced improved compliance with workers rights. Bilateral international agreements between transnational corporations (TNCs) and international union federations are seen as stronger tools than unilateral voluntary initiatives: But there is still a long way to go. Transparency, organised worker participation, union access to production premises and participation in standards development and monitoring, and inclusion of the whole supply chain, especially subcontractors, are among the crucial points. It is recommended to develop stronger instruments to control standard compliance and full respect for workers' rights.

Introduction

While corporate citizenship is being mainstreamed, there is a growing concern that transnational corporations (TNCs) maybe cannot assume the role of social development promotion assigned to them. This was clearly expressed by the UK magazine, The Economist, which devoted a January 2005 mid-section to a review of corporate social responsibility (CSR) review. The main conclusion was that selfish profit interest is what drives economic and social development, and that it is unnecessary to add other, social or environmental purposes. It concludes that "the business of business is business. No apology required." (The Economist, 2005)

A broad range of critical viewpoints are also expressed by other sectors. CSR is seen as a "greenwash" of corporate behaviour; a strategy to undermine collective bargaining or nicknamed "corporate self-regulation". Some NGOs argue that TNCs represent enormous concentrations of power and their efforts to maximise profit regularly lead to an abuse of people and resources that no corporate self-control can prevent. Stronger governments and civil societies capable of inducing internationally binding regulations are required, they believe.[90]

Another critical viewpoint comes from developing country producers, who are forced to comply with several private voluntary standards if they wish to export their products. Without an internationally recognised, independent control system, neither they nor the consumers will benefit from such voluntary standards, they complain.

Though from very different perspectives, there is to some extent a common denominator in what the sceptics say: corporations are not democratically accountable, and should not be encouraged to make their own rules or social policy. They should rather comply with common rules developed by broader, democratic processes. Politicians and governments are needed to take the political responsibility and establish international rules. They may need the help of a stronger,

---

[90] A Greenpeace statement before the Johannesburg World Summit on Sustainable Development in 2002 argues that "resistance from governments and industry to legally binding rules on corporate accountability at the international level as well as at the national level only increases the public's perception of increasing corporate control of governments and creates suspicion regarding the real intentions of any corporate social and environmental programme". (Greenpeace, 2002)

better coordinated global civil society to be able to do so. The international trade union movement is an important stakeholder, representing workers´ interests in all parts of the globalised economy. But it has still not developed one common international strategy or position. Unions from the South are often confronted with a reality that differs quite considerably from the words of glossy CSR reports and official company policy. They seem generally to be more sceptical than unions from the North.

This article will look at some factors behind these different attitudes. First, it takes up the discussion of voluntary standards vs. internationally binding regulation, the criticism of outsourcing, transfer of risk and abuse of "sweatshop" factories in third world countries, and how workers in developing countries see the voluntary initiatives. Secondly, it looks at two cases from the supposedly high end of the scale of CSR: the banana giant Chiquita and the clothing producer Gildan, comparing the image they try to create regarding their practice in Latin America. Finally, the cases are discussed in a broader context, and some recommendations are given, aimed at stakeholders such as unions, donors and others.

The concepts of social responsibility, social accountability and corporate citizenship are used without further definition here. Being ideological rather than scientific concepts, the difference between them can be hard to define. For my part, I see corporate citizenship as the broader concept and as more politically problematic, because it implicitly assigns "citizens´ rights" to companies.

The reader should also know that my data on company practices have been collected mainly based on my work with local union capacity building concerning health, safety, environment and labour rights in Central America and the Caribbean region during the last six years.[91]

The UN and governments go voluntary

The only international organisations capable of adopting legally binding rules are the United Nations (UN) and World Trade Organization (WTO). But the UN seems to have stepped back from its regulatory role in later years. At the World Economic Forum in 1999, UN Secretary-General Kofi Annan challenged business leaders to join

---

[91] As union adviser in a programme run by the United Federation of Danish Workers (3F) and funded by the civil sector programme of the Danish governmental development aid agency, Danida.

an international initiative called "the Global Compact", which held its first Leaders Summit in June 2004. The Global Compact represents a strategic shift towards promoting voluntary international standards and evolves around ten basic principles of good business practice. It does not enforce or monitor the behaviour of companies, but relies on public accountability and self-interest to pursue the ten principles. (Global Compact, 2005). The tripartite ILO system seems to live in the shadow of this overall tendency.

Likewise, many governments promote deregulation and voluntary standards. With the current liberalisation of trade, a growing competition between governments to attract foreign investment is inevitable, especially in developing countries. By merely appealing to the goodwill of investors, they spur the so-called "race to the bottom", because low wages, highly flexible and weak regulation, as well as tax exemptions are main competitive factors. The WTO addresses tax and tariffs as part of trade, but generally not social, labour and environmental aspects. Thus, it seems obvious that international regulation is required to control social dumping.

TNCs, on the other hand, increase their influence over local communities. Comparing corporate turnover to national GNP, more than half of the world's top 100 economies are corporations. Big TNC investors in developing countries sometimes dominate export figures, food supply or local employment to a degree that makes their bargaining position extremely strong. Local managers may develop harmonious relations with the community and their workers, but are removed if they fail to deliver. Annual revenues determine their fate, not long-term environmental and social protection. The "triple bottom line" is a nice concept, but little doubt is left about the hierarchy between the three (Karliner, 2002).

Increasingly, powerful retailers and supermarket chains of the rich countries are also developing standards. *EurepGAP* is such a European initiative without union or NGO participation. It includes occupational health, safety, welfare and social responsibility issues, but not workers' rights in general (Eurepgap, 2003). Suppliers must comply to secure their contracts. Although weak in content, workers' representatives report a high monitoring activity.

Also, a general international social responsibility standard is under development in the International Standardization Organization (ISO) to supplement the management standards on quality (ISO9000 series) and environment (ISO14000 series).

Vulnerability, voluntary standards and framework agreements

Generally, transfer of cost-heavy parts of production to cheaper countries, outsourcing and branding are parallel processes. Branding implies trying to sell life-style, social group identity, quality and ethical consciousness together with the product. TNCs need to link positive values to the brand, which leaves them more vulnerable to criticism of unethical methods (Riisgaard, 2004).

A number of NGOs have had a certain impact on corporate behaviour through campaigns addressing reputation and influencing consumers' choice. TNCs try to protect their image against possible campaigns and maintain their reputation among shareholders and consumers precisely through the voluntary initiatives.

Another side of this coin is the permanent demand of cost and risk reduction that causes corporations to try and reduce liability and social responsibility. Outsourcing and subcontracting reduce social responsibility to an ever-shrinking part of the workforce and makes an evaluation of relationships with suppliers, contractors and subcontractors even more relevant as part of CSR.

Recently, international framework agreements between TNCs and international union entities have been a growing phenomenon. It is a logical response to the emerging internationalisation of labour markets, but experience is mixed. Compliance appears to be a problem. International enforcement mechanisms and sanctions do not exist, and part of the motivation of TNCs to sign such agreements is to keep unions from participating in campaigns against their behaviour. Developing country workers are not well informed about the content of these agreements and it seems to require a strong local union organisation to take advantage of such agreements (Riisgaard, 2003).

But unions are weak in most developing countries. Procedures and involvement at other levels may be necessary to guarantee the right to organise and to protect workers against prosecution. Bilateral framework agreements are obviously stronger tools than self-chosen voluntary standards, but in the absence of enforcement, they still have little impact.

Outsourcing, transfer of risk and double standards

The relocation of production from the industrialised to developing countries, opens the possibility of maintaining double standards and eventually losing the higher standards. Public criticism of double standards in the first place motivated corporate certification of standards compliance. Trade unions in the North actively contributed to this criticism.

TNCs often introduce higher social and environmental standards and better, possibly cleaner technology in developing countries. But there may also be negative effects:

1. The social level in the country of origin is challenged when jobs, income, useful qualifications and experience etc. among workers are lost. High levels of social dialogue, union organisation, democratic rights and workers' influence may also be lost.
2. Hazards are transferred from a community with higher educational level, accumulated knowledge and experience with the particular risk to a context with lower education, general industrial experience and lack of knowledge of the specific risk.
3. Transfer of technology from countries and areas with much higher social protection to areas with low social protection indicates more a fear of losing the job as "whistle-blower", who reacts to risks and danger signals (Nielsen, 1996; Teknologirådet, 1999).

Curbing the development of new, cleaner technology may be another negative effect of relocating production processes to low-cost countries. When the bulk-sewing processes moved to low-wage countries, a much-needed process of technological innovation was curbed. Repetitive strain injuries (RSIs), cotton dust and chemical hazards were among the targeted risks of pilot technological innovation projects that emerged in Japan, Canada and Europe (Hague, 2001; Messing, 1999). Studies, however, suggest, that it is the combination of transfer to developing countries and outsourcing, subcontracting etc. that is the real problem.

The weaker regulation and enforcement, lack of knowledge and experience, more generalised corruption etc imply both a possibility and a temptation for TNCs to allow and practise lower standards in developing countries. It is highly relevant to discuss possible ways to control this behaviour.

How do workers in developing countries see CSR?

Seen from the workers' perspective, CSR is a management initiative. Often the following happens: Before the visits of CSR auditing staff, soap, toilet paper and towels suddenly appear in the bathrooms. Workers say that these items disappear after the audit. They may receive new respiratory masks, gloves, and uniforms and are certainly instructed to wear them. The place is cleaned up and fixed. More permanent changes may include reconstruction of bathrooms, installation of washing machines, widening of buffer zones, a canteen etc.

Auditors interview workers individually. For lack of protection against reprisals, few criticise what goes on at the workplace when auditors are not there. Workers are easily fired for saying or doing something that may harm the likelihood of obtaining a certificate.

To the local workers, the power of TNCs over their working and living conditions may not be so easy to distinguish from that of earlier political dictators or semi-feudal landlords. TNCs create jobs and expectations of development, but dreams may suddenly be torn apart by decisions to lay off workers, outsource or move production. Subservient governments may allow companies to eliminate any internal workers organisation opposing such decisions.

CSR in the fresh fruit and clothing industries

In the following, we will look into recent, publicly criticised, practices of two TNCs from the high end of CSR: Chiquita in the fruit sector, and Gildan in the clothing sector. Although very different, there are similarities between the two cases: both are quality brand names, both own production units, and both have won prizes for social and environmental responsibility reporting. The cases are meant to indicate whether the introduction of CSR leads to social improvement or bad practices can be covered behind a smokescreen of CSR reporting, auditing and certification.

The Chiquita case

One of the most advanced examples of social responsibility reporting is that of the multinational banana company, Chiquita. In the 1990s, it started an unusual cooperation with the US-based NGO, Rainforest Alliance, to get its plantations certified according to the sustainability programme, Better Bananas.

Chiquita's strategy was to conquer a large part of the difficult but lucrative European market. One of the difficulties was that, contrary to the USA, the EU had a growing import of fair trade bananas competing with multinational ones. An NGO and union-led campaign against Chiquita in 1998 convinced the corporate executives that a more offensive strategy was needed.

Chiquita is known notoriously as the banana company with most unionised employees in Latin America. In 2001, it signed a regional framework agreement with the Latin American Coordination of Banana Workers Unions (COLSIBA) and the International Union of Food and Agricultural workers (IUF), which placed it among the top 30 multinationals from a union point of view. It was the first agreement with union organisations from the South and contains an adherence to the ILO conventions on freedom of association and right to collective bargaining. One of the crucial points is that independent Chiquita suppliers should comply with the same standards and that the company must inform the unions about business decisions that may seriously affect employment. Others are the establishment of an evaluation and mediation committee, and that unions should abstain from campaigning internationally against the company while the dispute-resolving methods of the agreement are not exhausted.

Chiquita is a member of the Social Accountability International (SAI, North American) and Ethical Trade Initiative (ETI, European), which both include labour rights in their standards. Among the banana TNCs, Chiquita has clearly chosen the most daring CSR strategy and stands out with a clearer adherence to environmental protection and workers' rights. In 2003, Chiquita Brands earned the first-ever CERES-ACCA[92] award for Outstanding Sustainability Reporting for its 2001 CSR report. In January 2005, Chiquita's PR officer in Europe, George Jaksch, announced that all of Chiquitas plantations had received certification for complying with the SA8000 standard.

The more problematic sides of the company's practice in Latin American countries are presented below. Apart from harassment and threats against unionists, which may be difficult to prove but are frequently reported by workers, the problems fall into three main areas:

---

[92] The Coalition of Environmentally Responsible Economies and the Association of Chartered Certified Accountants

1. A falling proportion of the Chiquita bananas come from unionised plantations with collective bargaining agreements.
2. Reduction of social levels of the collective bargaining agreements achieved through a tough bargaining line.
3. Problems in compliance with the health, safety and environment criteria.

A decreasing proportion of workers are organized and protected by collective bargaining agreements: This is achieved by outsourcing production to independent supplier plantations, by selling or closing a number of its plantations and through staff reductions. It is a general tendency that may be driven by the desire to get rid of unions or simply by general cost-reduction policies. The expansion of the banana export production during the latest ten years has mainly been located on the Pacific coast of Ecuador and Guatemala - areas where unions are practically extinct. Ecuador is the world's biggest banana exporter, while Guatemala grew to be the biggest supplier of bananas to the USA in 2004. An admirable effort to revive unionism is going on in Ecuador, but the level of union organisation still does not exceed 1% in the banana sector.

Chiquita sold all of its plantations in Colombia to the national company BANACOL in 2004. They were unionised and covered by a comprehensive system of collective bargaining agreements. The national union that organizes the banana workers, SINTRAINAGRO, and the international organisations behind the agreement with Chiquita, COLSIBA and IUF expressed serious concern that Chiquita did not comply with its obligations to inform the unions in due time according to the agreement. Workers are also concerned about selling the bananas to Chiquita in the future.

One of two Panamanian banana plantation conglomerates at Puerto Armuelles (five plantations covering 6,000 hectares) was sold to its 3,000 workers in July 2003. At the other, in Bocas del Toro, the company tried to reach a similar agreement according to the union but without success. Heavy rains and floods in January 2005 made the future uncertain for Chiquita workers in Panama and Costa Rica, and the workforce at Chiquita-owned plantations was reduced in both countries.

At Chiquita's Maya division (Honduras and Guatemala), the decline accelerated after Hurricane Mitch in 1998. In Guatemala, five unionised plantations were closed on the Atlantic coast in 2002-03 and four unions were lost. In Honduras, the number of organised workers fell from above 5,000 before Mitch to below 2,000 at the beginning of 2005 in the Tela Railroad Company, Chiquita's subsidiary. Meanwhile, the quantity of Chiquita bananas bought from independent and non-union plantations in Ecuador, Honduras and Guatemala has increased dramatically. Some 15,000 hectares of banana plantations that supply Chiquita bananas have been identified by observers on the Guatemalan south coast. While the unionised plantations produce some five million boxes, approximately 23 million boxes are produced at non-union farms on the south coast.

The policy of reducing Latin American farm ownership is clearly expressed in the annual report 2004: "Today, 33 percent of our bananas come from Chiquita-owned farms in Latin America, which is down from about 49 percent in 2001. Buying more bananas from independent growers increases our sourcing flexibility and reduces certain agricultural and weather risks."

This would not be a problem if the independent Chiquita suppliers met the demands of the Chiquita-COLSIBA-IUF framework agreement. But generally there has been little progress regarding compliance. Initially, a number of farms in Colombia became organised, and a total of two unions have been established at independent Chiquita supplier farms in Honduras. But little has happened in Costa Rica, Ecuador and Guatemala. Ongoing union negotiations with the Ecuadorian Chiquita supplier, Reybanpac (47 farms, approximately 10,000 workers), has not resulted in any new unions or agreements. Dismissals of unionised workers occur frequently, plantation workforce is divided into tiny companies (so-called tercerizadores), to exclude the possibility of forming a legal union, and private armed forces have been used against workers striking legally. This did not happen at a Chiquita supplier plantation, but has scared many workers from exerting their right to organise.

Guatemala seems to be even worse regarding violent methods. Workers at the south coast plantations are often told when hired that organising a union means losing their job and in some cases losing their life or the life of a family member. A high number of former Civil Self-defence patrols from the civil war are still armed, and the widespread criminal drug-trafficking also forms part of the violent environment. Some workers disappear and sometimes murder is disguised as a traffic accident.

Unions pressured to accept declining living and working conditions: As long as a deterioration of living conditions is achieved respecting the rules of collective bargaining, one may argue that this does not run counter to any rules of the game. It must be recognised that Chiquita negotiates, while other TNCs prefer more dictatorial methods. Nevertheless, what Chiquita does contradicts the impression they try to give through their CSR reports etc. To proclaim all of their plantations SA8000-certified while they reduce both the percentage of bananas harvested at their own plantations and the social conditions of the workers at these plantations comes close to misleading PR.

The Chiquita banana workers union in Panama that agreed to buy the plantations on a cooperative basis was forced to cut workers' social benefits. The other union was caught by surprise when Chiquita insisted on reducing social benefits in the latest collective bargaining agreement. The union thought that it was protected against deterioration of the agreement by law. However, after more than a year of negotiations under threats of plantation closures, it felt it had no alternative but to sign an unsatisfactory agreement. The process was similar in Costa Rica, Guatemala and Honduras. But while the Guatemalan banana workers were threatened in a very direct way, and five plantations actually closed, the Honduran union managed to get through the drawn-out negotiations without major losses of social benefits.

Insufficient management of the environment and working environment, and misleading information to workers: The latest available Chiquita social responsibility report at the moment of writing (Chiquita, 2002) mentions that workers' health and safety and the environment are areas of concern. Contrary to what is stipulated in the Better Bananas certification system, the use of pesticides increased because of the resistance of pests. Chiquita has promoted bipartite safety committees at the plantations and worked on an internal health and safety system, but unions have criticised that they were not involved during the elaboration of the management system. The introduction of a new occupational hazard at plantations in Honduras and Guatemala - the pesticide-impregnated plastic bag - illustrates some weaknesses of the certification systems.

The bags are treated with *chlorpyrifos,* which was banned for use in private homes in the USA in 2002 and is among the 12 chemicals that cause the highest number of intoxications and deaths in Central America, and thus targeted for stronger regulation (PLAGSALUD, 2001). It is a nerve poison and damaging to the environment.

Chiquita introduced these bags at their own plantations in Guatemala and Honduras in spite of worker protests. Inaccurate information and threats to close plantations were the means used to overcome the resistance. The Honduran Minister of Labour mediated in the conflict and formed an inter-institutional committee of government experts to decide if evidence supported the workers' complaints. Unsurprisingly, their conclusion favoured the company. The experts evaluated the risk exclusively based on WHO's LD50 value[93], which expresses the risk of dying from acute intoxication, but they ignored risk of any other harm to human health (Comisión interinstitucional, 2002).

Later, a study was made by the Swedish-financed regional SALTRA programme, with support from the United Federation of Danish Workers (3F). Highly qualified institutions from Costa Rica and Nicaragua did this first ever epidemiological study of *chlorpyrifos* in a tropical climate (Wesseling, 2004). Workers at ten Chiquita plantations in Honduras who worked with the bag were found to be exposed to *chlorpyrifos*, in spite of the use of personal protective equipment. Excess of symptoms corresponded with objective findings. The workers were found to be in a state of mild intoxication with a risk of permanent health damage. It was recommended to stop using the impregnated bag.

The results were presented to the company and the workers in October 2004, but management did not recognise its validity. Workers then threatened to stop working with the bag. The union and researchers informed the Honduran Minister of Labour and the aforementioned experts committee about the results. The company decided to abandon using the bag at the beginning of February 2005.

A main problem in this case is that four different systems of health and safety protection ignored scientific evidence, workers' concerns, obvious symptoms and open protest actions, and also underestimated the hazards of *chlorpyrifos*: 1) Chiquita's own OHS system, 2) the Better Bananas certification, 3) the SA8000 certification, and 4) the legal protection of workers' health and safety. Moreover, this shows the problematic side of certifications that do not include worker participation in the protection of their own health, safety and environment.

---

[93] LD50 = lethal dose for 50% of the population in animal experiments

Conclusive remarks to the Chiquita case

For Latin America taken as a whole, a growing part of Chiquita bananas are produced under conditions that do not meet the core ILO conventions or the certification programmes of Chiquita. A growing amount comes from the Guatemalan Pacific coast, where opposition to big landowners and union activity can be fatal. Chiquita has outsourced production and sold off farms, especially where the workers had achieved the best social conditions through collective bargaining. Although the regional agreement stipulates a Chiquita responsibility for suppliers' compliance with the standards, evidence from Ecuador, Costa Rica and Guatemala shows that this is far from the reality.

The company still negotiates with workers' unions unlike most banana companies. This may contribute to maintaining the social standards where unions are strong, as the latest bargaining results in Honduras show. Nevertheless, some workers have been forced to accept wage or social benefit reductions under threats of plantation closures, while farms have been certified for meeting SA8000 standards. Pesticide consumption has increased, including the most toxic pesticides, although reduction is part of the voluntary standards. Chiquita claimed to have a high level of workers' health and safety protection, but tried to force workers to work with a highly hazardous pesticide.

A contradiction between declared principles and practice in Latin America, especially concerning enforcement of standards at suppliers' farms, is found. Some local union leaders call the certificates manipulation. Misinforming consumers about the social, environmental and labour rights practice should not be named responsible business performance.

The Gildan case

Caused by transfer of the main parts of the clothing industry to low-wage countries, an early development of NGOs and other watchdogs criticising "sweatshops"[94] drove the business to introduce voluntary certification schemes. Well-known brands like NIKE, Walt Disney and Reebok needed to clean their brand names. Since then, a number of

---

[94] "Sweatshop" signifies a workplace with bad working conditions, unregulated work load and low wages – in short, exploitation. It is used in the USA to characterise foreign as well as domestic companies; in the latter case normally with migrant workers.

initiatives have come forward and compete for audit compliance along the production chain. The main ones are listed below:

FLA: The Fair Labor Association was a product of President Clinton's 1996 Apparel Industry Partnership initiative, formed in 1998. Unions left the initiative saying that the FLA's code of conduct was incomprehensive. Over 175 colleges and universities are affiliated.[95] It has an NGO Advisory Council. Since June 2003, the FLA has released the results of audits on the internet (FLA, 2005).

WRAP: The Worldwide Responsible Apparel Production emerged as a business alternative to the FLA and claims to have over 700 member companies[96]. In total, 1,300 factories participate, but it has no union participation. Labour and NGO leaders criticise it for being a closed system and lowering international standards.

WRC: The Workers Rights Consortium was founded in April 2000 by students' organisations and university administrations in the USA. It has an advisory committee with labour rights experts, as well as NGO and union representatives. Its influence is based on the role of universities as customers.

FWF: The Fair Wear Foundation is a Dutch organisation founded in 1999 by the FNV union confederation and the Clean Clothes Campaign. Employers' organisations participate. The FWF's Code of Labour Practices for the Garment Industry is aligned to the model codes of the international Clean Clothes Campaign and the ICFTU (International Confederation of Free Trade Unions). Fully operational in 2004.

SAI: The Social Accountability International, which is the North American organisation behind the SA8000 standard, with, as mentioned above, union board participation.

ETI: The Ethical Trade Initiative, which is a UK-based alliance promoting ethical trade and labour rights, also with union board participation.

---

[95] It includes brand names like Adidas-Salomon, Eddie Bauer, GEAR for Sports, Gildan Activewear, Liz Claiborne, New Era Cap, Nordstrom, Nike, Patagonia, Puma, Reebok, Phillips-Van Heusen and Zephyr Graf-X.

[96] It includes manufacturers like Sara Lee Corporation, Jockey International, VF Corporation (with brands like Lee, Wrangler, Rustler, Riders, Britannia and Chic Jeans), Russell Corporation, OshKosh B'Gosh, Tropical Sportswear International, Gerber Childrenswear. These are mainly brands distributed by supermarket chains.

A joint initiative for one globally recognised code of conduct involves the Clean Clothes Campaign (CCC), ETI, FLA, FWF, SAI and WRC[97] (Joint Initiative, 2005).

There are several NGOs involved in campaigning against violations of workers' rights in this industry, the most important in this case being: the National Labor Committee (NLC, USA), the Maquila Solidarity Network (MSN, Canada), American Students Against Sweatshops (ASAS, founding member of WRC), the Clean Clothes Campaign (CCC, mainly European campaign network), and Oxfam International (which has launched a campaign covering the clothing industry, but is primarily involved with food production).

Non-compliance in the clothing industry

The Canadian-based TNC Gildan Activewear owns production units in the clothing industry and has one of the most ambitious CSR programmes. Much like Chiquita, it received an Award for Excellence in Corporate Social and Ethical Responsibility in 2003.[98] It has its own code and adheres to both the WRAP and FLA systems.

Gildan's practice was accused of being like that of other maquila (assembly) producers. Generally, many methods are applied to avoid unions in this industry. Discrimination, harassment, firings, blacklisting, and even death threats are reported by union activists. Even being at the better end of the scale can be far from enough to comply with, for example, the core labour standards.

The public non-compliance case started in November 2002, when the 24th Gildan El Progresso (a fully owned apparel factory in Honduras) fired 42 workers, of whom 39 had filed a request for certification of a union ten days before they were fired. The first public reaction came from the Canadian NGO, Maquila Solidarity Network (MSN) in May 2003 based on research at both wholly owned and contracted Gildan factories in Central America and Mexico. Some US institutional customers (among them WRC members) called on Gildan to reinstate fired workers, give a written guarantee that they are free to organise a union without retaliation, and accept an independent

---

[97] Brands that attended its January 2005 meeting included Adidas, Expresso, Gap Inc., Gsus, Hess Naturtextilien, O'Neill, Marks & Spencer, Nike, Otto Versand and Puma.

[98] It was given by the Canadian International Development Agency and the Canadian Producers and Exporters Association.

investigation of their Honduras facilities. Gildan defended the lay-offs saying they were caused by seasonal slowdown. They declared that written information to workers would be ineffective because of workers' "low educational levels".

In response to threats of legal action against the organisation, MSN informed Gildan that it stood by the findings. Gildan offered to meet with several of the institutional purchasers (colleges and universities) or fly them to Honduras to visit factories. A significant Gildan investor, the Solidarity Fund of the Quebec Federation of Labour, which manages Quebec union members' pension investments, sent two representatives to investigate the case. They found that the workers were fired for union activity.

Next, Gildan applied for FLA membership and was formally accepted as a participating company on 22 October 2003. The Canadian network acknowledged this as a step forward, but was not satisfied. They were concerned by the length of time it might take before there was an FLA audit of even one Gildan facility. The FLA did not require Gildan to take immediate action to address worker rights violations.

Meanwhile, the American NGO, the National Labor Committee (NLC), released a new report on worker rights violations at the AAA/Alejandro Apparel contract factory in Honduras, which sells 75% of its production to Gildan. A total of 42 workers were fired for trying to organise a union. Other complaints included long workdays and working environment problems (NLC, 2003).

Purchasers were urged to voice their concerns and request that Gildan a) cooperate with an independent investigation, b) communicate both verbally and in writing their commitment to respect workers' rights to employees, and c) offer to reinstate fired union members at both the criticised facilities. Purchasers were asked to abstain from terminating contracts, as the campaign objective was to improve conditions and promote decent jobs, not to make the company leave Honduras. According to a later WRC report, on 30 October, Gildan El Progreso fired two employees for efforts to establish a union.

On 4 November 2003, 37 more union supporters were fired according to documents provided by the union federation, FITH (Federación Independiente de Trabajadores de Honduras). One of the workers dismissed was six months' pregnant. Due to Gildan's subsequent refusal to reinstate the union organisers, the Canadian Solidarity Fund sold off its Gildan shares and also took its representative off the company's board. The Fund owned shares worth approximately $90 million.

In January 2004, the WRC and FLA received a complaint from the Maquila Solidarity Network and Canadian Labour Congress, supported by FITH, about the El Progreso factory concerning wages, hours of work, freedom of association, harassment and abuse. The WRC team was denied access to the premises when it tried to investigate the complaints, but the FLA carried out its audit. Both organisations found that labour rights were violated and joint discussions with Gildan were initiated. In a July 2004 report, the WCR finds Gildan unwilling to remediate the violations of labour legislation and codes of conduct. The freedom of association was clearly violated; evidence suggested overwhelmingly that women had been sexually harassed and abused by the company doctor; and illegal practices concerning wages and working hours were confirmed. It was confirmed that women's rights had been violated with respect to firings, denial of sick leave to pregnant women etc.

At a July 12 meeting, convoked to discuss remediation, Gildan's CEO announced the company's decision to close the factory 11 weeks later, claiming that the decision was "absolutely unrelated" to the investigation of worker rights violations etc. Gildan admitted afterwards that the timing of the announcement was unfortunate and expressed regret for the unintended disrespect (Gildan, 2004). On 27 July, Gildan's FLA-status was placed under a 90-day special review.

Gildan's El Progreso factory closed down in September. On 26 October, it was decided at an FLA Board to remove Gildan from its list of participating companies; an unprecedented step in the FLA's history. Conditions for re-instatement of Gildan were decided, among them a system of internal training and monitoring of freedom of association, and a constructive dialogue with North and Central American NGOs. Gildan's status as a participating company in the FLA was re-established on 10 December, 2004. Talks with WRC continued.

On 19 January 2005, the company finally agreed to implement a corrective action plan to meet its obligations as supplier to the institutions affiliated to the WRC. It would offer reasonable job opportunities for laid-off workers at various production sites, reinstate workers fired for exerting their labour rights in 2002 and 2003, and pay the wages of the 39 workers fired for union activity from the date of their dismissal to the day of the closure of the factory, while publicly admitting it had been a violation of their rights. It agreed to train their administration and supervisors in complying with the freedom of association. However, the plan to end the dispute with the WRC went further. Gildan promised to give priority to hiring ex-workers from its closed El Progreso factory in another maquila factory, to providing these workers with free transportation, and to covering the costs of re-housing for all ex-workers from the El Progreso plant and their dependents who agreed to live where the company would open a new factory. Gildan agreed to cooperate with a Honduran NGO to verify implementation. The WRC found this to bring Gildan in concordance with the codes of conduct of member institutions (WRC, 2005).

Conclusive remarks to the Gildan case

With the Honduran Ministry of Labour as the only exception, all external reviews found workers rights violations at the El Progreso Gildan factory, although they were initially denied by the company. Institutional investors and customers had to intervene, and one big investor withdrew its $90 million capital from the company because of Gildan's reluctance to take adequate action. In an unprecedented move, the FLA withdrew Gildan´s status as a participating company, while Gildan's failure to comply with (WRC) codes of conduct signified a loss of institutional customers. Even then, it did not admit its violations nor offer full compensation and rehabilitation to affected workers.

Throughout the case, the company avoided cooperation with the relevant union federation, FITH, nor was it proposed by the involved organisations. The relatively positive outcome was obtained through great efforts and cooperation, in which strong international pressure was exerted. It cannot be called responsible business behaviour when so much negative publicity and action is needed to make the company admit violations and comply with the most basic workers' rights.

Discussion

So, is CSR mainly a smokescreen or a way to improve social relations and conditions? The cases do not suggest any of the two, but rather that CSR may be a tool that can be used to achieve both things, depending on the will and actions of stakeholders. The two cases confirm that even at the high end of the CSR scale, voluntary standards are not enough to guarantee workers rights, protection of social standards, workers' health or the environment.

Local labour authorities have little capacity to assess worker complaints and the enforcement of labour laws is generally insufficient to guarantee workers' rights.

The cases seem to confirm that NGO-led campaigns can influence consumers in the rich countries to some extent and force companies to reconsider their behaviour. In both cases, cooperation between unions and NGOs to influence corporations from the inside and outside played an important role.

Unions in developing countries generally do not have access to communication with institutional customers, retailers and individual consumers and are in their initial phases too weak to constitute a real bargaining strength. The union movements of developing countries are often not united and strong enough to launch broader struggles to protect labour rights, but need international or political support.

Although Chiquita is among the multinationals that accept and negotiate with unions, the overall tendency is to diminish union-organised production and buy growing quantities from suppliers without enforcing labour rights at their production units. This reflects a general tendency of TNCs to avoid unions as actors in their voluntary monitoring and auditing schemes. They prefer NGOs to their own workers' elected representatives, as was seen in the Gildan case. Some TNCs even see NGOs as the alternative to unions.

Generally, consulting workers collectively is not a part of voluntary CSR systems. Local unions are not involved in the elaboration of the codes, nor asked for a statement for the annual report. Technical staff develop priorities and plans, pretending to know what is best for workers. CSR reflects a somehow paternalistic sort of mentality that contradicts democratic labour rights. Historically, workers have won the right to organise with the aim of influencing and improving their conditions in essentially non-democratic, privately owned companies. Once workers are organised, their right to exert influence takes the form of collective bargaining, more permanent committees of dialogue and negotiation (e.g. health and safety) or even statutory worker representation on company boards.

A crucial element is the workers' right to elect their representatives and democratically discuss common positions free from employer interference. To be able to remain anonymous while expressing criticism and complaints to the employer is only possible when union representatives are legally protected against firings and other reprisals and where this protection is enforced. Workers' critical observations are unlikely to be communicated to management where this is not the case. With high unemployment and no unemployment benefits, why would workers risk their job to voice their opinion?

Better democratic control of TNCs seems necessary both from within and from the outside. The international union movement can help transform self-chosen standards to negotiated framework agreements with internal as well as international workers' control. As known from traffic offences, it cannot be left to offenders to set their own rules, monitor compliance with them, or decide the penalty for breaching them. It is often argued that commercial "traffic" functions differently because supply and demand take care of regulation. Consumers' "free choice" in the supermarket can be compared to monitoring, while failing demand can be compared to punishment. This is based on the assumption that consumers have free access to alternative information and react adequately to it. In practice, it depends on voluntary efforts whether consumers are adequately informed and react to the information.

Both the right of consumers to know the truth about the products and the democratic rights of workers to organise and collectively negotiate their conditions are at stake. A healthy corporate development may be more probable if these rights are promoted. It could help curb unfair competition based on false statements and cover-ups.

Recommendations

Based on the cases and observations presented, the following are recommendations to donors, unions, TNCs and governments:

Develop worker -participation in internal decision-making: Corporate citizenship might be a misleading concept if you start to think of corporations as citizens. Corporations contain multiple interests. Three main parties have legitimate authority and constitute the classic tripartite labour market model: management, unions and government. The tendency is to downplay the tripartite model. Democracy should, on the contrary, be built on workers' participation in corporate decision-making through their unions. This should be seen as a part of democracy.

Participation of unions in CSR systems: Improved methods of corporate social accountability should be developed and implemented to overcome the weaknesses presented in this article. Local and international union organisations should participate in the elaboration of policy, certification criteria and monitoring systems. There should be public access to reliable, union-controlled information throughout the production chain.

Corporations should open up access for unions to contractors, subcontractors and suppliers. This should be incorporated into standard supply contracts and include the obligation of suppliers to provide comprehensive information to the workers concerning their labour rights. The workers should be involved on a collective basis as unions, they should be asked to express their joint position to auditors, and they should have the opportunity to express their viewpoints in annual corporate reports.

Strengthen civil society and cooperate with authorities: Donors should support representative organisations to empower civil society (workers, unions, NGOs) and local regulatory and supervisory authorities to counterbalance corporate power. Cooperation between unions and labour inspection authorities with the support of NGOs can improve the quality and objectivity of the work of all parties and help fight corruption. Donors should include social, labour and environmental clauses in all their own development aid and loan contracts.

Strengthening control and enforcement at the international level: Stronger unions at the higher end of the commercial chain, NGOs, governments in importing countries, and consumers could provide some strength to an otherwise weak enforcement system. Alliances between these stakeholders to control and improve corporate behaviour may achieve better results than CSR alone. The union movement is in favour of better regulation and strengthened collective bargaining. To achieve this, the tripartite ILO should be strengthened in its regulatory role. The core labour rights should become part of all trade agreements.

Promoting international framework agreements may contribute positively, especially if systems of tripartite control and enforcement are introduced. To lift collective bargaining up to a global level is not an easy exercise. The Nordic and the EU model, involving the parties of the labour market so deeply in its regulation, cannot be transposed to the international level overnight, because of historic and cultural differences. But a social dialogue model based on international framework agreements with TNCs and sector-based employer and employee organisations should be considered to be a "third leg" of international regulation, covering the gap between legally binding and voluntary standards.

The international union movement can provide some inside, worker-controlled, information by building direct links between unions in developing countries and workers in the higher end of the distribution chain. Retail workers' unions could build a link to consumers. To play this role, it must develop reliable information systems based on confidence between the different links in the chain. When basic rights are obviously violated in developing countries, a legal right to react throughout the chain should be established to provide more effective sanctions.

What unions can do: A stable and reliable labour force in a well-functioning society is among the conditions for long-term business success. Allowing the workers to act in an organised and democratic way, expressing their collective positions through independent unions, is not only to grant them their rights; it is investing in the development of employees that think critically and devote themselves to democratic decision-making. It can help the company improve quality, productivity, environmental performance, customer service, and enhance both corporate citizenship and business performance.

Unfortunately, a union-organised workforce is an offer that few TNCs accept, although it could bring order to chaotic labour relations where contracts, complaints, wage claims etc. are individual. Union federations offer worker training, information and support to local union activity. In this respect, nevertheless, Danish, Norwegian, Swedish, Spanish, Belgian, Dutch and US labour organisations implement development aid projects with union capacity-building around issues such as dialogue, negotiations, international cooperation, technical training, gender equality, occupational health and safety, investigations etc. If accepted, this could support the implementing of CSR principles and strengthen companies' self-monitoring and sustainability.

Bibliography

Chiquita (2002). Social Responsibility Report.
www.chiquita.com/corpres/CR2002/2002-CRReport-English-FINAL.pdf

Chiquita (2004). Deliver Sustainable Growth. Chiquita Brands International 2004 Annual Report.
www.chiquita.com/chiquita/bottomline/Annuals/2004annual.pdf

COLSIBA. Coordinadora Latinoamericana de Sindicatos Bananeros. www.colsiba.org

Comisión Interinstitucional (2002). INFORME, Tegucigalpa, Honduras.

ETUC (2001, October). Corporate Social Responsibility in a legislative and contractual framework", Executive Committee.

Economist, The (2005, January) The Good Company. A Survey of Corporate Social Responsibility, 22.

Eurepgap (2005). International standards, food production, revised.
www.eurep.org/documents/webdocs/EUREPGAP_GR_FP_V2-1Jan04_update_22Feb05.pdf

FLA (2004). Tracking charts. Gildan.
www.fairlabor.org/all/transparency/charts_2004/27002901C.pdf

FNV (2004). Corporate Social Responsibility in a Global Perspective, Policy Plan 2004/07. FNV Mondiaal, Amsterdam.

Gildan (2004). Corporate Citizenship Report, Montreal, Canada. www.gildan.com

Greenpeace (2002). Call for a legally binding international instrument: eu.greenpeace.org/issues/corplia.htm

Hague, J. et al. (2001). Muscosceletical Disorders and Work Organisation in the European Clothing Industry, TUTB, Brussels.

Human Rights Watch (2002). Tainted Harvest, Child Labor and Obstacles to Organizing on Ecuador's Banana Plantations.
www.hrw.org/reports/2002/ecuador/

Joint Initiative on Corporate Accountability and Workers Rights (2005). www.jo-in.org/pub/latest.shtml)

Karliner, J. & Ted L. (2002). Corporations have too much power, CorpWatch and Global Exchange.
www.corpwatch.org/article.php?id=1728

Little, A.D. (2002). The Business Case for Corporate Citizenship.

Messing, K. (1999). Integrating Gender in Ergonomic Analysis, TUTB, Brussels.

National Labour Committee (2003).
www.sweatshopwatch.org/headlines/2003/msnupdate_nov03.html

Nielsen, J. (1996). Når farligt arbejde flytter, CASA.

PLAGSALUD (2001). Central America at a good pace, MASICA Review, PAHO/WHO

Riisgaard, L. (2003). Fagforeningsstrategier til sikring af Arbejderrettigheder indenfor Transnationale Selskaber. Roskilde Universitetscenter

Riisgaard L. (2004). "The IUF/COLSIBA-Chiquita framework agreement: a case study" ILO Working Paper, 94.
www.ilo.org/public/english/employment/multi/download/wd94.pdf

Riisgaard, L. (2002). "Un estudio piloto del conocimiento y la aplicación del acuerdo entre COLSIBA /UITA y Chiquita." Prepared for the Danish General Workers Union in Managua.

Raagaard, T. (2004). Dansk pres giver bedre bananer, Forbrugerbladet Tænk&Test, 47.

Raagaard T. (2005). Kritik af banangigant, Forbrugerbladet Tænk&Test, 52.

Sopisco News (2005, September) Mercado Bananero de USA.

Teknologirådet (1999). Farlig teknologi. Miljoeregulering ved samhandel med udviklingslande, Teknologiraadet.

Taylor, J. G & Scharlin, P.J. (2004). Smart Alliance. How a global corporation and environmental activists transformed a tarnished brand, Yale University Press.

UN Global Compact. www.unglobalcompact.org

Wesseling, I. et al. (2004). Efectos de clorpirifos sobre la salud de los trabajadores bananeros de La Lima, Honduras, SALTRA, IRET, Costa Rica (unpublished).

Workers Rights Consortium (2005). WRC, January 25 statement www.workersrights.org)

CHAPTER 11

DEVELOPMENT FINANCE INSTITUTIONS AND CORPORATE CITIZENSHIP

EXPERIENCES FROM THE INDUSTRIALISATION FUND FOR DEVELOPING COUNTRIES

Esben Rahbek Pedersen

Ph.D. Fellow, Copenhagen Business School, Denmark

Mahad Huniche[99]

Business Development Specialist, Nordic Consulting Group, Denmark

Abstract

Each year, development finance institutions (DFIs) commit billions of euros to private sector investments in developing countries. However, their ability to promote corporate citizenship has gone widely unnoticed in academia. This paper tries to remedy this neglect by discussing how DFIs can make a contribution to the economic, social and environmental development in low-income countries. The Danish Industrialisation Fund for Developing Countries (IFU) serves as an example to illustrate the processes and practices of DFIs.

---

[99] The authors would like to thank IFU for providing relevant data regarding the projects and contributing to the description of IFU's social and environmental initiatives. The input of IFU has been of inestimable importance for the making of this chapter.

Introduction

The private sector is increasingly seen as an engine of employment, income, investment and growth (Gibbon & Schulpen 2002, p. 1; UN 1999, p. 31).[100] In consequence, a wide range of international organisations, development banks, bilateral donor agencies and venture funds are now introducing various credit instruments, partnership programmes, business infrastructure components etc. in the attempt to stimulate private sector development in developing countries.

These initiatives - in general termed private sector development (PSD) programmes – are based on the underlying assumption that economic growth in the private sector is crucial in reaching development objectives - above all poverty reduction (cf. Kragh et al. 2000, p. 319; Schulpen & Gibbon 2001, p. 16). However, realising that economic development does not necessarily mean sustainable development, organisations involved in PSD programmes are increasingly combining economic instruments with social and environmental components.

This chapter describes how a Danish development finance institution, IFU, deals with social and environmental issues when supporting private companies' investments in developing countries. The objective is to analyse how IFU makes corporate citizenship operational and, more generally, discuss how DFIs can contribute to the improvement of social and environmental standards in developing countries. However, before going into a detailed presentation of IFU's social and environmental initiatives, we will begin with an introduction of DFIs and their role in promoting private sector development in developing countries.

Development Finance Institutions and the Private Sector in Developing Countries

Foreign direct investment (FDI) can be an important source of economic growth in developing countries (OECD 2002, p. 5).[101]

---

[100] The private sector can be defined as: "(…) a basic organising principle for economic activity where private ownership is an important factor, where markets and competition drive production and where private initiative and risk-taking set activities in motion" (OECD 1995, p. 10).

[101] FDI is usually defined as: "(…) a form of international inter-firm cooperation that involves a significant equity stake in, or effective management control of, foreign enterprises" (de Mello 1997, p. 4). Moreover, FDI includes: "(…) other,

Moreover, provided that the recipient countries are capable of absorbing the foreign investments, FDI can also contribute to poverty reduction, competition, knowledge and technology transfer etc. (ibid.). However, many developing countries find it difficult to attract FDI because investors often consider developing countries as more risky compared to relatively 'safe' markets in industrialised countries (NMFA 2003, p. 15; Schulpen & Gibbon 2001, p. 93). Corruption, political instability, inadequate infrastructure, inflation etc. create an insecure business environment that reduces the share of FDI that goes to less developed countries. The lack of investments is an important barrier to economic growth, which in turn makes it difficult to reach the overall development objective of reducing poverty in developing countries.

The purpose of DFIs is to provide long-term finance for private sector projects in developing countries and transitional economies that fall outside the arena of the commercial banking sector and/or where the risk of the projects or the country in question makes investments more demanding for the business community.[102] Today, there is a whole industry of bilateral and multilateral DFIs that offers equity, quasi-equity, loans and guarantees to private sector projects in developing countries. The most significant multilateral DFI is undoubtedly the International Finance Corporation (IFC), whereas OPIC (USA), CDC (UK), DEG (Germany) and FMO (Netherlands) are among the more important bilateral DFIs.

Unlike traditional finance institutions, DFIs are not only about profit. Return from investments is not distributed between the owners but placed in new investments or accumulated as reserves (DMFA 2004, p. 30-31). Instead, the underlying rationale of DFIs is that FDI will eventually generate positive development impacts in terms of economic growth, innovation, job creation, poverty reduction etc. However, DFIs are aware that certain conditions have to be met before the positive impacts from FDI can be materialised. For instance, countries with relatively small technology gaps and a human resource base capable of absorbing the positive spill-over effects are more likely to experience economic growth as a consequence of the FDI (de Mello

---

broader forms of non-equity cooperation involving the supply of tangible and intangible assets by a foreign enterprise to a domestic firm without foreign control. These broader collaborative associations include most types of quasi-investment arrangements (…), joint ventures with limited foreign equity participation, and R&D cooperation" (ibid.).
[102] Source: www.edfi.be

1997). Moreover, open economies with few trade barriers and a good investment climate tend to generate more positive impacts from FDI than countries with a poor business climate, large technology gaps and a human resource base that is not educated to make use of foreign investments. In conclusion, the net impact of FDI ultimately depends on a wide range of firm, industry, and nation-specific factors, such as governmental policies, infrastructure, investment motives, entry modes, corporate strategies etc. (cf. Moran 1999; NMFA 2003; de Mello 1997, p. 4).

DFIs also want to ensure that economic growth leads to socially and environmentally sustainable development in the recipient countries. In consequence, terms like 'CSR' and 'corporate citizenship' are beginning to take hold in the development finance community, and an increasing number of DFIs have over the last decade formulated social and environmental policies and introduced facilities to support sustainable development, improve working conditions, promote human rights etc.

Among them is IFU. In the following sections, we will describe how IFU is dealing with corporate citizenship and discuss some of the challenges facing DFIs who are trying to stimulate social and environmental improvements in developing countries[103]. The discussions are supplemented with information from external evaluations of IFU.

The Industrialisation Fund for Developing Countries (IFU)

IFU was founded in 1967 and is part of the Danish International Investment Funds, which besides IFU also includes The Investment Fund for Central and Eastern Europe (IØ) and The Investment Fund for Emerging Markets (IFV). No new investments are allowed in IFV and the capital should be retransferred to the Danish State once the assets become liquid. IFU offers capital and advice on the implementation and operation of joint ventures between partners in Denmark and developing countries. To be eligible for IFU financing, all projects have to be commercially viable and financed in part by a

---

[103] In accordance with IFC, we will define corporate citizenship as: "(...) the proactive management of the social, environmental and labour dimensions of a company's business practices" (Source: www.ifc.org).

private Danish company. From 1967 to 2004, IFU has been involved in more than 528 projects in 71 countries (IFU 2005a).

IFU projects can be divided into three phases: - the project preparation, the investment and the exit phase (see Figure 11.1 below). Before IFU and a Danish company reach a binding agreement, the company formulates an investment proposal that is subjected to a screening process in order to ensure that the project complies with IFU's policies and guidelines. A feasibility study is often prepared and the business partners formulate a business plan for the project (Andersen 2004, p. 18). During the project preparation phase, IFU may also assist the Danish company in mobilising additional financing for the project from other DFIs. This phase is completed when IFU and the business partners sign a shareholders' agreement or a loan agreement[104].

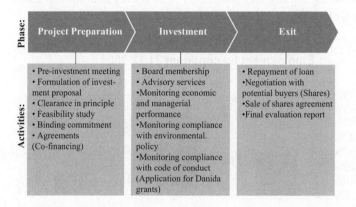

Figure 11:1 Overview of phases in an IFU project

During the investment period, IFU's investment officers monitor and evaluate the project at regular intervals. These evaluations include the economic and managerial performance as well as environmental and social aspects. If IFU is shareholder or lender in the project, a representative for IFU often participates as a board member or as an observer in the work of the board of directors. For projects in eligible countries, partners may also apply through IFU for Danida (Danish International Development Assistance) grants to cover, for example, education and training of project employees as well as environmental and occupational health and safety improvements. IFU's policy is to

---

[104] Source: www.ifu.dk

exit from a project when it has become duly consolidated, normally 5-10 years after project implementation.

The Development Impact of IFU Projects

The central development objective of IFU is to promote economic activity in developing countries in collaboration with Danish trade and industry. Increasing economic growth is expected to contribute to poverty reduction: - the primary objective of all development assistance (Schulpen & Gibbon 2000, p. 16). Job creation is, of course, central in this regard and IFU estimates that projects supported by the Fund from 1967 to 2003 have created approximately 99,995 jobs, primarily in Asia (IFU 2005a). The difference is primarily caused by the fact that IFU has supported more projects in Asia compared to the other regions. In total, 49% of the projects have been carried out in Asia (including Turkey and Malta), 31% in Africa and 20% in Latin America (IFU 2005a).

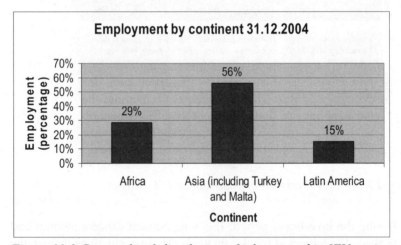

Figure 11:2 Geographical distribution of jobs created in IFU projects (IFU 2005a)

Even though the projects supported by IFU have generated quite a few jobs in developing countries, the number in itself says little about the quality of the jobs or the social and environmental impacts of the project companies' activities. In consequence, job creation as a development objective has to be seen in relation to other issues, such as working conditions, environmental protection, technological transfer, as well as training and education (cf. Kragh et al. 2000, p. 321; NMFA 2003, p. 29). IFU has tried to integrate some of these issues in the project preparation and investment phase by developing a number of social and environmental initiatives. Of special importance are the environmental policy and the code of conduct that were introduced in 1996 and 1998 respectively. In the following sections, we will discuss the two policies in turn.

IFU's Environmental Policy

The objective of IFU's environmental policy is to improve the environment in IFU-financed projects by minimising possible adverse environmental effects and to promote positive impacts. This applies to both the external environment (e.g. soil, water, air, and the health and safety of the local population) and the working environment (health and safety of employees) (IFU 2001, p. 1-4).

IFU has established a set of pre- and post-investment procedures in order to make sure that the project companies comply with the environmental policy. The first indispensable requirement is that all projects are in accordance with the environmental rules and regulations of the host country. Secondly, the Danish partner has to make a so-called "Best Judgement Declaration" on the environmental impact of the project, confirming whether the project company's production and other activities are carried out in accordance with Danish environmental rules and regulations[105], whilst all substantial deviations should be justified and accepted by IFU. The results from the assessment are used to establish whether IFU may – and in the affirmative – on what conditions IFU is prepared to participate in the project. The post-investment procedure involves the preparation of an annual environmental status report, which also includes human health and safety (security and accidents). This management of the project company continuously assesses whether the environmental performance remains at an acceptable level (IFU 2001, p. 1-4).

---

[105] Moreover, IFU carries out an environmental categorization of the project company in one of the World Bank's three classes: - A, B or C. Category A means that the project may have diverse and significant (external) environmental impacts, which could be irreversible. B-categorised projects may have specific (external) environmental effects. Few, if any, of these impacts are irreversible. Category C implies that the project has negligible, insignificant or minimal environmental impacts (IFU 2001, p. 3). The large majority of IFU's current portfolio are B projects (151). Moreover, there are 6 A projects and 29 C projects (IFU 2004b, p. 15).

The introduction of the environmental policy is likely to have a positive impact on the environmental performance in the IFU projects. As seen from the figures below, the large majority of the projects have a fair, good or excellent environmental performance. However, the net impact of the environmental policy is difficult to assess, because a wide range of factors affect the environmental standards in the project companies, such as expectations to the future, business culture, industry, size, geography etc. (cf. DMFA 2004, p. 53-54; IFU 1999a, p. 31-34).

External environment

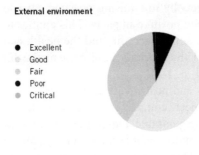

- ● Excellent
- ○ Good
- ○ Fair
- ● Poor
- ◐ Critical

Occupational Health and Safety (OHS)

- ● Excellent
- ○ Good
- ○ Fair
- ● Poor
- ◐ Critical

Figure 11:3 Environmental performance of IFU projects (IFU 2005a, p. 16)

IFU's Code of Conduct

Soon after the introduction of the environmental policy in 1996, IFU realised that enhancing economic growth, development and a more equitable income distribution required a focus on both the environmental and social aspects of investments. This in turn created a need for a more systematic approach to address social issues and lead to the formulation of the Code of Conduct in 1998. The objective of IFU's Code of Conduct is to increase awareness of matters related to business ethics, social responsibility, human rights, occupational health and safety, and external environment (IFU 1999b). IFU's Code of Conduct is a set of general principles, where it is stated that concrete guidelines and policies are formulated in dialogue with the relevant stakeholders. However, it is made clear that IFU shall utilise the framework established by international organisations and agreements such as:

- The United Nation's Universal Declaration of Human Rights, 10 December 1948, including the International Covenant on Civil and Political Rights (UN 1966) and the International Covenant on Economic, Social and Cultural Rights (UN 1966)
- The Convention for the Protection of Human Rights and Fundamental Freedoms, Council of Europe, 4 November 1950
- ILO Conventions Nos. 29 (Protection against forced labour), 87 (Protection of freedom of association), 98 (Protection of the right to collective bargaining), 100 (Equal remuneration for men and women), 105 (Abolition of forced labour), 111 (Non-discrimination concerning employment) and 138 (Protection against child labour)
- The OECD Convention on Combating Bribery of Foreign Public Officials in International Business Transactions, 17 December 1997.

In the appraisal of projects and through board membership or as observer in the project companies, IFU seeks to promote the principles in the abovementioned Declaration, Covenants and Conventions. Moreover, IFU's investment officer evaluates the project company's compliance with the Code of Conduct on an annual basis in the so-called Annual Conduct Review. The evaluation is based on 13 indicators relevant to human rights, including child labour, gender equality, forced labour etc.

The requirements in the Code of Conduct are likely to have a positive impact on the policies and practices of the project companies. However, as with the environmental policy, the net impact of IFU's Code of Conduct on the social performance in the project companies is difficult to verify (DMFA 2004, p. 54). What can be concluded is that IFU experiences only few social and environmental problems and that most projects comply with the Code of Conduct (see Figure 11:4 below).

Esben Rahbek Pedersen and Mahad Huniche

Code of Conduct

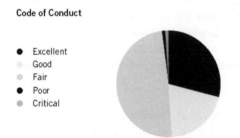

● Excellent
○ Good
○ Fair
● Poor
○ Critical

Figure 11:4 Code of Conduct performance of IFU projects (IFU 2005a, p. 16)

Recently, IFU has been involved in the development of a new tool designed to help companies detect potential human rights violations. The tool is named Human Rights Compliance Assessment (HRCA) and is expected to be released in 2005. Since 1999, it has been under development by the Human Rights & Business Programme at the Danish Institute for Human Rights (DIHR), and is a joint venture between the Danish Institute for Human Rights, the Confederation of Danish Industries (DI), and the Danish Industrialisation Fund for Developing Countries (IFU), with the support of the Danish government (Danida). The aim of this cooperation has been to develop a widely accessible resource tool to help companies deal with human rights issues relevant for their particular operations. When the full HRCA is released, it will be the most comprehensive tool on the market defining company responsibility towards human rights.

The entire tool runs on a database containing over 350 questions and 1,000 corresponding human rights indicators, developed from the Universal Declaration of Human Rights, the 1966 Dual Covenants, and over 80 other major human rights treaties and conventions. The full HRCA will be an interactive computer programme that will allow the companies to select and modify the information in the database to suit their type of business and area of operations. The standards and indicators will be updated on an annual basis, based on feedback from both company users and human rights groups, to ensure that the tool addresses the real life problems faced by companies and to reflect changes/developments in the international human rights law.

A Quick Check of the HRCA was published in November 2004.[106] The Quick Check comprises approximately 10% of all the questions contained in the entire HRCA database and relates to some of the most essential human rights issues a company must consider in relation to its activities. This check was developed in cooperation with a group of development finance institutions, including IFU, to provide companies and investment funds with a condensed assessment of key human rights issues.

The Quick Check covers violations in relation to the following three areas:

1. Employment Practices – concerning the rights of individuals employed by the company, or seeking employment with the company
2. Community Impact – concerning the rights of individuals residing in societies (including societies defined by political, cultural or geographic boundaries) which are affected by company activities or products
3. Supply Chain Management – concerning the rights of individuals affected by business partners' operations, whether as employees, local residents or other stakeholders, and includes corruption/bribery and management of the supply chain.

IFU expects to apply the Quick Check as from mid-2005.

Dilemmas of DFIs

As indicated in the previous sections, projects supported by IFU seem to have generated a number of positive development impacts (cf. DMFA 2004, p. 10). However, that does not imply that the activities of IFU and other DFIs are friction-free and exempted of conflicts, dilemmas and diverging interests. For instance, based on the NCG evaluation conducted in late 2004, IFU were criticised by the Danish Economic Council (DEC) for primarily subsidising Danish companies' investments in well-advanced developing countries. Furthermore, it was argued that the Danish companies supported by IFU often have the international experience and financial capacity to undertake the investments on their own (DEC 2004).

---

[106] The Quick Check is free on the net, see: www.humanrightsbusiness.org

However, things might be a little more complex than that. Admittedly, IFU's support to companies contains an element of industrial policy, since it reduces some of the risk from investing in countries that are generally perceived as 'risky' (see also next section). The question is, however, whether the achievement of industrial and development objectives is always mutually exclusive? Moreover, the statement that IFU primarily supports advanced developing countries is a little oversimplified. Projects supported by IFU must be located in developing countries on the OECD's list of development aid recipients, and per capita income may not exceed USD 5,115 (2004). Therefore, these countries are not all that advanced. Moreover, IFU's portfolio is not simply a mirror of the investment patterns in Denmark. For instance, IFU has a significantly higher engagement in Africa compared to the Danish FDI in general (Hansen 2004, p. 123, 140).

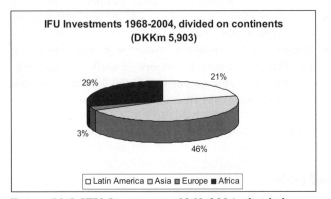

Figure 11:5 IFU Investments 1968-2004, divided on continents (IFU 2005a)

However, what is probably more interesting than these principal discussions regarding the nature of IFU is that it might actually be disadvantageous for IFU to only support relatively inexperienced companies in the poorest developing counties. Not only would it result in a drastic reduction in IFU's activities, but IFU would also be likely to perform miserably - both from an economic and development perspective. This brings us to some of the dilemmas facing DFIs supporting private sector investments in developing countries.

The Geographical Dilemma: Safe vs. Risky Investments

It is often assumed that companies gradually increase their international development to more and more distant markets (Hashai & Almor 2004, p. 467; Johanson & Vahlne 1990, p. 13). This is partly caused by the 'psychic distance' that can be defined as the:

"(…) factors such as differences in language, culture, political systems, etc., which disturb the flow of information between the firm and the market (…)" (Johanson & Vahlne 1990, p. 13).

As companies gradually accumulate foreign market knowledge and commitment, they will expand their activities to new countries with higher psychic distance (ibid.). In consequence, developing countries will find it difficult to attract FDI because most industrialised country companies will perceive these markets as too risky and uncertain.

DFIs also face this problem when trying to convince companies about the investment opportunities in developing countries. For instance, it was concluded in the evaluation of IFU that poorly developed countries in Africa made it difficult to attract FDI (DMFA 2004, p. 52). Likewise, the evaluation of the Finnish DFI, Finnfund (The Finnish Fund for Industrial Development Cooperation), concluded that Finnish companies prefer to invest in 'safe' markets, which makes it difficult for Finnfund to convince them about the investment possibilities in the developing countries (Schulpen & Gibbon 2001, p. 93; Finnfund 1992). Last but not least, an analysis carried out by IFC (1996) found that industrialised country companies saw investments in developing countries as more risky than investments in other countries (IFC 1996).

The dilemma is that countries which need private sector development the most are also likely to be the countries that have the most difficulties in attracting FDI. Even though this perception does not always reflect the actual risk when operating on such a market, foreign companies will need some incentives before they are prepared to invest in developing countries. DFIs may provide such incentives to participate with risk capital and share market knowledge with companies who want to invest in developing countries. As noted in the evaluation of the Norwegian DFI, Norfund (Norwegian Investment Fund for Developing Countries):

"Part of the hesitation of private investors to invest in developing countries derives from a natural slowness in entering into new

271

markets and from risk anticipation exceeding actual risk. DFIs may in this respect (through both portfolio management and direct involvement) act as frontrunners by having more knowledge of the market, thereby reducing the gap between perceived and actual risk and reducing the time for making investment decisions" (NMFA 2003, p. 15).

The Size Dilemma: Multinational Corporations (MNCs) vs. Small and Medium-Sized Enterprises (SMEs)

Provided that foreign market knowledge and commitment are important determinants of the internationalisation process, it is also reasonable to expect MNCs to perform better than SMEs in developing countries because the latter have neither the necessary resources nor the international experience to commit themselves to physically distant markets. At least, this seems to be the conclusion from the various evaluations and analyses of IFU in the last decade. Already in 1998, it was concluded in the 30-year report of IFU that projects with large Danish partners performed better than projects with small Danish partners (IFU 1998, p. 53). These findings were later supported by the comparative assessment of six DFIs that was made in relation to the evaluation of IFU. All DFIs unanimously agreed that the financial performance of SME projects was below average (DMFA 2004, p. 25). Today, there is still a substantial difference between the performance of small and large projects. As seen in Figure 11:6 below, the internal rate of return (IRR) of SME projects is significantly lower than projects involving large partners. Moreover, SME projects have higher mortality rate data from IFU estimates that approximately 5% of all projects involving large partners are closed during the first 10-15 years, while for SME projects the figure is approximately 50%.

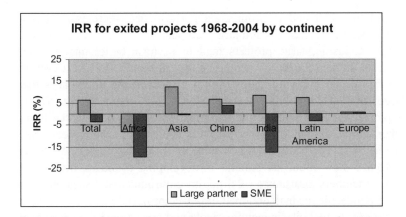

Figure 11:6 Performance of SMEs and 'large' projects (IFU 2005a, p. 39)

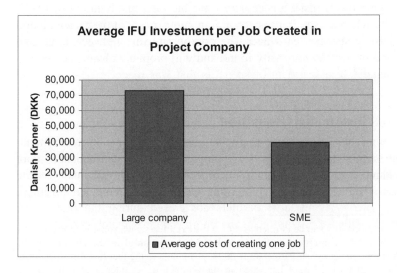

Figure 11:7 Average IFU Investment per Job Created in Project Company

Looking at the development impacts, the costs of creating a job is also determined by the size of the projects. As seen from Figure 11:7, the average IFU investment per job created is significantly lower in SME projects. This could be due to the fact that larger projects with large companies are more capital-intensive. However, the indirect job effects working through suppliers etc. may be higher for larger projects. With regard to social and environmental performance, there is no major difference between SMEs and large companies.

In conclusion, large projects tend to perform better than smaller projects. In consequence, it would be logical for IFU to invest only in large projects involving major MNCs. However, the dilemma is that large projects involving major MNCs are more likely to be implemented even without the participation of IFU or other DFIs. In other words, the 'additionality' of DFIs decreases as the project's size increases.[107] The need for IFU's services - e.g. risk capital, expertise and know-how about investments in developing countries, training of board members, assistance of firms on environmental issues etc. - is more noticeable in small and medium-sized projects.

In order to be both financially viable and have a positive net impact in developing countries, IFU and other DFIs must include both profitability and development concerns in their portfolio decisions. Large projects make a necessary contribution to the bottom line of the DFI, whereas small projects are in most need of risk capital and advisory services. However, the appropriate mix between large and small projects is not easily found and will probably always be open to debate[108].

Conclusion and Discussion

The private sector is increasingly seen as an engine of employment, investment and growth in developing countries. In consequence, more and more governments in low-income countries try to stimulate private sector development by promoting privatisation, commercialisation,

---

[107] Additionality can be defined as: "(...) the extent to which something happens as a result of an intervention that would not have occurred in the absence of the intervention" (English Partnerships 2004, p. 1). Due to the fact that it is difficult to know what would have happened in the absence of an intervention, measuring additionality becomes very difficult and sometimes even speculative (Gibbon & Schulpen 2002, p. 17). This also goes for DFIs. For instance, in the evaluation of IFU in 2004, the evaluation team and the IFU's board differed in their understanding of the additionality dimensions of IFU's activities (DMFA 2004, p. 78). Among other things, IFU found that an analysis of positive impacts should have included more elements, such as: "a) Improvement of business plans and feasibility studies; b) Guidance on obtaining local approvals and c) Enhancing project bankability and securing access to external financing" (ibid.).

[108] According to IFU, the number of SME projects has increased in the last decade. From 1968 to 1994, IFU invested in 264 projects, of which 56% involved large Danish companies. The picture changed from 1995 to 2004 and SMEs now account for 58% of all IFU projects.

foreign direct investments etc. By the same token, numerous international organisations, development banks, bilateral donor agencies and venture capital funds have recently introduced a wide range of credit instruments, business partnership programmes, enabling environment programmes etc. (cf. Kragh et al. 2000, p. 319).

Based on a short presentation of the background for the growing appreciation of the private sector in the donor community, the article has described how DFIs can promote social and environmental improvements in developing countries. The hope was to shed some light on how investors can be actively involved in the making of good 'corporate citizens'.

IFU was used as a case example to illustrate the role of DFIs in promoting corporate citizenship. Even though it is difficult to measure the net impact of IFU, the results indicated that IFU - and DFIs more generally - can have a positive impact on the social and environmental performance in private sector projects in developing countries, e.g. by introducing environmental policies and codes of conduct. That does not mean that DFIs are automatically above reproach. DFIs face a number of dilemmas when investing in developing countries that put some limits on their efficiency and 'additionality'.

What cannot be questioned, however, is that DFIs are increasingly adopting corporate citizenship initiatives and will probably continue to do so in the future: both as a safeguard against outside criticism and as a proactive means to promote social and environmental improvements in developing countries.[109] Even though the corporate citizenship literature has paid practically no attention to DFIs, DFIs seem to have paid enough attention to corporate citizenship to introduce a wide range of social and environmental policies that are likely to have some positive development impacts.

---

[109] For instance, a comparative analysis of six DFIs in relation to the evaluation of IFU concluded that all DFIs unanimously agreed that the environmental policies and codes of conduct were important to the achievement of their objectives (DMFA 2004).

Bibliography

Andersen, B. M. (2004). Investeringsfonden som sparringspartner: Vurdering af muligheder og faldgruber er nødvendige når IFU og IØ deltager i projekter i udviklings- og i østlande, Dansk Projektledelse, 9[3], p. 18-19.

De Mello, L.R. (1997). Foreign Direct Investment in Developing Countries and Growth: A Selective Survey, The Journal of Development Studies, 34[1], p. 1-34.

DEC (2004). Danish Economy, Autumn 2004: English Summary, Copenhagen, Danish Economic Council (DEC), Chapter II: International Outsourcing. http://www.dors.dk/english/index.htm

DMFA (2004). Evaluation: The Industrialization Fund for Developing Countries, Copenhagen, Danish Ministry of Foreign Affairs (DMFA)/Danish International Development Agency (DANIDA).

English Partnerships (2004). Additionality Guide: A Standard Approach to Assessing the Additional Impact of Projects, London, English Partnerships: The National Regeneration Agency, Office of the Deputy Prime Minister
www.englishpartnerships.co.uk/additionality

FINNFUND (1992). Joint Ventures and Aid Evaluation of Finnfund, Helsinki, Ministry for Foreign Affairs, Department for International Development Cooperation, Report of Evaluation Study, 1992[3]. http://global.finland.fi/julkaisut/evaluoinnit/eval_94/r92_3.html

Gibbon, J. & Schulpen, L. (2002). Comparative Appraisal of Multilateral and Bilateral Approaches to Financing Private Sector Development in Development in Developing Countries, Helsinki, United Nations University (UNO)/World Institute for Development Economics Research (WIDER), Discussion Paper, 2002[112].

Hansen, M.W. (2004). Danske virksomheders etableringsmønster i lavtlønslande, p. 121-140 in DI (2004): Guide til outsourcing og etablering, Copenhagen, Dansk Industri (DI).

Hashai, N. & Almor, T. (2004). Gradually internationalizing 'born global' firms: an oxymoron?, International Business Review, 13[4], p. 465-484.

IFC (1996). International Joint Ventures in Developing Countries: Happy Marriages? Washington DC, International Finance Corporation (IFC). Discussion Paper, 29.

IFU (1998). IFU 30-year report 1967-1997, Copenhagen, The Industrialization Fund for Developing Countries (IFU). http://www.ifu.dk/ifu/5-year-report/30yearSummary_uk.pdf

IFU (1999a). Foreign Direct Investment and the Environment, Copehnhagen, The Industrialization Fund for Developing Countries (IFU).
http://www.ifu.dk/EnvironmentalReview/Envir_Review98_99.pdf

IFU (1999b). Code of Conduct, Copenhagen, The Industrialization Fund for Developing Countries (IFU). http://www.ifu.dk/common/cc.doc

IFU (2001). Environmental Policy, Copenhagen, The Industrialization Fund for Developing Countries (IFU). http://www.ifu.dk/EnvironmentalPolicy/EnvironmentalPolicy.doc

IFU (2004a). Reaching project no. 500: Investments worth DKK 50bn and 85,000 new jobs in developing countries, Copenhagen, 26 March 2004, IFU. http://www.ifu.dk/ifu/ifu_default.htm

IFU (2005a): Annual Report 2004. Copenhagen, The Industrialization Fund for Developing Countries (IFU).

Johanson, J. & Vahlne, J. E. (1990). The Mechanism of Internationalisation, International Marketing Review, 7[4], p. 11-24.

Kragh, M. V., Mortensen, J. B., Schaumborg-Müller, H. & Slente, H.P. (2000). Foreign aid and private sector development, p. 312-331 in Tarp, F. (ed.): Foreign aid and development. London, Routledge.

Moran, T.H. (1999). Foreign Direct Investment and Development: a Reassessment of the Evidence and Policy Implications, p. 41-55 in OECD: Foreign direct investment, development and corporate responsibility. Paris, Organisation for Economic Cooperation and Development (OECD).

NMFA (2003). Evaluation of the Norwegian Investment Fund for Developing Countries (Norfund), Oslo, Norwegian Ministry of Foreign Affairs (NMFA), Evaluation Report, 1.

OECD (1995). Private Sector Development – A Guide to Donor Support, Development Assistance Committee (DAC), Paris, Organisation for Economic Cooperation and Development (OECD).

OECD (2002). Foreign Direct Investment for Development: Maximising Benefits, Minimising Costs, Overview, Paris, Organisation for Economic Cooperation and Development (OECD).

Schulpen, L. & Gibbon, P. (2001). Private Sector Development: Policies, Practices and Problems, Copenhagen, Centre for Development Research (CDR), CDR Policy Paper. www.cdr.dk

UN (1999). Looking Ahead - A Common Country Assessment of Viet Nam, Hanoi, United Nations (UN), December.